ORGANIZATIONAL CHANGE & GENDER EQUITY

ORGANIZATIONAL
CHANGE
& GENDER
EQUITY

International Perspectives on Fathers and Mothers at the Workplace

EDITORS

Linda L. Haas
Philip Hwang
Graeme Russell

Sage Publications, Inc.
International Educational and Professional Publisher
Thousand Oaks ▪ London ▪ New Delhi

For information:

Sage Publications, Inc.
2455 Teller Road
Thousand Oaks, California 91320
E-mail: order@sagepub.com

Sage Publications Ltd.
6 Bonhill Street
London EC2A 4PU
United Kingdom

Sage Publications India Pvt. Ltd.
M-32 Market
Greater Kailash I
New Delhi 110 048 India

Printed in the United States of America

Library of Congress Cataloging-in-Publication Data

Main entry under title:

Organizational change and gender equity: International perspectives
on fathers and mothers at the workpace / Edited by Linda L. Haas, Philip Hwang, Graeme Russell.
        p. cm.
    Includes index.
    ISBN 0-7619-1044-1 (cloth)
    ISBN 0-7619-1045-X (paperback)
      1. Organizational change. 2. Work and family. 3. Parents—Employment.
    4. Sexual division of labor. I. Haas, Linda. II. Hwang, Philip O.
    III. Russell, Graeme, 1947-
      HD58.8 .O7289 1999
      331.25—dc21   99-6398

00 01 02 03 04 05 06 7 6 5 4 3 2 1

Acquiring Editor:	Harry Briggs
Editorial Assistant:	MaryAnn Vail
Production Editor:	Wendy Westgate
Editorial Assistant:	Nevair Kabakian
Typesetter/Designer:	Marion Warren
Indexer:	Jean Casalegno

Contents

PART II   WORKPLACE PROGRAMS AND POLICIES   77

PART III ORGANIZATIONAL CHANGE AND GENDER EQUITY   163

Preface

The Ford Foundation has a long-term commitment to promoting women's advancement, children's healthy development, and an equitable society. Since the early 1970s, the foundation has supported programs to advance the status of women and to address equity and fairness in the workplace. About a decade ago, the foundation developed a new initiative to address these challenges. In a program paper entitled "Work and Family Responsibilities: Achieving a Balance," the foundation explained that its program would rest on the assumption that society wants men and women to be able to make commitments to both family and work responsibilities. We sense that women and men may need more choices than they have today and that expanding available options might contribute to steadier performance at work and stronger families.

A set of projects was undertaken in the 1990s to advance gender equity by focusing on the interaction of work and family responsibilities in the context of large work organizations and by experimenting with processes of institutional change. These collaborative action research projects at three major U.S. corporations involved research teams working with company managers and employees to examine the way work is carried out and how new approaches to working could both meet business goals and help individuals address family and personal needs. In this approach, examination of work practices through a "work-family lens" released positive energy to devise better ways to meet the company's goals and individuals' personal needs. The successful results of these projects have been reported in the foundation's publication "Relinking Life and Work: Toward a Better Future" (authored by Lotte Bailyn and Rhona Rapoport, who are also contributors to this volume).

The Ford Foundation has also been involved in helping to fund research on corporate culture and fatherhood in Swedish corporations (initiated by Linda

Haas and Philip Hwang, who are both editors of and have chapters in this book) and in helping Haas and Hwang establish a network of international scholars who are interested in work-family linkages. We saw this as an opportunity to gain a deeper understanding about how these work-family and gender issues are being addressed in other societies, which vary in governmental commitment to gender equality. The network of scholars developed by Haas and Hwang in turn decided to collaborate in writing this book.

This book addresses the challenges that are just beginning to emerge and that I expect will occupy us—not just in the United States but in many industrialized societies—as we enter the 21st century. It is an incontrovertible fact that in societies all over the world, during the last 50 years, women have entered the paid workforce in increasingly large numbers. This has both been caused by and resulted in new laws guaranteeing women's equality in many spheres. Although in a few quarters there is still debate about whether this is good or not, the reality of this major shift in women's roles has been generally accepted. The discussion has now shifted to trying to deal with the consequences of these changes for individual men and women, children and families, workplaces, and other societal and community institutions.

As this volume amply documents, much attention has focused on changing the workplace—first by recruiting greater numbers of women, then by instituting equal opportunity laws and family benefit policies and programs, and now by implementing changes in organizational leadership and corporate culture. Whereas work organizations *can* help shape the broader cultural norms of the society, they also simultaneously reflect the societal consensus of the times.

Although change has occurred in cultural norms, it is a slow and incremental process. For example, as women have increasingly moved into the world of work, men have increased their activity in the family in most industrialized societies by at least a little bit. However, it is clear that women cannot continue to shoulder the dual burden of the "second shift" so well articulated by sociologist Arlie Hochschild. Income inequality, which has always existed, is increasing. We are also becoming a society in which time is limited and, hence, a valuable commodity. The trade-off between income and time has never been possible at the lower end of the income scale and appears to be increasingly difficult now for higher-income families as well. This shortage of income and time has led to a frenetic family life across the income spectrum. A serious challenge for the future is to devise ways for more people—not only women—to take on a greater share of family caregiving, including husbands, partners, employers, community organizations, and governments. We may need to develop innovative solutions and institutions that we have not yet imagined.

I would like to share what I have learned from this volume in the hope that these personal reflections will help us get "out of the box" of our own thinking and lead us to new ways of thinking about and addressing these challenges. First, governmental policy promoting women's advancement is neces-sary but not sufficient. In many societies, constitutions and laws have been revised to guarantee women equality and to prohibit discrimination in many spheres. This is an essential step in advancing women's status, and, as already noted, significant gains have been achieved as a result. Nevertheless, in every society around the globe, women are still disadvantaged in comparison with men on most economic and social indicators. Public leadership remains primar-ily a male preserve, whereas family caregiving continues to be primarily a female one.

Second, transformation of gender roles and cultural norms takes a very long time. For example, achieving a substantial increase in the proportion of men in Sweden who take parental leave took more than 25 years. This gradual change occurred in the context of explicit and strong government policy and commit-ment both to gender equity and the male parenting role. Yet gender equity remains elusive. Men's work is still valued over women's work, and fostering women's economic independence is not sufficient to shift gender roles in the family.

Third, the ideology and practice of gender equity has yet to be adequately developed and articulated to become a sufficiently strong motivator for men to change the balance between work and family in their own lives. Women's movements have focused on the need for men to be supportive of women's changing roles but perhaps with insufficient emphasis on what men gain from this shift. Rather, the discussion has focused on increasing women's public roles and concomitantly on what men give up. There has been less discussion of what men might gain from gender equity—more active and deeper engagement with their partners and families, particularly their children. Thus, women's exhorta-tions along with government policy may not be enough. Perhaps men them-selves need to be visible as leaders and facilitators for other men to bring about significant shifts in parenting and family commitment. This may mean recon-ceptualizing the gender equity paradigm. In a society in which men and women are truly equal, they still may engage differently at home and at work. How can we articulate roles that are equitable but not the same?

Finally, it is not surprising, therefore, that sustaining the link between work and family and gender equity is still difficult. By challenging both the tradi-tional division of labor between women at home and men at work and the excessive priority of work over family and community not only for women but also for men, we are seeking a far-reaching transformation in cultural norms and practices.

One of the key learnings from this volume for me was not only to link family with gender equity but also to be explicit about society's commitment to children. One interesting aspect about Sweden's progress in advancing gender equity is that such progress that has been achieved is the result of not only a societal commitment to equality between men and women but also a very explicit commitment by men and women to children.

A second key insight for me was that, although much work had been done to shatter the old notion of the "ideal worker" and the "organization man," which the late William Whyte so poignantly described in the 1950s, much less has been written outside of feminist theory about changing our notions of the "ideal mother," and there is little literature on or discussion of an "ideal father" or even the "ideal parent." There is much work to be done here.

Perhaps if we start from an understanding about the realities of the lives of mothers, fathers, and other caregivers today, at the beginning of the 21st century, and then consider the needs of families, particularly children, as well as the communities that families live in, we will be in a better position to articulate both an unfinished agenda of women's equality and new approaches to gender equity in the home, the workplace, and the broader community.

June H. Zeitlin
Director, Gender and Institutional Change Project
The Ford Foundation

Introduction

LINDA L. HAAS
PHILIP HWANG
GRAEME RUSSELL

Until recently, work and family were regarded as separate spheres of social life, with little effect on each other. The difficulties of combining work and family were less recognizable than they are today because fewer women were in the labor force while children were young, and men could rely on women to be primarily responsible for housework and child care. This has now dramatically changed. In most advanced industrialized societies, the roles of men and women have become more similar. Women are becoming as likely as men to be in the paid labor force, even during their early childbearing years, and are often interested in occupying the full range of occupations at all levels of organizational hierarchies. Men are also increasingly more engaged in taking on an active role in family life, especially in regard to developing close relations with children (Hayghe, 1990; Hwang & Lamb, 1997).

Women's mass entrance into the paid labor force and companies' growing reliance on female labor have encouraged some companies to pay more attention to how employees manage responsibility for family life. Corporations are also now asked to deal with situations in which men want to spend more time caring for family members. Competition in the world market has made companies anxious about productivity and labor costs, and many have been forced to reduce the size of their workforces. New incentives for maintaining individuals' organizational commitment and for boosting individuals' productivity must be found. One type of incentive is a more family-friendly work environment (Bowen, 1988; Morgan & Milliken, 1992).

Social scientists in several countries are now engaged in research projects that focus on how companies are changing to help individuals combine work and family roles, in a way that would yield benefits to work organizations, make progress toward the goal of gender equity, and contribute to the well-being of employees and their families. In all, 19 scholars contributed to this volume, representing three continents and a wide range of basic and applied disciplines, including anthropology, business, economics, education, law, psychology, social work, and sociology. Although most chapter authors have academic affiliations, most have also been substantially involved in direct work with companies on gender equity and/or work-family issues. Some authors are highly placed professionals in government and research organizations interested in issues affecting women, men, and families. All together, this is a unique group of individuals who are highly experienced and knowledgeable about the topics they write about; they are committed to high standards of excellence in terms of the collection and reporting of research findings and are interested in the practical application of research. Each chapter highlights pioneering work by the authors. As an added benefit, each chapter makes accessible to an international audience research findings on specific societies that might be difficult for individuals outside those societies to obtain.

THE IMPORTANCE OF THIS BOOK

There are several books already published that discuss work-family issues. Most works describe how individuals (especially career women) cope with balancing work and family roles in particular cultural settings; such studies typically do not make strong connections between individuals' abilities to juggle multiple roles and the social context in which the juggling act takes place.

This book is different from most of those that have come before it because of its simultaneous emphasis on three research-based themes. The first theme is that work-family issues must be considered from a gender perspective; otherwise, changes in work practices are unlikely to facilitate women's and men's reconciliation of work and family responsibilities. The second theme is that work-family linkages must be regarded as socially constructed—that is, as deeply embedded in social institutions, especially in the culture of work organizations. The third theme, related closely to the second, is that work-family linkages and work organizations themselves must be considered in their social context; they are influenced by what happens in the external social environment. Therefore, an international perspective on organizational change and gender equity can help uncover the cultural values and norms that perpetuate or undermine gendered practices in work organizations. Each of these themes is discussed more below.

GENDER EQUITY

Some books on work-family linkages take for granted gender differences in orientations toward family and work and, subsequently, companies' rationale for reinforcing such differences. This book does not take gender for granted but seeks instead to explore its impact. Many chapters focus on the persistence of "gendered practices" within work organizations, such as the tendency for women and men to occupy different jobs based on presumptions about their interests and abilities. Such practices go along with commonly held assumptions about male-female differences and also help to reproduce such differences (Acker, 1997).

We have based our study of work-family linkages (following Bailyn, 1993) on the idea that such linkages must be gender equitable. Gender equity would exist when it is taken for granted that both men and women are entitled to compete for the whole range of positions within companies and when it is accepted that both male and female employees are responsible for family income provision and child care. It has often been assumed that work-family issues are "women's issues," something companies need to pay attention to only if they want to recruit or retain valued female employees. However, viewing work-family programs and policies like this can single women out in a way that leads to discrimination in recruitment and the development of "mommy tracks" in corporations that jeopardize women's attempts to earn high incomes or move into jobs commensurate with their interests and abilities. It can also reinforce the notion that men should prioritize work over family (Glass & Estes, 1997; Lewis & Cooper, 1996).

Work-family programs and policies that are based on the idea of gender equity seem likely to have greater potential to benefit companies than those that single out mothers of young children as beneficiaries. When women's job opportunities are not influenced by presumptions about their work commitment or responsibilities for family care, companies can take advantage of women's full range of skills and talents. When men do not have to make difficult decisions about dividing their loyalty and time between job and family, companies may gain workers whose high quality of life and experience developing close relationships with family members make them more productive. Although much more research is needed, it seems probable that a "business case" can be made for companies' actively seeking ways to help employees of both sexes combine work and family roles, especially if a long-term orientation toward investing in employees' potential is adopted. Moreover, gender equitable family-work policies and programs based in the workplace seem likely to yield significant benefits for families. When women have equal employment opportunity, they will earn higher incomes; with higher incomes, families have greater economic stability, which is an extremely important determinant of children's well-being and the quality of family relationships. When both men and women are encouraged to participate in caregiving of children and elders, then these dependent groups' needs are more likely to be met.

THE SOCIAL CONSTRUCTION OF WORK-FAMILY LINKAGES

Another important point in our work is that we are interested in exploring, not taking for granted, how connections between work and family spheres and individuals' work and family roles are socially constructed. Social construction of work-family linkages occurs at many different levels and in various areas of social life. In this work, we focus on how the cultures of work organizations shape individuals' choices and options regarding combining work and family roles.

We look at work organizations as having "cultures" that can facilitate or hinder mothers' and fathers' balancing of work and family responsibilities (following Bowen, 1988). To say that work organizations have cultures implies that there are shared values and norms concerning behavior that shape how management reacts to employees' need for flexibility for family purposes and how employees act, not just toward their jobs but also toward their families. The overall work organization has a "culture," and individual categories of workers or sections of the workplace may in turn have their own "subcultures."

The cultures in most work organizations in advanced industrial societies have developed in ways that contribute to widespread discrimination against women, especially women seeking jobs considered nontraditional or at the higher ends of organizational hierarchies. Much of this discrimination is based on the assumption, now outdated, that women are not as work oriented as men or that women lack the necessary qualifications for employment. Likewise, organizational cultures have developed in ways that encourage men to be more loyal to the organization than to their families, to feel that earning family income is sufficient to demonstrate love for family members, and to think that their identities and sense of success are tied up more with their jobs and its rewards than with their families. Men who want to be active fathers, or who need to provide care for ill or disabled spouses or parents, also experience discrimination, based on the assumption, now outdated, that men are not as family oriented as women or that men lack the qualifications to provide caregiving.

Organizational cultures have stability and are therefore typically resistant to change. Many individuals have a stake in traditional ways of running organizations, whereas others' behaviors have become so habituated that they cannot imagine change. Many aspects of organizational culture are visible (e.g., written policies for parental leave), but most are so taken for granted that they are "invisible." The invisible aspects of organizational culture arise from thousands of small decisions made by individuals at all levels of the organizational hierarchy; these decisions then form a network of informal rules and regulations that regulate employees' behavior as much as formal rules and regulations can. The informal culture can reinforce tradition after the organization has formally decided to make a break with the past.

Although organizational cultures are resistant to change, as social constructions they are fluid and dynamic. They are deeply rooted but not intractable. Organizations must adapt to the social environment to survive. Organizational cultures are consequently influenced by external social forces (e.g., global economic competition, national government policy, demographic and economic trends) and internal social forces, ambiguities, and contradictions (e.g., lower workforce productivity as a result of family concerns, younger men's desire to spend more time with their families, women who want high management positions without working overtime; Hearn, 1998; Milliken, Dutton, & Beyer, 1990; Trice & Beyer, 1993). A dominant concern reflected in the chapters in this volume is how gender equity comes about through organizational change. Many chapters address the subject of what helps organizations decide to take responsibility for helping their employees with managing caregiving roles and what (and who) drives organizational innovation. Change in organizational cultures requires replacing old values and norms for behavior with new ones. Some writers take up what the transformation to a gender equitable work organization would involve in terms of new shared values and norms for behavior.

THE SIGNIFICANCE OF AN
INTERNATIONAL PERSPECTIVE

To understand the social construction of work-family linkages, the book also takes up the impact of societal culture on beliefs about gender and the culture of work organizations. This calls for an examination of how national social policies (or the lack of them) put constraints on, or provide encouragement for, men's and women's sharing of breadwinning and child care roles as well as the development of gender equitable work-family policies and practices within work organizations. Work organizations do not exist in a social vacuum but are embedded in local communities that may or may not have resources for families to use in solving work-family dilemmas (e.g., day care, counseling, elder care). Work organizations are also under the jurisdiction of regional and national governments, and sometimes even of international organizations (such as the

United Nations or the European Union). These governing bodies can set standards for work organizations in such areas as equal employment opportunity for women, equal pay, work hours, and family leave, and they can provide needed services for working families. Several chapters in this book consider the impact of community resources and government legislation on individual women's and men's interests and abilities to combine work and family and on work organizations' attitudes and behavior toward working mothers and fathers.

To examine more closely how cultural practices influence, reproduce, and change organizational culture and gender relations, this book looks at the issue of organizational change and gender equity from a cross-national perspective. We present research findings from a range of societies where researchers have been actively involved in understanding the conditions under which companies will elect to promote family well-being and gender equity. Not only is a range of societies covered, but the authors themselves come from an even wider range of cultural backgrounds. Added insight arises from the fact that several writing teams have "mixed" membership; at least one team member has pursued the topic from the "insider's perspective" (i.e., he or she grew up in the society being studied), while at least one other team member has adopted the "outsider's perspective" (i.e., he or she did not grow up in the society that is being studied).

An international perspective is vital to the study of gender equity and work-family balance. Nearly all modern societies are faced or will soon be faced with the challenge of integrating the spheres of work and family. By looking at several societies at one time, we can learn about challenges held in common and explore how solutions might or might not work across country lines.

The first society focused on in each section of the book is the United States. This society, the largest of those studied, has had a history of encouraging working parents to rely on their own resources for balancing work and family roles. The government has hesitated to provide resources like subsidized child care, and, until recently, employers assumed that workers left their family responsibilities at the workplace door. Companies interested in recruiting and retaining the best workers have increasingly offered a wide array of benefits to working parents. Typically, such programs officially are gender neutral but informally are assumed to be of interest only to women. Employees who take advantage of programs face the prospect of being considered disloyal to the company, so usage rates for programs tend to be small. Many workers lack formal access to any work-family benefits because they are part of a growing portion of the labor force that lacks job security; these individuals work on contract, short term, or when called; this is part of an international trend (also evident in the United Kingdom and Australia) referred to as "casualization." In the United States, the individuals most likely to bring about organizational change in the direction of gender equity seem likely to be employed by work organizations as high-level managers, especially in human resources. To be successful, they must make a strong business case for companies' paying greater attention to workers' need for flexibility.

The second society that receives attention in this volume is the United Kingdom. In this nation, mothers of young children have had low employment rates because of strong beliefs that children suffer from maternal employment. This has very recently changed, however, as more mothers have left the home to work at least part-time jobs. The United Kingdom, as part of the European Union (EU), has been "encouraged" to develop more government supports for working parents, but it has resisted until recently when it became the last EU nation to adopt the "social charter." Very few supports like day care or paid parental leave have been developed as of yet, but there are signs that the United Kingdom would like to make rapid progress and learn from its European neighbors that have had work-family supports in place for a long time. Concerns about changing men's roles, however, remain unstated, because work-family issues are seen (as they are in the United States) as a woman's issue and not significantly tied up with the issue of equal employment opportunity. In the United Kingdom, the driving forces for change seem likely to involve nonprofit organizations interested in this issue and labor party activists.

The third society we consider is Australia. Australia has many of the same trends in women's and men's labor force participation as the United States, such as increasing numbers of mothers of young children entering the labor market. And like the United States and the United Kingdom, the government has been fairly slow to put into place a large network of programs supportive of working parents and children. Changes in workplace policies and programs have recently come about because of the efforts of trade unions, which help to replace existing policies by making a legal case for change (e.g., in the case of parental leave). Attempts to enforce women's legal rights for economic employment opportunity have also been linked to improving workplace supports for parents, although little attention is paid to fathers still.

The last society covered is Sweden (with some information provided on its neighbor Denmark). Sweden has been the most "advanced" society of those covered here in terms of the extent of family-friendly policies and programs and its commitment to the goal of gender equity. The government has historically been the driving force for change, partly out of an ideological concern for the well-being of children. Unlike elsewhere, a strong emphasis has been placed on changing men's roles so that they share breadwinning and caregiving responsibilities with women. However, a weak economy has forced Sweden to pay more attention to the needs of work organizations, and work organizations themselves have been slow to dramatically change their cultures to be more gender equitable. Further progress toward the goal of gender equity seems unlikely unless businesses more critically evaluate how the structure of work helps to perpetuate differences between men and women and reinforce the traditional gender-based division of labor for income provision and child care. Strong trade unions and a large number of activist women are beginning to organize themselves to help work organizations do this.

THE PLAN OF THE BOOK

The book is divided into three main parts. The first part takes up what is known about mothers and fathers at the workplace, to explore problems working parents have that workplace practices and policies can worsen or solve. In addition to discussing trends in labor force participation, authors in this section explore how gender affects mothers' and fathers' status in the labor market, participation in unpaid family work, and attitudes toward combining work and family roles.

The next part of the book covers workplace programs and policies relevant to work-family and gender issues in each of the four societies. These include efforts to promote women's economic opportunity, efforts to provide substitute care for children while their parents work, and policies that offer parents some flexibility to take time from work to take care of family responsibilities. Reasons for the way such programs and policies have developed in each society are described, and predictions about the future development of gender equitable work-family policies are made. Some emphasis is placed on identifying aspects of organizational culture that resist and/or facilitate change.

The last part of the book encompasses case studies of organizations undergoing change. Each chapter offers rich insight and details of the difficulty of bringing about gender equity; together, the chapters yield insights and hypotheses for future study, in terms of the processes by which individual companies come to address work-family issues and the specific conditions under which organizational change is more likely to result in gender equitable work-family policies. The shape gender equitable organizational cultures might take in the future is mainly discussed in chapters in this part.

Each part of the book is preceded by a preface written by one of the editors. These prefaces highlight how the chapters in that part explore the three main theses on which the book project was based as well as the lessons we might draw from a cross-cultural examination of work-family issues.

REFERENCES

Acker, J. (1997). Introduction. In L. Rantalaiho & T. Heikanen (Eds.), *Gendered practices in working life* (pp. ix-xi). London: Macmillan.
Bailyn, L. (1993). *Breaking the mold: Women, men, and time in the new corporate world.* New York: Free Press.

Bowen, G. (1988). Effects of organizational culture on fatherhood. In F. Bozett & S. Hanson (Eds.), *Fatherhood and families in cultural context* (pp. 187-217). New York: Springer.

Glass, J., & Estes, S. (1997). The family responsive workplace. *Annual Review of Sociology, 23,* 289-313.

Hayghe, H. (1990, March). Family members in the workforce. *Monthly Labor Review, 113,* 14-19.

Hearn, J. (1998). On ambiguity, contradiction, and paradox in gendered organizations. *Gender, Work, and Organization, 5,* 1-4.

Hwang, P., & Lamb, M. (1997). Father involvement. *International Journal of Behavioral Development, 21,* 621-632.

Lewis, S., & Cooper, C. (1996). *Balancing the work-family interface.* London: Sage.

Milliken, F., Dutton, J., & Beyer, J. (1990). Understanding organizational adaptation to change: The case of work-family issues. *Human Resource Planning, 13,* 91-106.

Morgan, H., & Milliken, F. (1992). Keys to action: Understanding differences in organizations' response to work and family issues. *Human Resources Management, 31,* 227-248.

Trice, H., & Beyer, J. (1993). *The cultures of work organizations.* Englewood Cliffs, NJ: Prentice Hall.

PART I

Mothers and Fathers at the Workplace

O nce upon a time, men were considered the ones responsible for providing income for the family, but most families in industrial societies today fit the model of the "dual-breadwinner" family, in which both husbands and wives are in the paid labor force, even when they have children. The transition to the dual-breadwinner model for family life has important consequences for the way work organizations operate and the way families organize their internal activities, such as housework and child care.

This part of the book provides information on the changing employment situations of mothers and fathers in the United States, the United Kingdom, Australia, and Sweden. There are important differences between these four societies in terms of women's participation in the labor market (e.g., mothers' likelihood of being employed when their children are small, women's participation in part-time work). However, there are striking similarities as well, regarding the forces that have played a significant role in encouraging more women to work; women's access to well-paid jobs at all levels of the occupational hierarchy; and men's tendency to work overtime, even when they have small children. Women's employment still remains more strongly affected by parenthood than does men's in all societies studied.

These chapters point out, however, that women's and men's attitudes toward employment are changing, in response to their concerns about being adequately involved in family life. Both sexes say they would like to work fewer hours and are reluctant to take on more responsibility at work while their children are young. Employees are also increasingly being faced with responsibility for the caregiving of disabled or aging parents; so far, they have had to make their own work adjustments to meet these new responsibilities. The needs of workers to reconcile employment with family seems likely to influence their choice of jobs and to put pressure on work organizations to offer them more flexibility throughout the life course.

In understanding the employment situations of mothers and fathers in modern society, it is important to note that there are significant class differences that have implications for parents' abilities to fulfill their responsibilities for providing income and care for their children. In the societies reported on here, two categories of families appear to be increasing in number, at each end of the social-class continuum. Julia Brannen labels these as "work rich" and "work poor" families. In "work rich" households, couples struggle to combine long hours of paid employment, usually in managerial or professional jobs that place high demands on employees, with their responsibilities for children. These couples can successfully fulfill the breadwinning role but potentially at the cost of fulfilling their roles as good parents. In "work poor" families, one or both partners are unemployed or struggle to fulfill the breadwinning role in jobs that are short term, part-time, or poorly paid. These couples' inability to adequately fulfill their breadwinning roles spills over in a negative way in their relationships with their children. Current economic trends that involve frequent company restructuring, movement of adequately paid jobs to developing countries, and replacing people with machines means that there are less jobs "in the middle" for parents to take. Continuing economic discrimination against women also undermines some couples' (and certainly single mothers') ability to achieve a reasonable economic standard of living. In some societies described here, the government has stepped in to help "work poor" families; in others, "work rich" families have received more support.

Another important topic in this part is dual-breadwinner families' division of labor for unpaid work. Here we find a significant discrepancy between parents' expectations and their behavior. Although there are important national differences, most parents in these societies believe couples should share domestic work; however, they do not practice this themselves. In most families in these countries, couples solve the problem of how to care for children and the home by agreeing on an arrangement in which the woman works part-time or at least does not work overtime pursuing a demanding profession or career. Such "agreements," however, are made in the context of women's lesser ability to earn as much as men in the labor market. In each society covered here, women's ability to steer family negotiations varies by their relative position in the labor market.

Men's participation in domestic work, especially child care, appears to have increased in the societies that are described here, but women remain primarily responsible for children's well-being. Men appear to have slightly increased their involvement in household work, whereas working mothers have dramatically decreased their involvement. An "equitable" domestic arrangement appears to be defined by couples as one in which each partner puts in about the same overall amount of time of paid work hours and unpaid domestic work hours *combined*. This situation, however, is a reality in some countries more than others; to some extent, this is related to the supply of "long" part-time jobs for women as well as the society's ideology about gender equality.

The impact of combining work and family roles on individuals' sense of well-being and job performance is also discussed in this part of the book. Although the availability of work-family benefits and having a supportive supervisor and coworkers are important for an individual's ability to successfully manage to combine both roles, evidence provided here points even more directly at how aspects of organizational culture influence an individual's psychological well-being. Characteristics of work, including job demands and job pressures, turn out to be very important predictors of an individual's level of well-being, and well-being contributes in turn to job performance. This suggests that work organizations will need to examine patterns of working in a more comprehensive way if they are to enhance the productivity of working parents.

These are the main issues that get taken up in this part. Specifically, chapter authors address the following key questions:

1. How are the work conditions of mothers and fathers changing and why?

2. To what extent do couples share responsibility for breadwinning and child care roles, and what facilitates or discourages such sharing?

3. How do traditional workplace policies and practices influence mothers' and fathers' abilities to combine breadwinning and child care roles and therefore become productive employees?

2

Employed Mothers and Fathers in the United States

Understanding How Work and Family Life Fit Together

ELLEN GALINSKY

JENNIFER E. SWANBERG

The study of work and family life is relatively new. Many studies have been exploratory, seeking to identify the work and family factors most strongly associated with various outcomes, including work-family conflict (Burke, Weir, & DuWors, 1979; Crouter, 1984; Hughes & Galinsky, 1988; Keith & Schafer, 1980; Piotrkowski & Katz, 1983; Voydanoff, 1988); role strain (Bohen & Viveros-Long, 1981); job satisfaction (Repetti & Cosmas, 1991); psychological well-being (Barnett & Baruch, 1985; Barnett & Marshall, 1991; Repetti, 1987);

AUTHORS' NOTE: The authors acknowledge the important contributions of James T. Bond in developing the conceptual model that explains the relationship between work and family life, and for reading and comments on earlier drafts. Support for writing this chapter was provided by the Ford Foundation. Support for the 1997 National Study of the Changing Workforce was provided by KPMG Peat Marwick, LLP; Allstate Insurance Company; the Boeing Company; Ceridan; Citibank, N.A.; the Commonwealth Fund; Fannie Mae; GE Fund; IBM Corporation; Johnson & Johnson; Merck & Co., Inc.; Mobil Corporation; NCR Corporation; Salt River Project; Xerox Corporation; and WFD.

marital relations (Hughes, Galinsky, & Morris, 1992; Repetti, 1989); and parenting satisfaction and children's development (Greenberger, Goldberg, Hamill, O'Neil, & Payne, 1989; Greenberger, O'Neil, & Nagel, 1994; Howes et al., 1995; Kohn, 1969; Kohn & Schooler, 1973; Lerner & Galambos, 1985; Menaghan & Parcel, 1990; O'Neil, 1992; Piotrkowski & Crits-Cristoph, 1982; Piotrkowski & Katz, 1983).

Other studies have probed theory, addressing the question of whether multiple roles enhance or deplete psychological well-being, especially among employed mothers (Barnett & Marshall, 1992; Baruch & Barnett, 1987; Marks, 1977). For the most part, the research to date has been based on the notion of separate spheres, conceptualizing work and family as distinct aspects of life, bridged by feelings of conflict or interference (Barnett, 1997). Recently, there has been a call for understanding the overlapping worlds of work and family, for developing and testing theories of how these experiences fit together (Barnett, 1997).

In this chapter, we address three questions: (a) How do work and family life affect employed parents' personal well-being and job performance? (b) How have the characteristics of employed parents' jobs and workplaces changed over the past 5 to 20 years? (c) How have employed parents' lives off the job and attitudes toward work changed over time?

The chapter draws primarily on data from the 1997 National Study of the Changing Workforce (NSCW), a research program of the Families and Work Institute that surveys representative samples of the nation's labor force every 5 years. It also provides a historical perspective by comparing data from 1997 with data from the 1992 NSCW survey and from the U.S. Department of Labor's 1977 Quality of Employment Survey (QES).

The sample size for the 1997 NSCW was 1,316 wage and salaried workers (635 women and 681 men) who had children under 18 years of age living with them at least half the year. The sample from the 1992 NSCW was 1,233 employed parents (632 women and 601 men) with children under 18. The sample from the 1977 QES was 618 employed parents (244 women and 374 men) with children under 18. Because each study has a slightly different sampling framework, we restrict the samples so that they are identical for the purpose of making comparisons. When comparing the 1992 NSCW and the 1997 NSCW, we reduce the 1997 sample to include only workers 18 to 64 years old. Similarly, when making comparisons between the 1997 NSCW and the 1977 QES, we reduce the 1997 sample to employees 18 years and older who were working 20 or more hours per week and were interviewed in English.

HOW WORK AND FAMILY FACTORS AFFECT
WELL-BEING AND JOB PERFORMANCE

Model, Hypotheses, and Measures

To address the question of how work and family factors affect parents' personal well-being and job performance, we developed a conceptual model (see Figure 2.1) based on the following hypotheses:

Hypothesis #1: Good quality jobs and supportive workplace environments enhance workers' personal well-being and quality of life off the job, as indicated by reduced feelings of job burnout and job-to-home spillover.

Hypothesis #2: Demanding and hectic jobs jeopardize workers' personal well-being and quality of life off the job, as indicated by elevated feelings of job burnout and job-to-home spillover.

Hypothesis #3: Supportive workplace environments offer some protection against the negative effects of demanding jobs.

Hypothesis #4: Some employed parents may be more susceptible than others to job burnout and negative job-to-home spillover because of the particular circumstances of their lives off the job.

Hypothesis #5: Employed parents who experience greater job burnout and negative job-to-home spillover also experience more negative spillover from their home lives into their jobs, which limits job performance.

Hypothesis #6: Negative spillover from home to job is also a product of the characteristics of employed parents' lives off the job, household demographics, employment status of spouse, dependent care responsibilities and problems, socioeconomic status, and so forth.

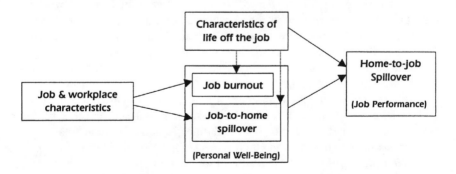

Figure 2.1. Conceptual Model

We measure the constructs in our conceptual model in the following ways. *Employee demographics* included age, gender, race/ethnicity, education, occupation, and years in the labor force, which were controlled for in all analyses. *Job characteristics* included earnings and fringe benefits, job demands, and job quality. *Earnings* were estimated on an hourly basis for the respondent's main job; *benefits* were represented by counts of traditional and dependent care benefits offered.

Job demands included the number of paid and unpaid hours worked at the parent's main job, number of nights away from home on business, frequency of paid or unpaid overtime with little or no notice, having a nonstandard work schedule, frequency of bringing work home, and job pressures. *Job quality* included five factors: job autonomy, learning opportunities on the job, meaningfulness of work, opportunities to advance, and job security. *Workplace characteristics* included flexible work arrangements, supervisor support, supportiveness of workplace culture, positive coworker relations, lack of discrimination, and respect on the job.

Personal well-being included *job burnout* and *job-to-home spillover. Job burnout* was measured by asking employees how often in the past 3 months they had felt emotionally drained by their jobs, "used up" at the end of the workday, stressed out by work, and tired when facing another workday. *Job-to-home spillover* was measured by asking how often in the past 3 months their jobs had caused them to lack time for themselves, lack time for family or other important people in their lives, lack energy to do things with family or others, not get everything done at home, and not be in as good a mood as they would have liked. Both job burnout and job-to-home composite measures were strongly correlated with general measures of personal well-being (i.e., stress, coping, and life satisfaction; Bond, Galinsky, & Swanberg, 1998) but are more robust for purposes of our explanatory analyses and have the advantage of being directly linked to work in the minds of employees.

Characteristics of life off the job that were measured included working multiple jobs, hours worked at job(s) other than main job, commute time to main job, marital status, parental status (having children under 18 and under 13), living in a dual-earner or single-earner household, frequency of breakdowns in child care arrangements, perceived quality of child care arrangements for children, perceived quality of child care arrangements for respondent, elder care responsibilities in past year and past time off work to provide elder care, current elder care responsibilities and time taken to provide current care, having both child care and elder care responsibilities, amount of time for self on workdays and nonworkdays, and total projected household earnings for 1997.

Home-to-job spillover, our indicator of job performance, was defined as the frequency in the past 3 months that the employees' family or personal lives had kept them from getting their work done on time at the job, taking on extra work, doing as good a job at work as they could, and concentrating on their jobs, and drained them of the energy needed to do their jobs.

To test our hypotheses, we conducted multiple linear regression analyses on unweighted data. We controlled for basic employee demographics, then earnings and fringe benefits. Additional variables were entered in blocks—job demands, job quality, workplace support—and tested independently of one another, rather than hierarchically.

Explaining Job Burnout and Job-to-Home Spillover

The most important determinants of job burnout among working parents in our sample were having a job with high demands, having a job of poor quality, and being employed at a workplace that was perceived to be unsupportive. These three variables together explained one third (32%) of the variance in parents' job burnout, with each being about equal in importance. The same three characteristics were significantly related to the other measure of well-being— job-to-home spillover—to about the same extent (variance explained was 30%). In this case, job demands and workplace support were more important than job quality, which was still an important determinant. These findings lend support to our first two hypotheses. To test the third hypothesis, that a supportive workplace might buffer the impact of job demands on well-being, we controlled for workplace support before evaluating the effects of job demands on well-being variables. Although the relationship between demands and well-being became less strong, it was still significant, which supported our hypothesis.

Next, we evaluated our fourth hypothesis that some employed parents might be more susceptible than others to feelings of job burnout and negative job-to-home spillover. We addressed this question by determining whether characteristics of life off the job explained any additional variance in job burnout and negative spillover from job to home when job and workplace factors were held constant. Employed parents who more often experienced breakdowns in their regular child care arrangements, had lost time from work because of elder care responsibilities, and spent more time commuting to and from work were more likely than others to report job burnout (based on the significance of partial correlations). However, these characteristics of life off the job explained very little (2%) of the variation in job burnout when job demands and workplace support were held constant.

Employed parents who perceived the quality of their child care arrangements to be low, experienced more breakdowns in their regular child care arrangements, spent more time commuting, had less time for themselves, had lower household incomes, and had children under 13 years old were more likely than others to report negative spillover from their jobs into their personal lives (based on the significance of partial correlations). But taken together, these off-the-job factors explained only 3% of the variance in negative spillover from job to home when job demands and workplace support were held constant.

Explaining Home-to-Job Spillover

Following the conceptual model outlined in Figure 2.1, we examined how characteristics of life off the job, job burnout, and job-to-home spillover were related to home-to-job spillover, our indicator of job performance. Variables representing characteristics of life off the job were tested as a block independently of the block containing job burnout and job-to-home spillover, while controlling for employee demographics. Employee demographic covariates explained only 4% of the variance in home-to-job spillover, with spillover being somewhat greater among nonminority mothers than other parents.

Although life-off-the-job factors were expected to be powerful predictors of spillover from home to job, they accounted for only 7% of the variance in home-to-job spillover. Experiencing more frequent breakdowns in regular child care arrangements, being dissatisfied with the quality of current child care arrangements, and having more than one job were the only significant individual predictors of negative home-to-job spillover. In contrast, employed parents who experienced less job burnout and less negative spillover from job to home reported much less negative spillover from their personal and family lives to their jobs than others did. Our indexes of job burnout and job-to-home spillover explained 18% of the variance in spillover from home to job, more than 2½ times the amount explained by characteristics of life off the job.

Our findings, then, suggest a chain effect, in which excessive job demands lead to job burnout and job-to-home spillover, which, in turn, lead to home-to-job spillover, which then diminishes job performance. To some extent, supportive workplaces protect employed parents from the negative effects of highly demanding jobs, but supportive workplaces are not enough. Job demands and the demands of life off the job must be manageable for employed parents if they are to be able to preserve personal well-being and perform their jobs effectively.

CHANGES IN EMPLOYED
PARENTS' JOB CIRCUMSTANCES

Given the importance of job demands, job quality, and workplace support for the well-being and productivity of employed parents, our next set of analyses involved an investigation of how these factors have changed over time. To address this question, we analyzed data from the same three surveys described above. We report historical comparisons only when identical questions were asked in each survey.

Job Demands Today and in the Past

We found that most employed parents (86%) had full-time jobs with regular daytime schedules at their main or only job. However, fathers were more likely than mothers to work full-time (96% vs. 76%). Three fourths (74%) of mothers and fathers worked regular daytime schedules at their main or only job, while one fourth (26%) of mothers and fathers worked evenings, nights, rotating, split, or variable shifts. The proportion of employed parents working nonstandard shifts did not change between 1992 and 1997.

Employed fathers with children under 18 worked longer hours than employed mothers when looking at paid and unpaid hours at all jobs (50.9 vs. 41.4 hours per week). Fathers' total work time had increased 3.1 hours per week in the past 20 years, whereas mothers' time had increased more, by 5.2 hours.

In 1997, employed fathers spent an average of 3 nights away from home on business travel over the past 3 months, compared with only 1 night for mothers. These numbers had not changed since 1992. Among fathers in 1997, 21% were required to put in overtime with little or no notice once a week or more, compared with only 13% of mothers. Fewer fathers (14%), but a bigger proportion of mothers (25%), reported never having to work overtime with little or no notice.

Almost one third of parents spent time on a weekly basis doing work at home that was directly related to their main job. The proportion of parents bringing work home from the job once a week or more had increased by 11% since 1977, while the proportion never bringing work home from the job had decreased by 17%. This change may have been abetted by a shift toward new technologies, such as portable computers, home computers, home fax, and e-mail capability.

Job pressures had increased substantially over the past 20 years, as indicated on all three items used to measure this construct. More than two thirds (68%) of parents in 1997 agreed with the statement "My job requires that I work very fast," which was a 10% increase since 1977 (when 58% of workers agreed). Even more mothers and fathers (88%) agreed that "My job requires that I work very hard," up from 71% in 1977. The biggest change in employees' perceptions of job pressures related to time. In 1997, 62% of parents agreed that "I never seem to have enough time to get everything done on my job," whereas in 1977, 41% of parents thought this way.

Job Quality Today and in the Past

Most employed parents felt they had some measure of job autonomy. Compared with parents in 1977, mothers and fathers 20 years later reported more freedom to decide what they did on their jobs (73% vs. 57%), more responsibility for deciding how their jobs got done (86% vs. 78%), and more say in what happened on their jobs (72% vs. 62%).

Most employees also had jobs that provided learning opportunities. The proportion of mothers and fathers with jobs that required them to keep learning new things had increased by 7% since 1977, while the proportion with jobs that required them to be creative had increased by 14%. Parents in 1997 were also more likely to feel that their jobs allowed them to use their own skills and abilities—an increase of 15% from 1977. Most employed parents (91%) reported that their jobs were meaningful to them, which was an increase of 6% since 1977.

An increasing number of employed parents reported job insecurity. Almost 3 in 10 employed mothers and fathers (29%) thought it was somewhat or very likely that during the next couple of years they would lose their current job and have to look for another. Fathers were just as likely as mothers to feel this way. In contrast, only 15% of employed parents in 1977 thought it was somewhat or very likely they would lose their job in the next couple of years and have to find a new one with another employer (14% lower than in 1997).

Compensation and Fringe Benefits
Today and in the Past

Total household income had not changed significantly from 1977 to 1997. Expressed in 1997 dollars, it remained at $57,594 for employed parents over the 20-year period. The majority of parents had access to traditional fringe benefits. In decreasing order of frequency, these included personal health insurance coverage (reported by 86%), family health insurance coverage (84%), paid holidays (84%), paid vacation (83%), a pension or retirement plan (77%), and paid time off for personal illness (75%).

However, only a minority of mothers and fathers had access to dependent care benefits, including dependent care assistance plans (available to 31%), elder care information and referral services (23%), child care information and referral services (20%), financial assistance for purchasing child care services (13%), and on- or near-site child services (12%). Historical comparisons with the data from the 1992 survey could be made for only five benefits. Of these, only access to elder care information and referral services had improved over the past 5 years, up from 10% in 1992. Access to the other four types of benefits had not changed, which included personal health insurance coverage, family health insurance coverage, child care information and referral services, and employer-sponsored or near-site child care centers.

Supportive Workplaces Today and in the Past

In the 1997 survey, two fifths (43%) of employed mothers and fathers reported that they had traditional flextime; that is, they were able to choose, within some range of hours, when they began and ended their workdays. Only one in four had daily flextime, in which they could change daily schedules as needed. Almost two thirds (63%) of employed parents found it relatively easy to take time off during the workday to address family or personal matters. However, only half had been able to take a few days off from work to care for sick children without losing pay, forfeiting vacation time, or fabricating some excuse for missing work.

Almost all (94%) of mothers and fathers in companies of all sizes said that women were able to take maternity leave to recuperate from childbirth without jeopardizing their jobs, and 80% reported that men could also take some time off when they became fathers. The majority (60%) of mothers and fathers working part-time believed they could switch to full-time work if they wanted to, while far fewer parents (38%) who worked full-time said they could switch to part-time. More than one fourth (28%) of parents spent at least part of their regular workweek working at home, while another 7% said they would be allowed to do so if they wanted to.

Most parents felt that their immediate supervisors were quite supportive, with between 76% and 94% agreeing with nine statements describing various dimensions of supervisor support related to performance of the job and personal or family needs (see Table 2.1). Mothers and fathers were equally likely to believe that their supervisors were supportive. We found that, on six of the eight items, parents interviewed in 1997 viewed their supervisors as somewhat more supportive than did mothers and fathers interviewed 5 years earlier. Although most of the differences between 1997 and 1992 were small, taken as a whole they suggested a change in employees' perceptions that was driven by actual increases in supervisor support over the past 5 years. The most dramatic change was that more parents in 1997 (76%) than in 1992 (66%) felt comfortable bringing up personal and family issues with their supervisors. There was no change with respect to supervisors' accommodating parents' family or business matters or in supervisors' having realistic expectations of parents, perhaps because the vast majority of supervisors (90+%) were reported to be highly supportive in both years.

Two thirds of mothers and fathers believed that their workplace cultures were supportive, with no change over the 5-year interval. Most parents had positive relationships with coworkers. Ninety percent of mothers and fathers felt that they were a part of the group of people they worked with, and 89% looked forward to being with the people they worked with each day.

TABLE 2.1 Working Parents' Perceptions of Supervisor Support: National Changing Workforce Survey, 1997 ($N = 1,316$)

Supervisor Support Items	Percentage of Parents Agreeing
My supervisor keeps me informed of the things I need to know to do my job well.	87
My supervisor has expectations of my performance on the job that are realistic.	92
My supervisor recognizes when I do a good job.	88
My supervisor is supportive when I have a work problem.	91
My supervisor is fair and doesn't show favoritism in responding to employees' personal or family needs.	83

CHANGES IN PARENTS' TIME USE AND WORK ATTITUDES

Time Use

Given the fact that job demands have increased considerably over the past 20 years, we thought it was worthwhile to explore how families were managing, in terms of how they spent their time and how they felt about work. We examined how employed parents spent their time at home on workdays by asking respondents to estimate the amount of time they spent in an average weekday in three broadly defined activities: caring for and doing things with children, household chores, and personal activities.

Married mothers in 1997 spent significantly more time than married fathers doing things and caring for children on workdays (3.2 hours vs. 2.3 hours). Likewise, mothers spent significantly more time with their children than fathers did on days off work (8.3 vs. 6.4 hours). However, this gap between married mothers and fathers had narrowed considerably in 20 years. Although the amount of time mothers spent with children had not changed, fathers had significantly increased the amount of time they spent with children. Married mothers' time estimates for their partners did not differ significantly from the amount of time fathers themselves reported spending, giving us some confidence in these self-reported figures. Because mothers have managed to preserve their time with children despite working longer paid hours and fathers have increased their time with children, and families have fewer children today than they did 20 years ago, it appears that children are receiving somewhat more attention from their employed parents than was the case two decades ago.

Employed mothers also spent more time on household chores than fathers did. However, as with the care of children, there have been dramatic shifts over 20 years. The difference between mothers and fathers was much greater in 1977 (2.5 hours per workday) than it was in 1997 (0.9 hours per workday). The amount of time mothers spent on household chores on workdays had declined by 36 minutes per day, whereas fathers' time had increased by 1 hour per day.

The additional time fathers and mothers were spending in paid and unpaid work seemed to be taking a toll on the time parents engaged in their own free-time activities. On average, married fathers in 1997 reported they had 1.2 hours for themselves on workdays; mothers reported 18 minutes less. The amount of time married parents had for their own personal activities had declined significantly over the 20 years. On average, married fathers in 1997 had 54 fewer minutes for themselves on workdays than fathers did in 1977, while mothers had 42 fewer minutes for themselves on workdays in 1997 compared with mothers surveyed in 1977.

Work Attitudes

Our findings indicate that families have accommodated themselves to the increase in job demands, with mothers preserving their time with the children and fathers increasing theirs. Mothers have decreased the amount of time they spend on household chores, while fathers have made up some of the difference. Both parents have cut back on time for themselves. Will families continue to absorb future increases in job demands?

To explore this question, we looked at parents' desires, in terms of both work hours and job responsibility. We found that many mothers and fathers wanted to work less. When asked about the number of hours they preferred to work each week, employed mothers reported that they would like to work 30.6 hours a week on average (compared with the 41.4 hours they actually worked), and employed fathers preferred working 38.8 hours weekly (compared with the 50.9 hours they actually worked), a substantial difference of 10.7 hours for mothers and 12.1 hours for fathers. All together, almost two thirds (65%) of parents preferred to work fewer hours for pay. This is a significant increase from just 5 years ago. The percentage of fathers wanting to work fewer hours had climbed from 54% in 1992 to 67% in 1997, while for mothers it had increased from 47% in 1992 to 63% in 1997.

In addition, we found that fewer parents wanted to take on more job-related responsibilities in the future. In 1992, 51% of employed mothers reported wanting greater job responsibility; by 1997, only 41% did. Among fathers, 64% wanted greater responsibility in 1992, dropping to 52% in 1997.

CONCLUSION

Employed mothers and fathers in 1997 were working longer, faster, and harder on the job and at home than they did 20 years previously. In response to the increased pace and pressures at work, our findings indicate that families had made accommodations. While preserving the amount of time they spent with children, mothers decreased the amount of time they spent on household chores and cut down on their own personal activities. Fathers increased the amount of time they spent on children and household chores and also cut down on the time they spent on free-time activities. Workplaces were reported by parents to be slightly more supportive than they used to be, but employed parents of both sexes were feeling the squeeze. They wanted to work less paid hours and were not as interested as they were before in assuming more responsibility in their jobs. Perhaps parents will push workplaces to deal with the mounting job pressure or will opt out of spending long hours at work. The extent to which parents believe they can afford to take these actions remains to be seen.

In the meantime, however, the findings from the 1997 National Study of the Changing Workforce have important implications for employers. Rather than viewing issues of work and family as a win-lose proposition, there is the potential for a win-win scenario. Our results suggest that employers who provide better-quality jobs, maintain supportive workplaces, and keep job demands at a reasonable level will retain employees who are more effective workers, people, and parents. These employers will clearly have a competitive edge over other employers in the near future.

REFERENCES

Barnett, R. (1997, September). *The shape of things to come: A new view of work/life for the next century.* Paper presented at the 1997 Work/Family Congress, New York.

Barnett, R., & Baruch, G. (1985). Women's involvement in multiple roles and psychological distress. *Journal of Personality and Social Psychology, 49,* 135-145.

Barnett, R., & Marshall, N. (1991). The relationship between women's work and family roles and their subjective well-being and psychological distress. In M. Frankenhaeuser, V. Lundberg, & M. Chesney (Eds.), *Women, work, and health: Stress and opportunities* (pp. 111-136). New York: Plenum.

Barnett, R., & Marshall, N. (1992). Worker and mother roles, spillover effects, and psychological distress. *Women & Health, 18,* 9-40.

Baruch, G., & Barnett, R. (1987). Role quality and psychological well-being. In F. Crosby (Ed.), *Spouse, parent, worker* (pp. 111-135). New Haven, CT: Yale University Press.

Bohen, H., & Viveros-Long, A. (1981). *Balancing jobs and family life: Do flexible work schedules help?* Philadelphia: Temple University Press.

Bond, J., Galinsky, E., & Swanberg, J. (1998). *The 1997 national study of the changing workforce.* New York: Families and Work Institute.

Burke, R., Weir, T., & DuWors, R. (1979). Type A behavior of administrators and wives' reports of marital satisfaction and well-being. *Journal of Applied Psychology, 64,* 57-65.

Crouter, A. (1984). Spillover from family to work: The neglected side of the work-family interface. *Human Relations, 37,* 425-442.

Greenberger, E., Goldberg, W., Hamill, S., O'Neil, R., & Payne, C. (1989). Contributions of a supportive work environment to parents' well-being and orientation to work. *American Journal of Community Psychology, 17,* 755-783.

Greenberger, E., O'Neil, R., & Nagel, S. (1994). Linking workplace and homeplace: Relations between the nature of adults' work and their parenting behaviors. *Developmental Psychology, 30,* 990-1002.

Howes, C., Sakai, L, Shinn, M., Phillips, D., Galinsky, E., & Whitebook, M. (1995). Race, social class, and maternal working conditions as influences on children's behavior in child care. *Journal of Applied Developmental Psychology, 16,* 107-124.

Hughes, D., & Galinsky, E. (1988). Balancing work and family life: Research and corporate application. In A. Gottfried (Ed.), *Maternal employment and children's development: Longitudinal research* (pp. 233-268). New York: Plenum.

Hughes, D., Galinsky, E., & Morris, A. (1992). The effects of job characteristics on marital quality: Specifying linking mechanisms. *Journal of Marriage and Family, 54,* 31-42.

Keith, P., & Schafer, R. (1980). Role strain and depression in two-job families. *Family Relations, 29,* 483-488.

Kohn, M. (1969). *Class and conformity: A study in values.* Homewood, IL: Dorsey Press.

Kohn, M., & Schooler, C. (1973). Occupational experience and psychological functioning: An assessment of reciprocal effects. *American Sociological Review, 38,* 97-118.

Lerner, J., & Galambos, N. (1985). Mother role satisfaction, mother-child interaction, and child temperament: A process model. *Developmental Psychology, 21,* 1157-1164.

Marks, S. (1977). Multiple roles and role strain: Some notes on human energy, time, and commitment. *American Sociological Review, 43,* 921-936.

Menaghan, E., & Parcel, T. (1990). Parental employment and family life: Research in the 1980's. *Journal of Marriage and the Family, 52,* 1079-1098.

O'Neil, R. (1992). *Maternal work experiences, psychological well-being, and achievement-fostering parents.* Unpublished manuscript, University of California, Los Angeles.

Piotrkowski, C., & Crits-Cristoph, P. (1982). Women's jobs and family adjustment. In J. Aldous (Ed.), *Two paychecks: Life in dual-earner families* (pp. 105-127). Beverly Hills, CA: Sage.

Piotrkowski, C., & Katz, M. (1983). Work experience and family relations among working-class and lower-middle-class families. *Research in the Interweave of Social Roles: Jobs and Families, 3,* 187-200.

Repetti, R. (1987). Individual and common components of the social environment at work and psychological well-being. *Journal of Personality and Social Psychology, 52,* 710-720.

Repetti, R. (1989). Effects of daily workload on subsequent behavior during marital interaction: The roles of social withdrawal and spouse support. *Journal of Personality and Social Psychology, 57,* 651-659.

Repetti, R., & Cosmas, K. (1991). The quality of the social environment at work and job satisfaction. *Journal of Applied Psychology, 21,* 840-854.

Voydanoff, P. (1988). Work role characteristics, family structure demands, and work/family conflict. *Journal of Marriage and the Family, 50,* 749-761.

3

Mothers and Fathers in the Workplace

The United Kingdom

JULIA BRANNEN

Since the 1960s, there has been a trend in the United Kingdom toward the greater integration of women into the workforce (Martin & Roberts, 1984). The increasing labour market participation of women, of mothers in particular, constitutes a change in time management, of both everyday time and life-course time. By the end of the 1970s, employment among mothers of children under 5 years was still at a very low level, with the great majority of women leaving the labour market and returning to part-time work once their children were at school (Martin & Roberts, 1984). This situation stands in marked contrast to some European countries where the employment rates of mothers of young children took off in the 1970s. In the United Kingdom, toward the end of the 1980s, this sequential pattern by which women organised their employment around childbirth and child rearing began to give way to a new set of strategies, with women interweaving employment between the births of their children. In general, over the past 20 years, mothers' labour market participation has been marked by several features: (a) a rather slow but rising level of full-time

AUTHOR'S NOTE: I wish to acknowledge the contribution made by Peter Moss, who was also responsible for the project Parental Employment Trends 1984-1994, carried out for the Department of Education and Employment, on which the chapter draws, and the work of Charlie Owen and Chris Wale, who were responsible for the statistical analysis.

EDITORS' NOTE: The author's use of British spellings has been retained.

employed mothers in *continuous* employment, returning to the same, largely higher-status jobs following maternity leave; (b) a heavy preponderance of mothers working *short part-time* hours in lower-status jobs that they fit around the school day; and (c) an increasing level of *unemployment* among lone mothers who are reliant on state benefits and are prevented from working part-time because of social security rules about earnings levels and prevented from full-time employment because of lack of child care.

In contrast, fathers' employment has been much less of a focus. Fathers have tended to have higher employment rates than other men. But by the end of the 1980s, their employment and working time strategies also showed signs of diversification. Full-time jobs for life supplemented by overtime and designed to bring in a "family" or "breadwinner" wage were beginning to disappear. Those still in the core labour force were working longer hours as the fear of job insecurity took hold. As manual work in the old manufacturing industries declined, many men became economically inactive, especially those in their 50s. At the same time, because of the decline in unskilled manual work and the resulting long-term unemployment, many younger men were not entering into family commitments (albeit some were technically fathers), whereas other men were financially responsible for two sets of family obligations, resulting from first and second marriages.

Increasingly, these changes have become significant at a household level, with a concentration of mothers and fathers in higher-status nonmanual jobs increasing their investment in employment by working longer hours and, in the case of fathers, longer full-time hours (i.e., overtime). Mothers at this occupational level tend to have partners who work in similar types of employment. This growing group of "work rich" households contrasts with "work poor" households in which both mothers and fathers are outside the labour market and with households in which lone mothers are unemployed (Brannen, Moss, Owen, & Wale, 1997; Gregg & Wadsworth, 1995).

The purpose of this chapter is to review trends in mothers' and fathers' participation in the U.K. labour market as well as mothers' and fathers' participation in household and caring work. It also covers the impact of parents' combining employment and family obligations.

MOTHERS AND FATHERS IN THE LABOUR MARKET, 1984-1994

Patterns of Employment

This chapter draws on recent secondary analysis of the Labour Force Survey (LFS) carried out with colleagues at Thomas Coram Research Unit (Brannen et al., 1997). The LFS is a national survey based on a sample of 60,000 households that has been carried out in England, Scotland, and Wales annually and, since 1991, quarterly. The analysis concentrates on men and women of working age (16-59 years for women and 16-64 for men). It compares women and men who are parents of at least one child still in full-time education (up to 18 years of age) who is resident in the household, and it contrasts the situation of these mothers and fathers with other men and women of working age. One particular contribution of the study was to refine the traditional analysis of working hours to take account of significant differences in the changing distribution of employment time; it distinguished between shorter and longer part-time employment (the former fewer than 16 hours per week and the latter 16-30 hours per week) and between shorter and longer full-time hours (30-40 hours and more than 40 hours, respectively).

This analysis indicates that the trends in mothers' and fathers' employment outlined above have continued into the 1990s. Evidence from this study and from studies of women returning to work soon after childbirth (McRae, 1991) point to a substantial change occurring in the 1980s and, more specifically, since the mid-1980s. Between 1984 and 1994, mothers' employment increased dramatically (from 49% to 59%), at twice the rate for other women; in contrast, fathers' employment fell slightly over the period. The strongest growth occurred in mothers' full-time employment and among women with children under 5 years of age, in which employment almost doubled from 27% to 45%. The latter increase is reflected in growing continuity in employment, with women resuming their former work within the statutory maternity leave period (of approximately 7 months).

Although the gap between mothers' and fathers' employment has been narrowing in the decade 1984 to 1994, mothers' integration into the labour market is much less than for fathers and other men. The difference is even more marked if working hours are taken into account. Fathers' volume of employment (defined as the total number of hours worked per week by all employed fathers) is more than double mothers' volume of employment. The continuing greater impact of children on mothers' employment patterns than on fathers' is also apparent if a *life-course perspective* is adopted and age-controlled comparisons are made. Among younger age groups of women, employment patterns diverge between women with and without children because of the impact of motherhood. By contrast, in the middle years, women's employment converges as the children of those who are mothers move into independence. (It is important to note that the number of mothers in the lowest age group—16 to 24 years—fell over the decade as a result of a trend toward later childbearing.) Among men, there is no such divergence, with fathers showing higher employment than men in general; the impact of children on their employment over the life course is constant and has changed little between 1984 and 1994.

Mothers' employment also continued to be strongly differentiated from fathers' in terms of their positions on the occupational hierarchy. Between 1984 and 1994, both mothers and fathers showed a marked occupational shift toward higher-status jobs, with the shift being more marked for mothers than for fathers; women with children under 5 years showed the fastest growth in higher-status occupations. Even so, in 1994, mothers' and fathers' *occupational profiles* were still very different. Employed fathers were twice as likely as employed mothers to be in professional and managerial occupations, while the position was reversed for semiskilled and unskilled manual occupations. More-over, women, especially those with a dependent child, were reported as twice as likely as men to be located in jobs without a fixed contract, many of which are part-time and lower status (Dex & McCulloch, 1995). While temporary work was more common among employed women than men, self-employment and shift work were much more concentrated among employed men.

Determinants of Employment

Our analysis suggests that not all mothers have similar chances of being integrated into the labour market. The characteristics that differentiate mothers' employment chances are not randomly distributed, as other research has also shown (Davies & Joshi, 1997; Dex, Joshi, & McCran, 1996; Harrop & Moss, 1995).

One of the most significant factors related to mothers' employment chances is *household composition*. Between 1984 and 1994, the employment situation of lone mothers deteriorated both in absolute terms and in relation to mothers living with male partners. While the employment rate for mothers with partners increased from a half to nearly two thirds, the employment rate for lone mothers fell back to just under two fifths.

A second characteristic that differentiates the employment chances of mothers is the *age of the youngest child*. Women with children under 5 years have substantially lower employment rates than other mothers. However, as already noted, the period 1984 to 1994 witnessed rapid increases in employment among mothers of young children and at a faster rate than for other mothers. In particular, full-time employment more than doubled among mothers of pre-school children. As already discussed, this increase in the employment of mothers with young children reflects the growth in use of maternity leave occurring over the 1980s and a proportionately greater increase in full-time compared with part-time working (see also McRae, 1991). Although mothers of three or more children are significantly less likely to be employed than mothers of one or two children, over the decade, the rate of employment change (across all employment categories) was much the same for mothers regardless of number of children.

A third characteristic is *educational qualifications*. The higher the educational qualifications, the more likely a mother is to be employed. Over the decade, levels of educational qualifications improved among women (see also Cortie, Laurie, & Dex, 1995; Dex et al., 1996), including women with dependent children. Employment rates increased fastest among the most highly qualified mothers and actually fell among the diminishing group of mothers with no educational qualifications. These changes were most apparent among mothers with a child under 5 years. Over the decade, the employment rate of college-educated mothers with a child of this age rose from just over two fifths to nearly three quarters, while the employment rate for mothers without a college degree hardly changed from just under a quarter. For women with some higher education, the highest rate of employment growth was for longer full-time hours, especially among those with a degree.

A fourth feature distinguishing mothers' employment chances relates to *ethnic background* (see also Sly, 1996). The highest levels of employment and the fastest growth in employment, especially full-time employment, occurred among white mothers, in contrast to low or negative growth rates among other ethnic groups.

Fifth, mothers' employment status is closely associated with *partners' employment and occupational status.* A mother is most likely to be employed if her partner is also employed. Only a quarter of mothers with an unemployed partner and only a third of mothers with an economically inactive partner were in the labour market; among mothers with a full-time employed partner, more than two thirds were in the labour force. Employment rates increased most over the decade among mothers whose partners were employed in full-time jobs; women with an economically inactive partner recorded no change in their level of employment. Overall, employment grew faster among mothers whose partners were in nonmanual employment than among mothers whose partners were in manual jobs.

The chances of employment also vary among fathers, and along very similar parameters to mothers. For example, in 1994, fathers were more likely to be employed if they were white, had only one or two children, had higher-education qualifications, lived in a two-parent household, and had an employed partner. Moreover, between 1984 and 1994, the differentiation increased in a number of cases. Most obvious, the employment position of lone fathers deteriorated even more than for lone mothers.

Extent of Employment

In terms of time, the working hours of both mothers and fathers have increased. There is evidence of a "ratchet" effect. Among mothers, we find rising rates of longer-hours part-time employment and of both shorter- and longer-hours full-time employment, but there is no change in the level of shorter-hours part-time employment. Short part-time employment is, as earlier noted, a typical characteristic of mothers' employment in Britain (in contrast with other European countries) and already at a high rate. The substantial increase in the average working hours of employed mothers is more marked than for other employed women. Again, the increase has been strongest for employed women with a child under 5 years. An average rise of 4 hours per week was recorded for these mothers, reflecting the particularly strong growth of full-time working in this group.

For fathers, the picture is more complex: a slight growth in part-time work, a fall in shorter-hours full-time work, and a slight rise in longer-hours full-time work, producing a modest overall increase in average weekly working hours, especially among those already working longer hours. Although the increase in fathers' hours was substantially less than for mothers' hours, the fact that it occurred at all is significant. On average, U.K. fathers work the longest hours of any fathers in the European Union, about 47 hours a week (this includes overtime and second jobs but takes no account of travel-to-work time; Brannen et al., 1997). But there is no sign that fathers are reducing their long working hours in response to the increased employment and working hours of mothers. Rather, the evidence from this study is that fathers overall made no adjustment; in 1994, they were working as long as, if not longer than, ever. This picture of fathers working long hours is confirmed by other studies (Ferri & Smith, 1996), with long hours particularly characteristic of fathers in managerial occupations. The net effect of this trend has been an increase in working hours at the household level as well as the individual level, to be discussed later.

Despite the considerable increase in full-time employment among women with children and the overall increase in the working hours of employed mothers between 1984 and 1994, it is clear that the *working hours' profiles* of mothers and fathers continue to differ greatly. In 1994, more than half of all fathers worked longer full-time hours, compared with fewer than one in ten mothers. Overall, employed fathers worked 20 hours a week more than employed mothers.

The hours that parents work vary by occupational group to a much greater extent among mothers than among fathers. Fathers working in professional and managerial jobs are more likely to work longer full-time hours than those in lower-status occupational groups. However, among mothers, part-time employment is concentrated in lower-status occupational groups, whereas mothers in professional and managerial jobs are much more likely to work full-time, both shorter and longer hours. Nearly three out of every five mothers employed in professional and managerial occupations work full-time, compared with just over a quarter of mothers employed in semiskilled manual work and one in ten mothers employed in unskilled manual work. The differentials are even greater if the comparison is restricted to longer-hours full-time work. The shift of both mothers and fathers into higher-status occupations is therefore contributing to an intensification of employment defined in terms of weekly working hours.

Consequences of Employment

The differential integration of mothers into the labour market is having major ramifications at the *household* level, concerning families' socioeconomic status. Social and economic inequalities arising from the occupations of male heads of households have shown themselves to be remarkably stable over time and the most significant discriminating factor in the United Kingdom in determining patterns of health (Smith, Bartley, & Blane, 1990; Whitehead, 1987) and educational achievement and political partisanship (Goldthorpe & Marshall, 1992). Nonetheless, mothers' employment is likely to exacerbate these inequalities. This is because household employment patterns cluster. As indicated, employed fathers are much more likely to have employed partners, just as nonemployed fathers are much more likely to have nonemployed partners. Indeed, according to the principle of "like attracting like," there is growing evidence of economic polarisation occurring between households.

By 1994, the dual-breadwinner family had become the norm among two-parent households with children; only one third consisted of single-breadwinner households. The great majority of two-parent households had an earner who was employed full-time, but it was more common for one parent to work part-time while one worked full-time than it was for both to work full-time. In contrast, the economic situation of lone parents is much more negative. Most lone parents do not have an additional earner contributing to their income, and lone parents are as likely to work part-time as they are full-time.

The polarisation of household employment is complicated by the distribution of working hours, which is related not only to the presence and number of household earners but also to the occupational and educational status of parents. Working hours, like employment itself, are not equally distributed across families. At one end of the household spectrum, there is a growing number of highly educated couples in which the woman is continuously employed and both partners work full-time, often for long hours, in jobs that reward them with high status and high income. At the other end of the household spectrum, there is also a growing number of "work poor" families, mostly headed by lone mothers who are not employed or have only a part-time job; they are dependent on state benefits and bring up their children on low incomes. In between, there are two groups of households: (a) the falling number of those with one full-time earner (single- and two-parent households) and (b) the slowly increasing number of households with one partner employed full-time and the other employed part-time.

THE DISTRIBUTION OF DOMESTIC
AND CHILD CARE OBLIGATIONS
AMONG MOTHERS AND FATHERS

Changing patterns of mothers' and fathers' employment are likely to affect household and caring work. This section reviews patterns of sharing domestic work in the United Kingdom.

Domestic Work

The increase in the number of households with young children and both parents in full-time employment has so far not led to a renegotiation of domestic roles between mothers and fathers in the United Kingdom (Brannen & Moss, 1991; Gregson & Lowe, 1994). The lengthening of working hours by both parents seems more likely to instead lead to households' increased hiring of domestic help (e.g., nannies and house cleaners). As other research has shown, such "bought in services" typically replace mothers' tasks—in other words, stereotypical female work (Gregson & Lowe, 1994). The net result of a trend toward the buying in of services is the creation of new jobs. These jobs mainly go to women and contribute to the growing differentiation in women's employment, with one group of high-status, employed mothers relying on the services of a second group of women in lower-status, poorly paid, and insecure employment. This trend may regenerate the servant classes, involving the displacement of domestic work from mothers to third parties whose labour is paid at low rates, often with no sick or holiday pay.

Although dual-earner households may transfer domestic work and caring to other women outside the household, not all such work can be transferred. Considerable gaps still remain in the relative contributions of women and men to unpaid work even when both are in full-time work. Recent evidence indicates that the largest gap is among couples with young children, with women spending 77 hours per week and men 68 hours in paid and unpaid work. Although these full-time employed women spent less time on paid work than men, this was more than compensated for by their greater amount of hours in unpaid work (Koudra, Church, & Murgatroyd, 1996).

Although domestic tasks may not be directly transferred within couples, there may be some renegotiation of time. Time-budget evidence from the mid-1970s to mid-1980s suggests that time spent in household work is declining for married women, whereas for men it has increased significantly, albeit from a very low base (Gershuny & Jones, 1987). Moreover, linking diary with work history data provides evidence that domestic practices have changed gradually following wives' entry into paid work (Gershuny, Godwin, & Jones, 1994). Although men may be contributing more in terms of time, gender stereotyping of tasks persists (Warde & Hetherington, 1993), and men's contribution remains small (Brannen, Moss, Poland, & Meszaros, 1994).

At the opposite end of the household spectrum from dual-breadwinner families are those families in which fathers are unemployed, a pattern typically associated with mothers' nonemployment. One study suggests that male unemployment does not lead to a renegotiation of the domestic workload (Morris, 1993), although a study of unemployed fathers with young children indicates a more varied picture (Wheelock, 1990). However, both studies agree that unemployed men's involvement in domestic work increases when women take on the breadwinner role.

Child Care

Although time-budget research suggests an increase in fathers' involvement in child care between the 1960s and 1980s (Gershuny & Jones, 1987), other evidence suggests that men are involved in the more pleasurable tasks, such as playing with children and taking them out (Wheelock, 1990). Brannen and Moss's longitudinal study of households with two full-time parents and young children showed that on every indicator of predictable and unpredictable child care demands—for example, taking time off when children were ill or making child care arrangements—mothers did more than fathers. Similarly, in relation to time spent in child care, mothers spent more time with children, including being the parent in sole charge (Brannen & Moss, 1991). The extent to which this is changing is presently unclear. What is clear is that men's increased involvement in child care tends to be confined to task performance rather than increased responsibility for children's well-being. Mothers remain the managers, organisers, and planners of domestic and caring work (Brannen et al., 1994).

Various explanations have been offered for the slow change in men's involvement in household and caring work. Some studies blame normative prescriptions for traditional motherhood and fatherhood, while others emphasise how men have more power in the family because they have relatively greater access to the resources of greater occupational status and earning power (Coverman, 1985). Less attention has been paid to how gender identities are constructed within partnerships, an issue that research is beginning to address (Brannen & Moss, 1991; Hochschild, 1989). The partnership context would seem to be important because empirical evidence suggests that women do not appear to express a great deal of dissatisfaction when men do not contribute in the home. Even though women say that men ought to contribute, dissatisfaction with their own household arrangement is seldom expressed. Brannen and Moss (1991) found that women resort to a number of strategies to avoid conflict with partners and to avoid personally confronting the fact that their households are not as egalitarian as they would like.

THE EFFECTS OF COMBINING
EMPLOYMENT AND FAMILY

In the absence of evidence indicating other than a marginal role for fathers in the care of their children and in domestic work, and given the lack of public child care provision in the United Kingdom, employed mothers resort to individual strategies for managing employment and domestic and caring obligations. This individualistic form of "coping" needs to be interpreted in the context of the fact that the responsibility for the dual-earner lifestyle and for children has rested largely with mothers and has been seen by them to be their responsibility.

At a practical level, mothers have managed and "juggled" time by cutting down on social activities, getting up early, cutting corners in housework, reorganising their schedules, and creating "quality time" for their children (Brannen & Moss, 1988; Lewis & Cooper, 1988; Sharpe, 1984; Yeandle, 1984). Mothers also have coped by adjusting their "mental set," which may be conceptualised as a cognitive compartmentalisation of the two worlds of work and home. For example, Brannen and Moss (1988) examined new mothers' resumption of employment following maternity leave and documented mothers' feelings of loss during their initial separation from their children. In the early days back at work, most mothers felt bereft and anxious. However, once they realised that their children were not unhappy with their caregivers, they soon adjusted and came to accept their negative feelings, although feelings of guilt did recur. Other studies of employed mothers' dilemmas suggest that feelings of guilt about working may result in mothers' overcompensating by spending more time with their children and excluding their partners (Cooper & Lewis, 1993).

In addition, there is a large amount of literature on the psychological outcomes for mothers, such as stress and role strain, which are associated with combining employment and family life (see Lewis & Cooper, 1988, for an overview). Given the range of possible outcomes, it is not surprising that the evidence is mixed. For example, while those with a heavy workload, notably mothers employed full-time, may experience some negative effects (e.g., tiredness), they may escape other outcomes such as boredom, loneliness, and low self-esteem (for reviews, see Brannen & Moss, 1991; Brannen et al., 1994). The evidence on mothers' mental health suggests that employment is only a contributory mediator of the negative aspects of domestic roles. Similarly, the relationship between women's employment and their physical health is mediated rather than determined by features of their employment situation and by the nature of their domestic and child care responsibilities. The literature on outcomes for fathers is significantly absent.

A major preoccupation in the literature and in social policy has been with the possible adverse effects of mothers' employment on young children. Most of the evidence that indicates negative effects, especially of early entry into day care on child development outcomes, is from the United States (see McGurk, Caplan, Hennessy, & Moss, 1993, for a review of the British and U.S. literature). The only existing longitudinal British study found few differences between children admitted early to day care and a comparison group of children cared for at home by parents (Melhuish, 1991). Factors related to day care itself, rather than to mothers' employment, might be significant for children's development.

By contrast, the effects on children of fathers' employment or unemployment have received little attention. Given the fact that nearly one in three children in the United Kingdom is now living in a household with no parent in employment (Department of Social Security, 1996) and that the proportion of families with children living in poverty has grown relative to other groups, this is a significant oversight. Similarly, the effects and implications of parental employment, either of mothers or fathers, on older children have received little attention, although the issue of the educational consequences of maternal employment has been a recent topic of debate in the media.

CONCLUSION

In this chapter, I have discussed the main trends in the employment of parents who have dependent children in the United Kingdom. These include the increasing integration of mothers of young children into the labour market, the increasing differentiation of employment chances of mothers and fathers, and a growing polarisation between "work rich" families and "work poor" families, the latter caused by the growth of nonemployed lone mothers.

Among families in which parents are employed, dual-earner lifestyles have become the norm, especially the middle course of the male breadwinner and wife employed part-time, and the two full-time earner family is growing rapidly. By contrast, the traditional pattern of male breadwinner and wife at home is in decline.

Despite the growth in numbers of mothers in the labour market, particularly those with young children, we have yet to witness any major change in the ways in which employment and family obligations are managed in the United Kingdom. No public support has been provided for employed parents and their children. Families that adopt the middle course of mother employed part-time and father full-time manage by creating a patchwork of largely informal support. In households with two full-time earners, fathers' investment in employment is high (typically working long hours). Mothers in these households typically retain the main responsibility for child care and domestic work and frequently replace their own time and labour with "bought in" services. In general, fathers in these families are more involved with and concerned about their children, in comparison with fathers in other types of families.

However, the dual-earner lifestyle appears to be increasing rather than diminishing fathers' involvement in employment, because they are spending longer hours in the workplace. One explanation for this lies in the development of the labour market, especially the climate of increasing job insecurity; another concerns normative notions of maternal care and responsibility that remain powerful and pervasive. This situation is reinforced by the fact that, in Britain, the number and proportion of lone-mother households is increasing, although there is considerable movement between the statuses of couple and single parenthood.

This chapter has concentrated on that part of the life course in which caring obligations are heaviest and the need for support is greatest, namely, when children are most dependent on their parents. As discussed, this is the period in which British mothers were traditionally least likely to be in the labour market and in which the current growth in employment is greatest.

The management of employment and family life obligations is, however, also affected by broader trends in employment. Employment careers are increasingly subject to a process of "condensation"; that is, they are compressed into a smaller proportion of the life course. The time spent in education and training has been extended, accompanied by later entry into the labour market. At the upper end of the life course, people tend to reduce their involvement in employment starting around age 55, which then lengthens the stage of retirement, especially as people live longer (Office for National Statistics, 1996).

Just as employment begins later in the life course, so does parenthood. Moreover, parenthood not only occurs later but lasts longer because young people are encouraged to remain in full-time education and continue to be financially dependent on their parents. As a consequence of these employment and life-course trends, the management of employment and family life obligations increasingly becomes an issue for the *middle* generation. This generation is also likely to have responsibility for older age groups at the same time that they are responsible for children and nonemployed young people. This "sandwich" generation, since it is most likely to be employed, is also the major contributor through tax and insurance to public welfare provision and pensions of the older generations. In short, the peak demands of employment and support for more dependent members of society increasingly coincide within the same period of the life course. Attention to how individuals are able to manage these peak demands is of importance not only to the individuals themselves but to children, employers, and policymakers.

REFERENCES

Brannen, J., & Moss, P. (1988). *New mothers at work: Employment and child care.* London: Unwin Hyman.

Brannen, J., & Moss, P. (1991). *Managing mothers: Dual earner households after maternity leave.* London: Unwin Hyman.

Brannen, J., Moss, P., Owen, C., & Wale, C. (1997). *Mothers, fathers, and employment: Parents and the labour market 1984-1994.* Sheffield, UK: Department for Education and Employment.

Brannen, J., Moss, P., Poland, G., & Meszaros, G. (1994). *Employment and family life: A review of research in the UK, 1980-94* (Research Series No. 41). London: Employment Department.

Cooper, C. L., & Lewis, S. (1993). *The workplace revolution.* London: Kogan Page.

Cortie, L., Laurie, H., & Dex, S. (1995). *Highly qualified women* (Research Series No. 50). London: Employment Department.

Coverman, S. (1985). Explaining husband's participation in domestic labour. *Sociological Quarterly, 26,* 81-97.

Davies, H., & Joshi, H. (1997). *Gender and income inequality in the UK 1968-1990: The feminisation of earning or of poverty?* London: Birkbeck College, Department of Economics, and City University.

Department of Social Security. (1996). *Households below average income: A statistical analysis 1979-1993.* London: Her Majesty's Stationery Office.

Dex, S., Joshi, H., & McCran, S. (1996). A widening gulf among Britain's mothers. *Oxford Review of Economic Policy, 12*(1), 65-75.

Dex, S., & McCulloch, A. (1995). *Flexible employment in Britain: A statistical analysis.* Manchester, UK: Equal Opportunities Commission.

Ferri, E., & Smith, K. (1996). *Parenting in the 1990s.* London: Family Policy Studies Centre.

Gershuny, J., Godwin, M., & Jones, S. (1994). The domestic labour revolution: A process of lagged adaptation? In M. Anderson, F. Bechofer, & J. Gershuny (Eds.), *The social and political economy of the household* (pp. 151-198). Oxford, UK: Oxford University Press.

Gershuny, J., & Jones, S. (1987). The changing work/leisure balance in Britain 1961-84. *Sociological Review Monograph, 33,* 9-50.

Goldthorpe, J., & Marshall, G. (1992). The promising future of class analysis: A response to recent critiques. *Sociology, 26,* 381-401.

Gregg, P., & Wadsworth, J. (1995). Gender, households, and access to employment. In J. Humphries & J. Rubery (Eds.), *The economics of equal opportunities.* Manchester, UK: Equal Opportunities Commission.

Gregson, N., & Lowe, M. (1994). Waged domestic labour and the renegotiation of the domestic division of labour within dual earner households. *Sociology, 28,*(1), 55-78.

Harrop, A., & Moss, P. (1995). Trends in parental employment. *Work, Employment, and Society, 9*(3), 421-444.

Hochschild, A. (1989). *The second shift: Working parents and the revolution at home.* Berkeley: University of California Press.

Koudra, M., Church, J., & Murgatroyd, L. (1996, Spring Issue B). Where have all the hours gone? Measuring time use in the UK. *Statistical News, 35,* 34-39.

Lewis, S., & Cooper, C. (1988). Stress in dual earner families. *Women and Work, 3,* 139-168.

Martin, J., & Roberts, C. (1984). *Women and employment: A lifetime perspective.* London: Her Majesty's Stationery Office.

McGurk, H., Caplan, M., Hennessy, E., & Moss, P. (1993). Controversy, theory, and social context in contemporary daycare research. *Journal of Child Psychology and Psychiatry, 34,* 3-23.

McRae, S. (1991). *Maternity rights in Britain: The PSI Report on the experience of women and employers.* London: Policy Studies Institute.

Melhuish, E. (1991). Research in daycare in Britain. In P. Moss & E. Melhuish (Eds.), *Current issues in daycare for young children.* London: Her Majesty's Stationery Office.

Morris, L. (1993). Domestic labour and employment status among married couples: A case study in Hartlepool. *Capital and Class, 49,* 37-52.

Office for National Statistics. (1996). *Population Trends, 84,* 47.

Sharpe, S. (1984). *Double identity: The lives of working mothers.* Harmondsworth, UK: Penguin.

Sly, F. (1996). Ethnic minority participation in the labour market: Trends from the Labour Force Survey 1984-1995. *Labour Market Trends, 104*(6), 259-270.

Smith, G., Bartley, M., & Blane, D. (1990). The Black Report on socio-economic inequalities in health 10 years on. *British Medical Journal, 301,* 373-377.

Warde, A., & Hetherington, K. (1993). A changing domestic division of labour? Issues of measurement and interpretation. *Work, Employment, and Society, 7,* 23-45.

Wheelock, J. (1990). *Husbands at home: The domestic economy in a post-industrial society.* London: Routledge.

Whitehead, M. (1987). *The health divide: Inequalities in health in the 1980s.* London: Health Education Council.

Yeandle, S. (1984). *Women's working lives: Patterns and strategies.* London: Tavistock.

4

Conflicting Commitments

Working Mothers and Fathers in Australia

HELEN GLEZER

ILENE WOLCOTT

As in other industrialised countries, Australian parents are confronting rapidly changing patterns of paid work opportunities and work time arrangements, as well as ways of combining work with family caregiving responsibilities. This chapter describes Australian mothers' and fathers' participation in the labour force. It then discusses the effects of family life on work, the effects of employment on family life, the division of labour regarding household labour, and parents' attitudes toward work and family. Finally, we consider Australians' progress toward adopting the dual-breadwinner model of family life.

WOMEN'S AND MEN'S LABOUR FORCE PARTICIPATION

In May 1998, women made up 43% of the Australian labour force. A comparison of men's and women's labour force participation rates between the 1960s and 1990s illustrates a pattern of convergence, with men's workforce participa-

---

EDITORS' NOTE: The authors' use of British spellings has been retained.

tion decreasing and women's workforce participation increasing. The overall labour force participation rate of all women increased from 36% in 1966 to 54% in 1998. Over this same time period, men's labour force participation rate decreased from 84% to 73%. The labour force participation rate for married women ages 25 to 34 (the early childbearing and child-rearing years) was 66% in 1998, which had more than doubled since 1966, when it was only 30% (Australian Bureau of Statistics [ABS], 1994, 1998a).

Although growing numbers of Australian women are in the labour force, they tend to be found in different jobs than men. More than three fourths of clerks and two thirds of salespersons and personal service workers were women in 1997. More than 88% of labourers and related workers and 90% of tradespersons were men. Although men and women were more equally represented in professional and semiprofessional categories, only 25% of managers and administrators were women (ABS, 1997). Decision making in families about paid work and family obligations may be influenced by these sex differences in earning potential and occupational opportunities. The degree of occupational segregation in Australia is shown in Table 4.1.

More than two fifths (43%) of women who were employed in May 1998 worked part-time, compared with only 12% of employed men (ABS, 1998a). During the main childbearing and child-rearing years, ages 25 to 44, a slightly higher percentage (48%) of employed women worked part-time. Almost three fourths (73%) of all part-time workers were female. Part-time workers tended to work what are sometimes called "short" hours; the average weekly work hours worked by all part-time workers in May 1998 was 15. While half of all Australian mothers worked part-time, half of all fathers regularly worked overtime (i.e., more than 40 hours) in 1998 (compared with one third of mothers; ABS, 1998b). Overall, fathers worked an average of 44 paid hours a week, compared with mothers' average of 38 (ABS, 1997).

When women work part-time, they tend to suffer from irregular work schedules, lower wages, and fewer training opportunities (Deery & Mahony, 1993; Jackson, 1996; Junor, Barlow, & Patterson, 1994; Probert, 1995; Still, 1996). Even women in management can have problems with part-time work. Still's (1996) study of the finance industry indicated that part-time women in management or with management career aspirations knew they had to pursue full-time employment to achieve their promotion goals. Crozier-Durham (1995) found that few workplaces have developed adequate strategies to accommodate part-time managers with family responsibilities. Women managers who worked part-time said that the key to their success was their own ability to be flexible— to alter their days of work, to take unfinished work home, to attend meetings at any time, and to be available and accessible when necessary.

Working part-time also has implications for women's ability to contribute to breadwinning. In couples with dependent children in which both partners

TABLE 4.1 Employed Persons by Occupation, May 1998

Occupation	% Females	% Males
Managers/Administrators	23	77
Professionals	49	51
Associate professionals	37	63
Tradespersons	10	90
Clerks/Sales/Service	72	28
Production/Transport	13	87
Labourers/related workers	37	63

SOURCE: Australian Bureau of Statistics (1998a).

worked full-time, women contributed an average of 43% of couples' earnings. When women worked part-time, the contribution was only 27% (ABS, 1995a).

THE IMPACT OF FAMILY ON WORK

Effects of Caregiving on Participation

One third of employed men and one third of employed women have dependent children under 15 years old. Of all couple families with dependent children, 59% have both parents in the labour force (ABS, 1998a). The age of the youngest child significantly affects mothers' workforce participation rates, but it does not affect men's. The labour force participation rates of mothers rise with the age of their youngest child, whereas men's stay constant at 95% (ABS, 1997). For example, in 1998, of mothers whose youngest child was under age 5, 50% of those in couple families and 39% of those who were lone parents were in the labour force. When the youngest child is school age (5-14 years), women's labour force participation goes dramatically up, to 72% for mothers with partners and 62% for lone mothers (Glezer & Wolcott, 1997).

Having caregiving responsibilities for elderly, disabled, or ill parents, spouses, and children also affects workforce participation, especially women's. About 70% of providers of personal care and home help for the aged, long-term ill, or disabled persons are in the labour force (ABS, 1994). According to a national survey of principal caregivers of people with disabilities, one third who are not in the labour force had been in paid employment before assuming their caregiving role (ABS, 1995b). Of those who left work to take on caregiving responsibilities, 42% were women ages 45 to 64, and 26% were women ages 25 to 44. Only 3% of men in the younger age group had left work to become a principal caregiver.

One of the main reasons women work part-time is to better manage work and family commitments, particularly when their children are young. In addition to affecting labour force participation, family responsibilities across the life course can require employees of both sexes to take time off from work or to make adjustments in their work. The amount employees need to alter their work for family reasons depends on family composition, the age of children, needs of elderly parents, whether the employee is a single parent, if the employee's partner works full- or part-time, or if there are other relatives who can assist. The amount of job flexibility and organisational constraints can also determine women's and men's ability to take time off for family responsibilities.

National survey data show how common it is for employees with dependent care responsibilities to have to take time off work. A national study of 2,642 persons in the labour force with dependent care responsibilities found that 58% had taken some time off to meet family responsibilities, for an average of 9.4 days during the previous 12 months (VandenHeuvel, 1993). There were no gender differences in the overall amount of time taken or in the amount of time mothers and fathers took off to care for children during school holidays or to care for their own elderly parents. However, although parents took off an average of 3.5 days per year to care for sick children, mothers were more likely to take this time off than were fathers (50% of mothers took time off to care for sick children vs. one third of fathers). On the other hand, more men (20%) had taken time off work to care for a partner than had women (9%).

Workers with family caregiving responsibilities often make or are willing to make other adjustments to work besides staying home. A major study of family caregivers asked respondents about the effects of caregiving on their occupational lives. Nearly one third of employed caregivers claimed that caregiving commitments caused repeated interruptions at their work, resulted in their having to work fewer hours, or both. Almost one quarter had taken periods of unpaid leave; 16% had taken less responsible jobs; and 13% had refused promotions (Schofield, Herrman, Bloch, Howe, & Singh, 1996).

Another study involving interviews with employees in several leading Australian corporations found that nearly three quarters of people with dependent children said that they would refuse a job or promotion if it decreased time available for family. Approximately two thirds of employees with dependent children and one half of middle managers indicated they would refuse a promotion if it threatened their partner's career (Russell, 1993). Difficulties with child care arrangements resulted in one fourth (24%) of working parents in Queensland saying they could not work flexibly at short notice; 21% said they could not work overtime; and 17% would not accept more responsibilities or promotion (Work and Child Care Advisory Service, 1994).

Women seem more likely than men to organise their work time to suit family demands. Wolcott and Glezer (1995) found that 62% of women working full-time and 56% working part-time rated no weekend or night work as an important aspect of working conditions, compared with only 37% of men.

Relocation is another employment decision individuals make with family considerations in mind. Wolcott and Glezer (1995) found that more than half of the parents said family reasons would prevent them from moving to a new location if this were necessary for their job. They resisted moving so that their partners could keep their jobs and because of anticipated increases in housing costs, a reluctance to change children's school, and a desire to remain near family members. Although women (67%) more than men (42%) thought their partner's job would deter them from relocating, the substantial proportion of men who would consider their partner's job in decisions to relocate indicates changes in the way women's employment in the family is perceived. These perceptions may reflect the importance of a second income as well as a shift in values. Case studies of relocation policies in several companies by Holmes (1996) supported the general view that it is still more often the wife's job that is "put on hold" when decisions are made about relocation. Companies that considered employees' family situation and provided a range of supports to family members found that such policies contributed to the successful outcome of relocations, for example, in terms of enhancing employee commitment.

THE IMPACT OF WORK ON FAMILY LIFE

Family responsibilities clearly affect individuals' participation in the labour market. Work also has an impact on family life. The majority of Australian families indicate that they cope fairly well with managing the dual roles of family caring and paid employment, probably because so many women work part-time. Most rate individual well-being and the quality of family relationships to be high and work conflict to be low.

Individual Well-Being

In Australia, paid work has positive effects on the psychological well-being of working parents, more so for women than for men. Two thirds of working women reported that employment had a positive effect on their self-esteem, compared with 56% of men (Wolcott & Glezer, 1995). A study of caregivers also found women to be more likely than men to say that employment had a positive effect on their self-esteem, because it was a source of relief and provided opportunity for another interest (Schofield et al., 1996). Women in paid work have been found to be more satisfied with their personal life, living standard, and life situation than nonemployed women (Wolcott & Glezer, 1995).

Parents were more likely to report that work had a positive effect on their life if they were satisfied with the hours they worked, if they felt a low degree of pressure and stress in life, if they were older (with older children), and if they were satisfied with their life as a whole. In addition, not working excessive hours and enjoying a sense of mastery and autonomy over their environment contributed to work's positive effects on fathers. Feeling less emotional distress and working part-time increased work's positive impact on mothers (Wolcott & Glezer, 1995).

Family Relationships

Employment has positive effects on family relationships in Australia. Only one third of men and one fourth of women working full-time felt that work had some negative effect on their relationship with their partner. Only one third of men and one third of women who worked full-time reported that they were often too tired to do things with their partner. More negative impacts of employment on parent-child relations were reported by two fifths of parents who worked full-time. Few parents, however, believed this effect was extreme. Of women employed full-time, 43% felt they did not have the energy to be a good parent, compared with 27% of full-time working men. Women who worked part-time were more likely than women who worked full-time to say that employment had a positive effect on their relations with their partner and with their children (Wolcott & Glezer, 1995).

Job-to-Family Spillover

A good balance between work and family priorities was reported to be achieved by almost half (45%) of working men and more than half (52%) of working women. Most parents appeared to prioritize family over work. Only one fourth of men (27%) admitted that they were more work-centred than family-centred, while one fifth of women described themselves as more interested in work than in family (Wolcott & Glezer, 1995).

The main factors affecting negative spillover of work into family life were similar for men and women. These included working long hours, being in a high-status occupation, and experiencing low work satisfaction. For men, being more work- than family-centred contributed to higher negative work spillover into family life, while for women, having a low sense of control over their lives and experiencing financial difficulties exacerbated negative feelings about balancing work and family commitments.

Australians' sense of being able to balance work and family, however, may be deteriorating. A 1995 study revealed that 26% of employees thought that their satisfaction with the balance between work and family had deteriorated (Department of Industrial Relations, 1996). Working time surveys show that the amount of hours that managers and professionals work is so great that it is likely that parents in these occupations will experience negative spillover of work into family life (ABS, 1998b). A report from the Industry Task Force on Leadership and Management Skills (1995) suggested that many women were leaving larger organisations to form their own small businesses because the dominant corporate culture is not seen as supportive of their career aspirations or of the balancing of work and family roles.

Both employers and policymakers emphasise that flexible working arrangements are the key to assisting men and women achieve a better balance between work and family life (Department of Industrial Relations, 1996). The majority of working parents appear to have access to flexible working hours if they need them, with more fathers (69%) than mothers (59%) reporting this (Wolcott & Glezer, 1995). However, some researchers have expressed concern that flexibility in working conditions and agreements may meet employers' production and service demands more than it meets family needs for schedules that enhance family life (Deery & Mahony, 1993; Probert, 1995).

SHARING HOUSEHOLD TASKS AND FAMILY CARE

Part of working parents' juggling act involves completion of household tasks and taking care of children. Australian surveys consistently find that domestic chores are still divided along gender lines (Bittman, 1995; Wolcott & Glezer, 1995). Bittman (1995) notes,

> Women work seven and a half times longer than men on laundry, ironing and clothes care, more than four times longer in cleaning, over three and a half times longer in the care of children and nearly three times longer in cooking. (p. 9)

House and outdoor maintenance remain men's domain, but these tasks, such as mowing the lawn, are more sporadic than the more daily tasks that women do, such as cooking and laundry. The time use survey also concluded that partnered men with children under 15 spent 11% of their day (2.6 hours) on household activities, whereas partnered women spent double the amount (22%) of their day (5.2 hours) on household activities (ABS, 1993). According to Bittman (1995), there are no "new men," and any changes that have taken place in how men and women share domestic tasks result from women's reducing their time performing household chores rather than from men's doing more around the house.

Between 1987 and 1992, however, both mothers and fathers reported spending more time with children. Goodnow and Bowes (1993) interviewed couples trying to avoid traditional gender-based domestic roles. They found that these couples organised their lives differently; meanings, expectations, and explanations about work influenced decisions and actions they made in regard to the domestic division of labour. A commitment to fairness, a capacity to compromise and to negotiate options, and a willingness to challenge stereotypes all appeared to be catalysts for change.

WORK VALUES AND WORK PRACTICES

From early in the 20th century until the 1970s, Australia had a wage-fixing system based on the sole-breadwinner model. By 1996, however, most Australians said they preferred the dual-breadwinner model. When asked in the Australian Family Life Course Study whether "A husband's job is to earn the money, a wife's is to look after the home and family," only 23% of both men and women agreed. Instead, the majority of men (65%) and women (69%) agreed that "Both partners should contribute to the household income." Women in the workforce (75%) were significantly more likely to support sharing the breadwinning role than women who were not in the workforce, but more than half of full-time housewives (52%) still subscribed to the dual-breadwinner ideal (Glezer & Wolcott, 1997). These results are consistent with similar industrialised countries, suggesting little popular support for the male-breadwinner/wife-homemaker model (Hakim, 1997).

Despite their ideological support for the dual-breadwinner model, the majority of respondents who were married or cohabiting (59% of men and 62% of women) admitted that it was the man who took the main responsibility for being the economic provider in their household. Only one third (34% of men and 30% of women) said the breadwinning responsibility was shared equally. (For 6% of the men and 8% of the women, the woman took the main responsibility for being the economic provider.)

Men's greater assumption of the breadwinning role seems to be related to the impact of childbearing on Australian women's employment patterns. Prior to becoming parents, the workforce patterns of men and women are similar, with both usually working full-time. It is at the time of the first birth that women usually start their pattern of interrupted workforce participation, either moving in or out of the labour force or shifting to part-time or casual employment (Rimmer & Rimmer, 1994). Half of all women who have been employed during pregnancy have not returned to employment within 18 months; when they do return to work, the majority work part-time (Glezer, 1988).

The women who return to employment sooner than other women after the first birth have high levels of education, high-status occupations, high incomes, strong work attachment, lower-earning husbands, and an attitude that substitute child care is not detrimental to young children (Glezer, 1988; Mitchell & Dowrick, 1994). Rimmer and Rimmer (1994), in their research on women's career breaks, found that women who took time out to care for children experienced a considerable decline in skills. Research by some of the major companies in Australia suggests that if companies provided child care and part-time working arrangements, women would return to work sooner after childbirth (Krautil, 1994).

Another important reason Australians do not live up to the dual-breadwinner model they admire is women's preference for part-time work. Research has consistently found a strong preference for part-time work among women with dependent children (Buchanan & Bearfield, 1996; Glezer, 1996; Glezer & Wolcott, 1997; Phau-Effinger, 1993; Wolcott & Glezer, 1995). Women's preferred work hours are strongly related to their actual hours in paid work. Figure 4.1 shows that few mothers (less than 8%) would prefer to not work at all. Most women (70+%), in various forms of part-time work, are satisfied with their part-time work hours. Only among women working full-time was there a high percentage of women (43%) wishing to work less (i.e., part-time). For working women with older children (youngest child ages 5-12), the results were quite similar.

Looking at unemployed women whose youngest child was under 18 years old, it was found that 44% preferred not being in paid work, with the percentage increasing to 53% for those with the youngest children under age 5. About two fifths (41%) of unemployed mothers with the youngest children preferred part-time employment. Very few (8%) wanted to work as many as 30 hours a week.

INTEGRATING WORK, VALUES, AND INCOME EARNING

A strong strand in work and family research directions in Australia has been the issue of reconciling preferences for flexible employment arrangements, particularly part-time work, with access to a secure and adequate income (Davidson, 1996; Probert, 1995). Cass (1995), for example, comments that retirement income policies "predicated on a gender-differentiated base of workforce participation, cannot provide equal outcomes for women while paid and unpaid work remain unequally allocated" (p. 57).

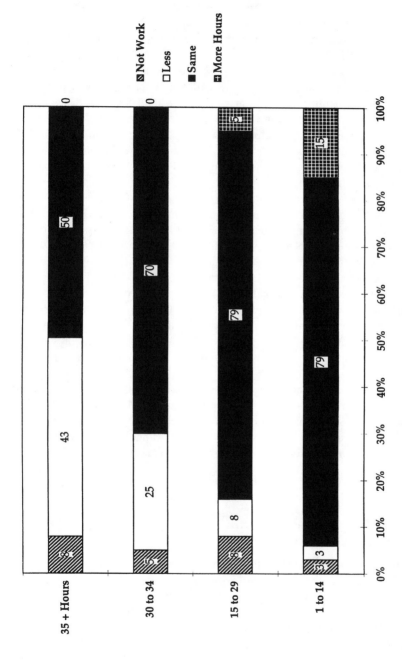

Figure 4.1. Current Versus Preferred Work Hours: Women With Youngest Child 0 to 4 Years (*N* = 156)
SOURCE: Glezer and Wolcott, Australian Family Life Course Study, AIFS (1997).

The debate sometimes takes the form of advocacy for increased social security payments to parents and partners who choose to remain at home as full-time family managers and caregivers versus support for increased government and employer provision of quality child care and elder care resources that facilitate women's participation in the labour force (Davidson, 1996). Buchanan and Bearfield (1996) proposed extending income support during transitions to parenthood and retirement as well as at times extending family caring for the ill and elderly. Probert (1995) has commented that such income supports are more likely to appeal to women with low education and workforce skills and can reinforce both gender stereotypes and women's income inequality. Affirming this position, Cass (1996) observed that, although these social security entitlements are not "officially gendered," the majority of people availing themselves of these family caring benefits are women.

Women's consistent preference for part-time work (however this is interpreted) reinforces the arguments made by these policy analysts that, in addition to improved employment benefits for part-time work, social security initiatives may need to compensate for part-time and interrupted employment careers over the life course. Economic and labour market trends that predict increasing casualisation of the workforce and a rise in part-time and lower-paid jobs for men as well as for women reinforce the need for such income support policies (Buchanan & Bearfield, 1996; Economic Planning and Advisory Council, 1996; Norris & Wooden, 1996). Mitchell and Dowrick (1994) have pointed out the importance of structuring tax incentives and social security benefits so that they do not discourage part-time work participation, particularly for low-income earners and lone parents, who otherwise might require complete government support.

There is little evidence that the majority of Australian men are actually dissatisfied with their assuming the primary breadwinner role and with women having a modified secondary income-earning role. Most women do not appear to desire any extreme social engineering to change this arrangement either (Probert & McDonald, 1996; Wolcott & Glezer, 1995).

Employers still generally assume that it will be their female employees with dependents, not their male employees, who will take advantage of flexible work conditions and make the necessary career adjustments responsibility for children requires. The availability of part-time work is often championed by employers as the means by which women employees can achieve a balance between work and family responsibilities (Wolcott, 1991, 1993).

Despite progress in legislation, changes in employer practices, and shifts in how men and women feel about sharing family responsibilities, it still appears that the achievement of a more integrated egalitarian sharing of work and family roles remains a vision rather than a reality in Australia. Mitchell and Dowrick (1994) contend that higher educational attainment by younger cohorts of women should lead to these women's increased workforce attachment during the childbearing years. These women have been socialised in a society going through major transitions in relation to gender roles and the labour market. It remains to be seen whether these younger women and their partners will realise this vision.

REFERENCES

Australian Bureau of Statistics. (1993). *How Australians use their time* (Cat. No. 4153.0). Canberra: Australian Government Printing Service.
Australian Bureau of Statistics. (1994). *Focus on families: Work and family responsibilities* (Cat. No. 4422.0). Canberra: Australian Government Printing Service.
Australian Bureau of Statistics. (1995a). Differences in men's and women's earnings. *Australian social trends: 1996* (Cat. No. 4102.0). Canberra: Australian Government Printing Service.
Australian Bureau of Statistics. (1995b). *Focus on families: Caring in families—support for persons who are older or have disabilities* (Cat. No. 4423.0). Canberra: Australian Government Printing Service.
Australian Bureau of Statistics. (1997, June). *The labour force Australia, June* (Cat. No. 6203.0). Canberra: Australian Government Printing Service.
Australian Bureau of Statistics. (1998a, May). *Labour force, Australia* (Cat. No. 6203.0). Canberra: Australian Government Printing Service.
Australian Bureau of Statistics. (1998b, August). *Working arrangements, Australia* (Cat. No. 6342.0). Canberra: Australian Government Printing Service.
Bittman, M. (1995). *Recent changes in unpaid work* (Australian Bureau of Statistics Cat. No. 4153.0). Canberra: Australian Government Printing Service.
Buchanan, J., & Bearfield, S. (1996). *Reforming work time: Alternatives to unemployment, casualisation, and excessive hours* (Unpublished Report). Melbourne and Sydney: Australian Centre for Industrial Relations Research and Training.
Cass, B. (1995). Gender in Australia's restructuring labour market and welfare state. In A. Edwards & S. Magarey (Eds.), *Women in a restructuring Australia: Work and welfare.* Sydney: Allen and Unwin.
Cass, B. (1996, May). *Summing up: Bridging paid and unpaid work—three future scenarios.* Paper presented at the Future of Work seminar, Australian Council of Social Service, Sydney.
Crozier-Durham, M. (1995). *Only so many hours: Flexible work at managerial levels.* Canberra, Australia: Department of Industrial Relations, Work and Family Unit.
Davidson, P. (1996, May). *Social security and the balance between caring and employment* [Issues Paper]. Sydney: Australian Council of Social Services.
Deery, S., & Mahony, A. (1993). *Temporal flexibility: Management strategies and employee preferences in the retail industry* (Working Paper No. 77). Melbourne: University of Melbourne, Department of Management and Industrial Relations.

Department of Industrial Relations. (1996). *Annual report 1995—enterprise bargaining in Australia: Developments under the Industrial Relations Reform Act.* Canberra: Australian Government Printing Service.

Economic Planning and Advisory Council. (1996, July). *Future labour market issues for Australia* (Commission Paper No. 12). Canberra: Australian Government Printing Service.

Glezer, H. (1988). *Maternity leave in Australia: Employee and employer experiences.* Melbourne: Australian Institute of Family Studies.

Glezer, H. (1996, February). *Pathways between paid work and parenting.* Paper presented at the seminar Bridging Paid and Unpaid Work: Strategies for the Future, Commission for the Future of Work, Sydney.

Glezer, H., & Wolcott, I. (1997). *Work and family values, preferences, and practice* (Australian Family Briefing No. 4). Melbourne: Australian Institute of Family Studies.

Goodnow, J., & Bowes, J. (1993). *Men, women, and household work.* Sydney: Oxford University Press.

Hakim, C. (1997). *Key issues in women's work: Female heterogeneity and the polarisation of women's employment.* London: Athlone.

Holmes, B. (1996). *Guide to family friendly relocations.* Canberra, Australia: Department of Industrial Relations, Work and Family Unit.

Industry Task Force on Leadership and Management Skills. (1995). *Enterprising nation: Renewing Australia's managers to meet the challenges of the Asia-Pacific century.* Canberra: Australian Government Printing Service.

Jackson, S. (1996). *The way forward: The future of work.* Melbourne: Brotherhood of St. Laurence.

Junor, A., Barlow, K., & Patterson, M. (1994). *Service productivity: Part-time workers and the finance sector workplace.* Canberra, Australia: Department of Industrial Relations, Equal Pay Unit.

Krautil, F. (1994, November). *Managing diversity in Esso Australia: Building a supportive workplace where women can achieve their potential.* Paper presented at the Australian Financial Review and Business Council of Australia Corporate Work and Family Awards, Sydney.

Mitchell, D., & Dowrick, S. (1994). *Women's increasing participation in the labour force: Implications for equity and efficiency* (Discussion Paper No. 308). Canberra: Australian National University, Centre for Economic Research.

Norris, K., & Wooden, M. (1996). The changing Australian labour market: An overview. In *The changing Australian labour market* (Economic Planning Advisory Commission Paper No. 11, pp. 1-14). Canberra: Australian Government Printing Service.

Phau-Effinger, B. (1993). Modernisation, culture, and part-time employment: The example of Finland and West Germany. *Work, Employment, and Society, 7,* 383-410.

Probert, B. (1995). *Part-time work and managerial strategy: Flexibility in the new industrial relations framework.* Canberra, Australia: Department of Employment, Education, and Training.

Probert, B., & McDonald, F. (1996). *The work generation: Work and identity in the nineties*. Melbourne: Brotherhood of St. Laurence.

Rimmer, R., & Rimmer, S. (1994). *More brilliant careers: The effect of career breaks on women's employment*. Canberra, Australia: Department of Employment, Education, and Training, Women's Bureau.

Russell, G. (1993, December). *Work and family audits of Australian workplaces: An employee perspective*. Paper presented at the conference "Work and family: The corporate challenge conference," sponsored by the Business Council of Australia and the *Australian Financial Review,* Melbourne.

Schofield, H., Herrman, H., Bloch, S., Howe, A., & Singh, B. (1996). A profile of Australian family caregivers: Diversity of roles and circumstances. *Australian and New Zealand Journal of Public Health, 21,* 59-66.

Still, L. (1996). *Brave new world? Women and part-time employment: The impact on career prospects and employment relations* (Working Paper No. 5, Women and Leadership Series). Perth, Western Australia: Edith Cowan University.

VandenHeuvel, A. (1993). *When roles overlap: Workers with family responsibilities*. Canberra: Department of Industrial Relations, Work and Family Unit, and Australian Institute of Family Studies.

Wolcott, I. (1991). *Work and family: Employers' views*. Melbourne: Australian Institute of Family Studies.

Wolcott, I. (1993). *A matter of give and take: Small business views of work and family*. Melbourne: Australian Institute of Family Studies.

Wolcott, I., & Glezer, H. (1995). *Work and family life: Achieving integration*. Melbourne: Australian Institute of Family Studies.

Work and Child Care Advisory Service. (1994). *The child care needs of working parents: A survey of Queensland workers*. Brisbane: Commonwealth of Australia.

5

Equality and Backlash

Family, Gender, and Social Policy in Sweden

ULLA BJÖRNBERG

This chapter examines the extent to which the ideal of the "dual-breadwinner" family in Sweden has been realised in a majority of Swedish families. This issue will first be investigated by looking at the attitudes that women and men have toward issues of reconciling work and family and the role they think the workplace and the government should take in helping individuals cope with multiple roles. Are Swedes as equal as the model advocates? Do individuals' perspectives on the issues of work and family vary by gender? How does social class affect men's and women's interest in combining work and family roles and their attitudes toward family policy?

Subsidised child care for working parents has been one of the main features of Swedish family policy, designed to help parents combine work and family roles. The second issue that will be discussed is parents' attitudes toward public child care. Again, the impact of gender and social class on attitudes is explored.

The third section of the chapter deals with equality within families from fathers' and mothers' perspectives. The types of adaptations parents have made in their work to accommodate responsibility for children are described, as is their use of formal family-leave benefits. The impact of occupational position

EDITORS' NOTE: The author's use of British spellings has been retained.

on parents' likelihood of making adjustments in their work for children's sake
is examined. The Swedish dual-breadwinner model is distinguished by its focus
on men and women sharing responsibility for child care as well as for providing
family income. Looking at fathers' and mothers' roles regarding child care is
therefore an appropriate way to explore how much of a gap exists between the
ideal and reality. The chapter concludes with a discussion of the future of the
dual-breadwinner model in Sweden given economic and political trends and
developments.

This chapter is based on results from a study of how employed parents
experience their lives in dual-breadwinner families in contemporary Sweden.
The study was carried out during the spring and autumn of 1992, at the
beginning of a major downturn in the labour market and in welfare provisions.
The sample consisted of 215 men and 455 women. All men were married or
cohabiting, while 146 of the women were single mothers living alone with their
children. To locate parents for the study, we obtained a random sample of
5-year-old children who lived in Göteborg and 13 additional urban and rural
municipalities around Göteborg on the west coast of Sweden. Using this list,
parents were contacted in their homes and interviewed. Of the parents in the
original sample, 80% chose to participate in interviews.

BACKGROUND ON THE SWEDISH MODEL

Before presenting results from the 1992 Göteborg parent survey, it is necessary
to present some background on Swedish family policy. (See also Haas &
Hwang, this volume, for further information on the development of Swedish
family policy.) During the past 30 years, Swedish family structure has been
affected by three important developments: an increase in women's labour force
participation, an increase in families' reliance on government benefits, and the
expansion of programs to help dual-breadwinner families.

Rise in Women's Labour Force Participation

The first important development is that more women, especially mothers,
have entered the labour market to provide households with a higher standard
of living. (Formerly, most families were based on the model of the "male-
breadwinner" family, in which men were responsible for income provision.)
Swedish women have not only joined the labour force in increasing numbers
and contributed a greater portion of family income, but they have also come to
be regarded as being as responsible as men for income earning. Thus, the
predominant Swedish family type today is the "dual-breadwinner" model.

An increase in women's involvement in the labour market coincided with
and was inextricably tied to the expansion of the Swedish welfare state. A large

number of jobs opened up for women in the public sector, which expanded greatly beginning in the mid-1970s. By the end of the 1980s, the percentage of women in the labour market was very close to men's.

At the beginning of the 1980s, only 20% of mothers with preschool-age children were employed full-time (Flood & Klevmarken, 1989), but over time, women have increased their employment hours, with the vast majority now employed in full-time jobs or in "long" part-time jobs of 30 to 34 hours per week. In the 1992 study, 43% of the mothers of 5-year-olds worked full-time. National data collected in 1990 found that working women in general averaged 34 hours of paid employment per week (Björklund, 1993). One major reason for this increase in women's hours is that incomes were reduced during the 1980s and prices were raised. One solution to this problem was for women to work more hours in paid work (Sundström, 1993).

Although women are almost as likely as men to be in the labour force, and they have similar educational levels, jobs are highly sex segregated in the Swedish labour market. Women are likely to have jobs at the bottom of the status hierarchy, in unskilled or semiskilled jobs in the service sector. In the 1992 study, more than one fourth of all male workers (27%) were in professional jobs, compared with only 10% of women. More than one third of female workers (35%) were classified as unskilled workers, compared with only 16% of men. This distribution corresponds closely to national figures (Statistiska Central-byrån, 1996).

Increased Reliance on Government Benefits

A second change affecting families in the past 30 years is their increased reliance on government benefits. Since the 1930s, Swedes have enjoyed the typical benefits of a "welfare state," including free or low-cost health care, free education, child allowance, means-tested housing allowance, and (since 1974) paid family leave. Since the 1970s, families have become more "dependent" on the state than ever before. Women in particular have become highly dependent on the public sector. Many are employed by the local government; about half of women work in the public sector, compared with only 16% of men. The government also typically provides women with benefits and rights that help them economically. Single-parent families are especially dependent on welfare benefits to establish a good living standard. Because of this support, the Swedish welfare state has been labeled "women friendly" (Hernes, 1987).

On the other hand, this dependency of women on the public sector has been feared to be potentially detrimental to women, because historically women did not occupy influential power positions within local authorities (who nowadays administer social services) and national political institutions. Today, however, women have obtained a number of positions within the established political institutions at both central and local levels. This happened as a consequence of a strong female political reaction against reductions of service positions and cuts in welfare since the end of the 1980s (Björnberg, 1993).

Expansion of Programs for
Dual-Breadwinner Families

The third change, closely allied with the first two, is that government policy has increasingly sought to support employed parents. It has done this by expanding the supply of subsidised, high-quality child care; mandating that employers must allow workers to take family leave; and providing no tax relief for households with homemakers.

Child Care

Public support for child care in Sweden is extremely strong, and access to child care has been considered a universal right granted to all children who need it. In 1995, this right was codified in law, and since then the municipalities have been obliged to provide child care for all children. One of the basic ideas of Alva Myrdal (a Swedish political activist who first formulated the ideology for publicly supported child care in the 1930s) was that families who do not have enough resources of their own should have access to common resources at a community level. She was primarily referring to children with poor parents and argued that public child care could play a double role, by giving these children a stimulating environment, toys to play with, and pedagogic guidance, while at the same time creating possibilities for women to work.

Today, working parents count on publicly subsidised child care services for their children to receive good care while they work. Nevertheless, support for child care is mostly related to ideological and pedagogical motives concerning the welfare and upbringing of children. Most people believe that the government should provide opportunities for the child to become socially integrated into a wider social setting than the family. It has been suggested by experts that parents' possibilities to provide children with stimulating activities and toys are differentially distributed, and child care provision accessible to everybody would provide a way to compensate children with scarce resources at home (Statens Offentliga Utredningar [SOU], 1972). Promoting the individual development of the child has been the basic motive for upholding quality in child care institutions—both the professional quality of preschool teachers and the physical environment in the centres. The preschool staff has been expected to give the children love as well as social training and to stimulate the intellectual capacities of the children (Kärrby & Giota, 1995).

Myrdal's ideas have been used in giving highest priority to children with particular needs of social support and stimulation—for example, those with problems developing social ties or with physical disabilities and children of single mothers. These children should be integrated into normal day care activities and not kept separate. In principle, children are not supposed to be denied access to child care facilities because of the unemployment of their parents or when their parents are on family leave because of the birth or adoption of a younger child. This point illustrates how day care centres were originally designed to support, not supplant, families in socialising their children.

In recent years, the government has supported parental participation in day care by subsidising the development of parent cooperatives, which have grown rapidly in number. Most people consider these to be "private" centres, although they are in fact heavily subsidised and supervised by public authorities. Because some children do not fit well into institutional settings, parents can choose to have their children cared for by public day care providers in the providers' or children's homes. These providers are employed by the municipalities, and they receive subsidies, toys, and supervision from the municipalities.

Parental Leave

Another government policy that has been structured in such a way to keep both mothers and fathers permanently attached to the labour market is paid parental leave after childbirth or adoption. (See Haas & Hwang, this volume, for a detailed description of this policy.) Recipients have job security during childbirth leaves, which makes it possible for women to remain attached to the labour market even when they give birth to children. During the 1980s, the birthrate increased, becoming one of the highest in Europe, helped along by the generous government leave policies. Women could stay at home for long periods while still being counted as belonging to the labour market and living up to the terms of the dual-breadwinner model.

The right for fathers to take paid parental leave was introduced in 1974. A comparison of the pattern of use of parental leave between 1981 and 1995 shows that there has been a steady increase in usage by fathers. By 1995, the number of fathers taking parental leave began to decrease. This may be because of a drop in coverage of loss of income from 90% to 75% (Riksförsäkringsverket [RFV], 1993, 1994, 1996). National data show that men with higher education and men who are married or cohabiting with a highly educated woman take parental leave more often than other fathers. The more similar in education and career aspirations the partners are, the more there is a tendency toward equal sharing. When the man earns much more than the woman, the likelihood for his taking parental leave decreases. Men who work in public services, especially in professions that are not male dominated, are taking a leading role (RFV, 1994).

The Development of the Equal-Status Contract

Some people believe that these three changes in Sweden have led to the development of a contract between private families and the government that has rendered the family less private than it is in most other countries. Moreover, these changes have to some extent reduced the status of the family, because it is the individual, rather than the family, that is the "unit" that receives benefits (Björnberg & Eydal, 1995).

Esping-Andersen (1990) has characterised Sweden as a "Social Democratic regime," which grants individual citizens universal and equal access to social services and social insurance, with payments that compensate for loss of income. Hirdman (1994) has suggested that, in Sweden, a gender dimension has been added to this Social Democratic model. She maintains that an "equal-status contract" developed during the years 1976 to 1990. According to this contract, women's status was to be improved to approach that of men's in the spheres of employment, family, and politics. Women should gain autonomy in society and in the family, as well as individual access to benefits, by being gainfully employed. For women to have an equal status in the labour market, they need an equal right to employment as well as an equal obligation to work to support their families and themselves. The equal-status contract also meant that women and men should be equally represented in all occupational categories and at all levels of the occupational hierarchy and that salaries should be based on competence and not on gender. Equal status within the family meant that rights and obligations were to be equally distributed, which included sharing domestic work and child care. Family members should have an equal standard of living within the family, and distribution of power and influence should be equal. Equal status within political life meant that women should be equally represented at all levels of government and vote as often as men.

The next section of the chapter will consider Swedish parents' perspectives on issues related to work and family and whether couples are as equal as the equal-status contract advocates.

SWEDISH PARENTS' PERSPECTIVES ON WORK AND FAMILY

In the Göteborg study, we asked parents about their views on several subjects, including proposed changes in family policy and day care, to discover whether they supported the equal-status contract.

Parents' Attitudes Toward Proposed
Changes in Family Policy

In 1992, when the Göteborg study was conducted, large cuts in welfare benefits precipitated by an economic recession were still to come. There were, however, lively discussions regarding family policy, and the debates focused on three questions:

1. How dependent should the family be on public provisions of transfers and services? Moderates and conservatives argued for the government to transfer more responsibility and choice to families, whereas Social Democrats and those on the Left wanted to retain or even expand services.

2. Can a 6-hour day be instituted for all employees? For decades, some women active in the political parties have advocated that a 6-hour day become the typical workday as a way to promote equality within the family (see Haas & Hwang, this volume). Now Swedish women tend to work 6-hour days at their own expense, whereas men work 8 hours or more. Employed parents of preschool-age children have the right to reduce their jobs to 6-hour days, but few men do so. The Social Democrats and Leftists now more strongly support the concept of a 6-hour day, especially since unemployment has risen. The moderate and conservative political parties remain opposed.

3. Should parents have a choice to stay at home with preschool-age children? The more conservative parties have long advocated a reform that would grant parents the right to stay home with their preschool-age children while being compensated financially. Because women typically make less money than men do, the assumption has been that this would mean that mothers would be the ones who stay home, a halfway return to the male-breadwinner model. The Leftist parties have vigorously opposed such a policy.

The 1992 study asked parents of 5-year-olds how they felt about these policy questions and other possible changes that would make work and family easier to combine. The analysis focused on how men's and women's attitudes might differ. (A more detailed presentation of the results of this analysis is presented in Björnberg, 1993.) A shortened wording of the questions and the distribution of the first ranked responses are presented in Table 5.1.

In general, parents' highest preferences were for measures aimed at improving work conditions. Both women and men expressed a wish for increased flexibility in working hours and shorter working hours. Thus, the general tendency was support for the dual-breadwinner model, central to the equal-status contract. But gender differences were highly significant regarding attitudes toward policies supporting tax relief and shorter working hours. Men wanted more public support for money to the household, whereas women

TABLE 5.1 Parents' Attitudes Toward Family Policy, 1991

"Taking the current Swedish family policies into consideration, what are the important areas in which new measures should be taken, according to your point of view? Rank the three most important." (Percentages are of men and women according to class and highest ranked alternative)

	Unskilled Workers, Men	Unskilled Workers, Women	Middle-Class Men	Middle-Class Women	Upper-Class Men	Upper-Class Women
Financial Support						
More money for families with children (e.g., tax relief)	17	13	22	11*	21	4*
Larger monetary subsidies for families with children (e.g., family allowances)	6	6	4	3	0	0
Child Care						
More child care places with public support	14	9	8	7	8	11
More alternatives within the child care system via privatisation	0	4	7	4	6	4
Working Conditions						
Shorter working hours with full wages for parents with children below 8 years of age	9	30*	23	34*	21	45*

TABLE 5.1 Continued

	Unskilled Workers, Men	Unskilled Workers, Women	Middle-Class Men	Middle-Class Women	Upper-Class Men	Upper-Class Women
Increased possibilities for flexibility in working life for families with children	20	10	8	13	14	22
Parental Support						
Parental leave allowances for more extensive period of time	10	13	12	17	6	9
Introduction of care allowances or parental care "wages"	17	13	11	8	20	4*
Other	7	2	5	3	4	1
Total	100%	100%	100%	100%	100%	100%
N	35	158	119	240	50	45

*Chi square tests showed values were significant at the .05.

wanted to work part-time with public support. The results reflect the different positions of men and women in work and family life. Men have stronger preferences for measures linked to male breadwinning.

These differences in gendered attitudes were not significantly influenced by differences in class position. However, within the middle and upper classes, women and men had highly divergent views. In these two classes, 20% of men but only 4% of women gave their highest ranking to tax relief. In the same stratum, 25% of men ranked an increased child care allowance as their strongest preferred alternative, compared with only 2% of women. Thus, men in high positions were strongly in favour of support for measures linked to breadwinning, whereas women strongly favoured policies designed to make work and family easier to combine.

These differences between women and men within the same social class reflect their different work-family situations. In this upper strata, women tend to have careers and work full-time; they regard their jobs as highly stressful, much as men do. Women's greater responsibility for children puts considerable pressure on them, so they highly value shorter working hours. Women with careers report (as do career men) that they already have flexible jobs, so enhanced flexibility is not much of an issue for this group.

The different attitudes of women in different class positions also reflect their work situations. Women in the working class have heavy jobs and are not working full-time to the same extent as women in high occupational strata. For working-class women, more flexible working hours, longer parental leave, and higher child care allowance were very attractive policy proposals and appeared more beneficial than proposals such as tax relief. Among men, unskilled workers were less in favour of shorter working hours than were men within other classes. This could be a reflection of the fact that unskilled workers had more insecure work positions and lower incomes than other men. Furthermore, male blue-collar workers often have more traditional views on family life and are less likely to favour ideas designed to promote equal responsibility for child care.

In general, researchers have found that women regard government policies that support families as more important than men do (Oskarsson & Wängnerud, 1995). This study shows that gender differences in attitudes toward policy changes are smaller when individuals are grouped by social class, but significant gender differences still persist.

Parents' Attitudes Toward Child Care

In the 1992 Göteborg study of families with 5-year-olds, 73% of families used public child care (which is very similar to the nation as a whole). Public child care was used more by parents in the higher occupational strata. Although both men and women appreciated public child care, women were more positive. Both men and women preferred professional staff to take care of their children, but men were more likely than women to say they would not mind depending on informal networks for child care.

Class differences in the use of public child care were also found when attitudes toward child care were investigated. The class differences were most sharp concerning attitudes toward how children under the age of 3 should be cared for. The higher their occupational strata, the more supportive men and women were of the idea that children under 3 should be taken care of by public child care. Women were more likely than men in the lower occupational strata to agree with this, too, which suggests that men's attitudes varied more by class than women's. In general, though, both men and women regarded the care of children as something worthy of societal support. These results support the view that Swedish society is one in which individuals are seen as having rights to benefits (Hernes, 1985).

PARENTS' ADAPTATIONS TO FAMILY AND WORK ROLES

Parents' Tendency to Alter Conditions of Work

In the public discourse, there is a high degree of agreement on the necessity for fathers to share parental responsibility. Taking parental leave is just one measure of paternal involvement. It has become more accepted that men should be able to leave work to pick up children from day care and that they should stay at home with a sick child. Still, many employers have not fully accepted the idea that fathers want to share parental leave with their partners. Many men experience difficulties taking parental leaves for longer periods of time. Negative attitudes from employers, workmates, relatives, and friends play an important role (Hwang, Eldén, & Fransson, 1984). A recent investigation of companies and their degree of "father friendliness" suggests that few companies are promoting fathers' active participation in child care and frequent use of mandated family-leave benefits (Haas & Hwang, 1995, this volume).

In the 1992 Göteborg study, it was discovered that almost two thirds of men (62%) had made some sort of restriction in their jobs because of their children. (Nearly all—87%—of women had made such adjustments.) This suggests that men, to a considerable extent, have adapted their work lives to their children's needs. The strategies men use are similar to those women use—they reduce work hours, refrain from taking on more responsibility at work, ask for more flexible working conditions, and reduce their amount of overtime (see Table 5.2).

There were some gender differences in work adaptations, however. Women were more likely than men to reduce their work hours, change to a more family-friendly job, reduce their overtime, and refrain from taking on more responsibility at work.

Class differences were also found. The higher the class position, the higher the percentage of men who said they had reduced their work hours, obtained more flexible work hours, and refrained from offers of taking more responsibility at work. No class differences were observed for two adaptations— changing to a family-friendly job and reducing overtime. These results point in

TABLE 5.2 Parents' Strategies for Combining Work and Family Roles, 1992

Replies to question "Have you made any adaptations in your job because of your children?" (Numbers are percentages who made adaptations)

	Unskilled Workers		Middle Class		Upper Class		Totals	
	Men	Women	Men	Women	Men	Women	Men	Women
Reduced work hours	17	62	20	72	34	71	24	68
Obtained flexible work hours	23	40	34	41	42	53	35	42
Refrained from career	6	27	18	31	26	38	17	30
Changed to family-friendly job	11	46	20	35	12	33	16	39
Reduced overtime	34	51	39	50	34	53	36	50
N	35	35	119	118	50	49	215	455

NOTE: Gender differences are significant (chi square p value = .0001) on all alternatives except for "obtained flexible work hours." Class differences between men are significant (chi square p value = .05) when unskilled workers are compared with upper-class men, except for the alternatives "changed to family-friendly job" and "reduced overtime."

the same direction as those findings concerning which men take parental leave (RFV, 1994). For men, adaptations of family and work are related to belonging to middle-class occupations, in which liberal attitudes prevail.

New Fathers, Old Partners

The results from the 1992 study suggest that men in high occupational strata, having jobs requiring high education with a comparatively high degree of flexibility, were more active than other men in wanting to develop themselves as fathers. Other researchers have also found that such men have high ambitions for both family and work (Edlund, Ahltorp, Andersson, & Klippestø, 1990; Lillieroth, 1992). In more and more jobs, social competence is required, which means that men's personal capacities have to be developed along with their professional and technical skills. Personal skills are developed in social relationships, including in close relationships with children. Many men have realised the advantages of caring for and spending time with their children. Men who had been asked about their motives to be active fathers often referred to a wish to develop themselves as people. They have assumed that contact with small children would help them to find new insights about themselves and to develop the emotional parts of their personality. Lamb and Oppenheim (1989), in a literature review on fathering, concluded that father involvement was inspired not by an ideal of equal partnership in parenting but by curiosity and a wish to have contact with the child. Ideology about equality in marriage had little influence on men's orientation toward fatherhood.

Mothers and "Home Stress"

Since the decades when the dual-breadwinner family was established as the preferred and most common family form in Sweden, we have seen a trend of decreased family stability. The number of divorces and separations is higher in families in which women are employed, compared with families in which women have chosen to be housewives (Axelsson, 1992). It is mainly women who take the initiative to divorce, and conflicts concerning home and family matters have been suggested as the main reasons for divorce (Koch-Nielsen, 1987; Wadsby & Svedin, 1993).

The health problems of women have also increased over the last decades, especially problems related to stress. More stressful work is an important explanation, but women's greater responsibility for the household and family also helps to explain their lower psychological health status compared with men (Hall, 1990; Lundberg, 1990; Moen, 1989).

The results of the 1992 study showed that mothers of 5-year-olds had a lower health status than fathers (see Björnberg, 1998). These mothers experienced lower psychological well-being and more symptoms of "home stress" than fathers did. *Home stress* was defined as stress experienced in connection with responsibilities for home and family. Women's work conditions did not have any significant effects on their experience of home stress. Home-stress levels were related to the amount of conflict in the family (regarding money, housework, and child rearing) and to parents' sense of control in their parenting role. Neither conflict nor lack of control was related to women's workload or number of children.

The results suggest that women's experience of home stress and lower psychological well-being must be understood in relation to gendered power relations. The social construction of the female gender presupposes that the woman will unconditionally assume responsibility for family and household, while the social construction of the male gender results in men's maintenance of autonomy and assurance that they can secure love, care, and service from women (Chodorow, 1978). The more women become adapted to the dual-breadwinner lifestyle, the more they would like to have their share of free time and autonomy. The division of labour and responsibilities in contemporary

Swedish families is an issue of drawing borderlines and setting limits for commitments and obligations between partners. Women prefer to share work more equally with men and would like men to perceive the situation the same way as they do. However, women often do not express these opinions openly, and, consequently, conflicts and home stress result (Björnberg, 1998).

THE FUTURE OF THE DUAL-BREADWINNER MODEL IN SWEDEN

This chapter has addressed the role of family policies in helping fathers and mothers reconcile employment and family life. The results of the 1992 Göteborg study show that patterns of adaptations of work and family have to be viewed in relation to gender and occupational position. In all families, women still carry more responsibility for child care and household chores, although these tasks are increasingly shared by men. Men in higher occupational strata seem more interested in balancing work and family roles than do men in lower strata. The more equal the partners are in terms of occupational status, the more likely they are to share.

It has to be stressed, however, that men's participation in the family is based on the terms that men have the informal power to dictate (Andersson, 1994; Roman, 1994). In all social strata, women still have to make more adaptations of their work to family life than men do. This is partly because of the fact that women typically have a lower occupational status than their male partners. Men's jobs are almost always regarded as more important, judged as carrying greater responsibility, and rewarded with higher wages. In most families, there is still a tacit mutual understanding that women are primarily responsible for the running of family life, even if both partners believe that they have agreed on the division of work and responsibilities on the basis of free choice (Haavind & Andeneas, 1994).

Another basic problem is that male conditions of life remain as norms for equal status. In all spheres of life, men are expected to give their highest priority to jobs, political matters, or other organised social activities, and not to let family obligations intervene. Women who engage in these activities have to abide by the same rules as men. When women are not able to adapt or cope, it is the women and not the expectations that are regarded as the problem.

The fact that women do a greater share of work within the family is often explained in terms of women being more family oriented than men. Family and work have been discussed in terms of a dualistic paradigm: Women have been regarded as more family oriented than men and men as more work oriented than women. This paradigm has been questioned in Sweden, and there is evidence to show that work and family orientations are not so gender polarised (Björnberg, 1998; Ellingsæter, 1995; Holter & Aarseth, 1993; Roman, 1994). Both men and women are oriented toward work and family in many different ways, and the spheres are highly integrated. Evidence from this study shows that men are interested in combining work and family roles, at least to a certain degree.

The results of the 1992 study suggest that a majority of both men and women feel that they manage fairly well to find a proper balance between family and paid work. Balancing, however, is more difficult in dual-career families, in which work demands are greatest, and is easiest in the public sector, in which jobs are more flexible. Moreover, women experience problems with psychological well-being and home stress, which are mainly related to the couple relationship and an unfair division of labour and money within the household.

There is no doubt that government policies aimed at making family and work easier to combine are important. Swedish policies that provide subsidised child care and paid parental leave are important steps and are regarded positively by parents. More flexibility in working hours and shorter working hours are highly desired among parents with small children, but they have yet to be realised at all occupational levels. Can the Swedish government continue to develop policies to help parents adapt to work and family roles given the current economic and political climate?

Several developments suggest that the Swedish government is pulling away from its commitment to the equal-status contract and the dual-breadwinner model. Perhaps the most important development relates to the economy. Sweden has suffered from a recession in the 1990s. For the first time since the 1930s depression, the unemployment rate has been more than 10%. Since 1990, women's labour force participation rate has dropped from 85% to 80%, while men's dropped from 95% to 85%. Women are less likely than men to suffer involuntary unemployment, because the largest reductions in jobs have occurred within the industrial sector. However, the unemployment rate is higher among mothers than among childless women (Statistiska Centralbyrån, 1996). Job insecurity among men can lead fathers to embrace their work roles to a greater degree, reducing their interest in and time for their children.

Women's jobs have also become more precarious. Declining revenues have led to cuts in social service jobs that women have traditionally held. There has been an increase in positions involving temporary employment and involuntary part-time work, which are occupied more by women than by men, and women often end up in jobs for which they are overqualified (Regnér, 1996). Single mothers in all educational categories have an even more precarious labour market position than married mothers (Björnberg, 1996).

There has also been a trend of women's being absent from work for child care purposes more than men are (Berlin, 1997). Since 1990, there has been a drop from 44% to 34% in the percentage of men taking temporary leave to care for a sick child. This change may be a result of the 1993 reduction in coverage of lost income from 90% to 75%. It hurts the household economy more when men (who earn more than women) stay at home with a sick child.

The Swedish welfare state has been built on the principles of full employment and everyone's right to employment; many benefits are directly tied to employment history. Because of the decline in employment, the government has had less tax revenues and been forced to cut citizen benefits. The Swedish welfare state has been based on the idea that entitlements should be provided at a high standard (Esping-Andersen, 1990). Since the recession began, the government has been forced to lower this standard. Reductions in benefits include the amount of subsidies for child care and the amount of compensation parents receive while on parental leave or when staying home for a sick child. In the area of child care, there have been several cost-cutting measures introduced, including centre closings, staff cuts, acceptance of higher caretaker-to-child ratios, operations budgets cuts, and increases in parents' fees. Day care for children with unemployed parents and after-school care for school-age children have been reduced.

There have been political changes in the way benefits are dispensed, which make it difficult for services to be retained or reinstated. Since the end of the 1980s, responsibilities for services have been decentralised to local municipalities. The national government's subsidies to municipalities have been cut, and the national government has banned the raising of municipal taxes. Municipalities have therefore been under pressure to reduce, rather than enhance, services.

The conditions for combining work and family will become more differentiated between women, because of their occupational status. Formal rights to parental leave and leave to care for a sick child will remain social citizenship rights, but the possibilities of using them will depend on negotiations with employers. Higher-status women may be in a better position to negotiate with employers than lower-status women. Some employed parents will hesitate to take advantage of their rights because they are afraid of losing their jobs, especially parents in temporary or insecure occupational positions.

It seems likely that the policies of employers regarding work and family will be more important in the future than will the formal rights mandated by government (see Haas & Hwang, this volume). It will be more risky for highly educated women to use the full extension of parental leave. This might mean a greater demand for child care for children under 1 year or more pressure on men to share parental leave. Parental leave will probably be used in shorter periods, as compensation for shorter work hours and flexible working conditions.

More irregular working hours and more temporary employment will require more flexible child care solutions, which might be difficult to obtain within the public child care system. Companies that rely on temporary workforces might have to supply child care solutions for those whose work hours do not fit the requirements of formal arrangements.

The widespread acceptance of the idea that women should have jobs and be breadwinners and that men should be active fathers means that both sexes are likely to remain interested in the development of policy measures that would help them combine work and family roles. In the 1992 study, an overwhelming majority of both men and women held the view that full-time housewives have low value in society and suffer from being dependent on their domestic partners (Björnberg, 1993). This attitude seems unlikely to change quickly, since the equal-status contract and the dual-breadwinner model have taken considerable time to become accepted in Sweden.

Overall, it appears that Swedish women are experiencing a backlash in their attempts to achieve equal participation in the labour market. The basis for this backlash is not because of a revival of a traditional family ideology in Sweden. Traditional gender discrimination is being revitalised by stiffer competition in the labour market, in which men are favoured. By earning more, men can set the conditions for participation in family life at the expense of women. General policies aimed at forcing employers to make work and family easier to reconcile could in fact produce more unequal conditions for women if employers see more risks than advantages in hiring women as employees.

REFERENCES

Andersson, G. (1994). *Leva för jobbet och jobba för livet. Om chefsfamiljernas vardag och samlevnadsformer* [Living for work and working for life. Everyday life and coexistence of families with men in management positions]. Stockholm: Symposion.

Axelsson, C. (1992). *Hemmafrun som försvann. Övergången till lönearbete bland gifta kvinnor i Sverige 1968-1981* [The vanished housewife. Transition to employment among married women in Sweden 1968-1981]. Stockholm: University of Stockholm, Swedish Institute for Social Research.

Berlin, E. (1997). Män tar allt mindre ansvar för sjuka barn [Men take less responsibility for sick children]. *Arbetsmiljö* [Work Environment], *11*, 3-4.

Björklund, A. (1993). *Utveckling av inkomstfördelning och arbetstider* [Development of income distribution and work hours]. Unpublished paper, University of Stockholm, Institute for Social Research.

Björnberg, U. (1993). Political parenthood among women and men in Sweden. In G. Hedlund & I. Pincus (Eds.), *Politics: A power base for women* (Report No. 3, pp. 5-39). Örebro, Sweden: Örebro University, Women's Studies Program.

Björnberg, U. (1996). Children's rights in dual earner family contexts in Sweden. *EUROSOCIAL Report, 61,* 101-120.

Björnberg, U. (1998). Psychological well-being among women with preschool children. In M. Chesney, K. Orth-Gomér, & N. Wenger (Eds.), *Women, stress, and heart disease.* Hillsdale, NJ: Lawrence Erlbaum.

74   MOTHERS AND FATHERS AT THE WORKPLACE

Björnberg, U., & Eydal, G. (1995). Family obligations in Sweden. In J. Millar & A. Warman (Eds.), *Defining family obligations in Europe* (Bath Social Policy Papers No. 23, pp. 359-378). Bath, UK: University of Bath.

Chodorow, N. (1978). *The reproduction of mothering.* Berkeley: University of California Press.

Edlund, C., Ahltorp, B., Andersson, G., & Klippestø, S. (1990). *Karriärer i kläm: Om chefen, familjen och företaget* [Careers in a squeeze: On managers, families, and companies]. Stockholm: Norstedts.

Ellingsæter, A. (1995). *Gender, work, and social change: Beyond dualistic thinking.* Oslo, Norway: Institute for Social Research.

Esping-Andersen, G. (1990). *Three worlds of welfare capitalism.* Cambridge, UK: Polity.

Flood, L., & Klevmarken, A. (1989). *Tidsanvändningen i Sverige 1984* [Time use in Sweden, 1984] (Memorandum 127). Göteborg, Sweden: Göteborg University, Department of National Economy.

Haas, L., & Hwang, P. (1995). Company culture and men's usage of family leave benefits in Sweden. *Family Relations, 44,* 28-36.

Haavind, H., & Andeneas, A. (1994). *Care and the responsibility for children: Creating the life of women creating themselves.* Paper presented at the Men's Families seminar, Copenhagen, Denmark.

Hall, E. (1990). *Women's work: An inquiry into the health effects of invisible and visible labor.* Stockholm: Karolinska Institutet.

Hernes, H. (1985). The welfare state citizenship of Scandinavian women. In K. Jones & A. Jónasdóttir (Eds.), *The political interests of gender: Developing theory and research with feminist face* (pp. 187-213). London: Sage.

Hernes, H. (1987). Women and the welfare state: The transition from private to public dependence. In S. Showstack (Ed.), *Women and the state* (pp. 72-92). London: Hutchinson.

Hirdman, Y. (1994). *Women from possibility to problem? Gender conflict in the welfare state: The Swedish model* (Research Report No. 3). Stockholm: Institute for Working Life Research.

Holter, Ö., & Aarseth, H. (1993). *Menns livssammanhang* [The male world]. Oslo, Norway: Ad Notam Gyldendal.

Hwang, P., Eldén, G., & Fransson, C. (1984). *Arbetsgivares och arbetskamraters attityder till pappaledighet* [Attitudes toward parental leave among employers and colleagues] (Report No. 1). Göteborg, Sweden: Göteborg University, Department of Psychology.

Kärrby, G., & Giota, J. (1995). Parental conceptions of quality in daycare centers in relation to quality measured by the ECERS. *Early Child Development and Care, 110,* 1-18.

Koch-Nielsen, I. (1987). *Skilsmisser* [Divorces] (Publication No. 118). Copenhagen, Denmark: Institute for Social Research.

Lamb, M., & Oppenheim, D. (1989). Fatherhood and father-child relationships. In S. Cath, A. Gurwitt, & L. Ginsberg (Eds.), *Fathers and their families* (pp. 11-26). Hilsdale Hove and London: Analytic Press.

Lillieroth, A. (1992). Intervjuer om chefskap, arbetsliv och privatliv [Interviews on managing, working life, and private life]. In J. Acker, A. Baude, U. Björnberg, E. Dahlström, G. Forsberg, L. Gönas, & H. Holter (Eds.), *Kvinnors och mäns liv och arbete* [Women's and men's lives and work] (pp. 41-54). Stockholm: SNS Förlag.

Lundberg, O. (1990). *Den ojämlika ohälsan: Om klass och könsskillnader i sjukledighet* [Unequal illness: Class and gender differences in sick leave]. Stockholm: Institutet för Social Forskning [Institute for Social Research].

Moen, P. (1989). *Working parents*. Madison: University of Wisconsin Press.

Oskarsson, M., & Wängnerud, L. (1995). *Kvinnor som väljare och valda* [Women as voters and the elected]. Lund, Sweden: Studentlitteratur.

Regnér, Å. (1996). *Hälften vore nog: Om kvinnor och män på 90-talets arbetsmarknad* [Half would be enough: Women and men in the labour market of the '90s] (Statens Offentliga Utredningar [Government Official Reports] No. 156). Stockholm: Gotab.

Riksförsäkringsverket [National Social Insurance Office]. (1993). *Vilka pappor kom hem? En rapport om uttaget av föräldrapenningen 1989 och 1990 för barn födda 1989* [Which fathers came home? A report on the use of parental leave 1989 and 1990 for children born 1989] (Report No. Is-I-3). Stockholm: Author.

Riksförsäkringsverket (1994). *Från moderskap till föräldraskap* [From motherhood to parenthood] (Report No. 1). Stockholm: Author.

Riksförsäkringsverket (1996). *Föräldrapenning 1995* [Parental leave 1995] (Report No. Is-I-8). Stockholm: Author.

Roman, C. (1994). *Lika på olika villkor: Könssegregering i kunskapsföretag.* [Equal on unequal terms: Gender segregation in companies within the information sector]. Stockholm: Symposion.

Statens Offentliga Utredningar. (1972). *Förskolan del 1: Betänkande angivet av 1968 års barnstugeutredning* [Nursery school part 1: Report from the 1968 investigation of child day care centres] (Report No. 26). Stockholm: Author.

Statistiska Centralbyrån. (1990). *Folk och bostadsräkningen 1990* [Population and housing counts 1990]. Stockholm: Author.

Statistiska Centralbyrån. (1996). *Arbetskraftsundersökningen årsmedetal 1996* [Labour force annual survey 1996]. Stockholm: Author.

Sundström, M. (1993). The growth in full time work among Swedish women in the 1980s. *Acta Sociologica, 36,* 139-150.

Wadsby, M., & Svedin, C. (1993). Skilsmässa: Bakgrund, orsaker och följder [Divorce: Background, causes, and consequences]. In A. Agell, B. Arve-Parès, & U. Björnberg (Eds.), *Om modernt familjeliv och familjeseparationer* [On modern family life and family separations] (pp. 177-186). Stockholm: Council for Social Research.

PART **II**

Workplace Programs
and Policies

A common criticism of organizational change processes is that those that focus almost exclusively on the development of policies and programs are almost always likely to result in limited outcomes. Instead, it is argued that genuine change will eventuate only if a more strategic, business-focused approach is adopted and if concerted efforts are made to change the internal culture of an organization. Programs and policies themselves will have little impact unless they are aligned with internal drivers of change. Nevertheless, it could be that programs and policies, if imposed externally through laws and regulations, could, over time, result in substantial internal change and the achievement of effective outcomes.

This type of argument is also evident in the gender equity and work-family areas. For many, the process of change began with external impositions (e.g., paid parental leave for women and men, affirmative action for women, and the International Labour Organisation Resolution 156 addressing the needs of workers with family responsibilities). However, the assumptions behind these laws and regulations or their intent vary markedly. These range from ensuring that women have equal employment opportunities to ensuring that the needs of children are cared for when parents are in paid employment. Gender equity—in both paid work and home life—has never been the major driver of workplace policies or programs. Sweden, however (as was noted in Chapter 5), has had a

broad policy focus on gender equity and ensuring that men have equal opportunities to share caregiving responsibilities with women.

Like the more general organizational change debate, the work-family and
gender equity discourse is now much more focused on business benefits and
organizational change. Most current commentaries on progress on work-family
issues and gender equity in the workplace emphasize two major shortcomings
of past approaches. First, there has been a lack of emphasis on gender equity
as a strategic business issue, and second, there has been a lack of emphasis on
changing the culture of organizations. These analyses challenge the extent to
which organizations have changed either to have a genuine focus on gender
equity or to become family friendly, and they point to the broader systemic and
organizational issues that need to be addressed for this to be achieved. This
argument is about the need to integrate gender equity and work-family into
strategic thinking within organizations.

These are the issues that provide the focus for this part. Specifically, chapters
address the following key questions:

1. What has been the history of the development of workplace programs and policies
   relevant to both work and family and gender equity?

2. What are the current trends in workplace programs and policies, and how can these
   be explained?

3. What programs and policies have been found to be effective in promoting gender
   equity?

4. What are the likely future directions in workplace programs and policies?

Given the very different approaches taken in the four countries (e.g., differences in the extent to which governments have been involved), these analyses
provide important insights into the process of change and the potential more
broadly based policies and programs have for producing changes in organizational and individual outcomes.

6

Workplace Programs and Policies That Address Work-Family and Gender Equity Issues in the United States

GARY L. BOWEN

Only a minority of wives are really successful at handling both a large agenda of social or civic obligations and their home duties, but everyone puts up such a good front that many a wife begins to feel that something is wanting in her that she is not the same. Determined to be as normal as anyone else, or a little more so, they take on a back-breaking load of duties—and a guilt feeling that they're not up to it. (Whyte, 1956, p. 363)

Many structural and normative changes have occurred in the fabric of work and family in U.S. society since the publication of Whyte's classical sociological volume titled *The Organization Man*, which was written at the height of the baby boom. Women's labor force rates have doubled; marriage rates have declined; cohabitation rates have increased; divorce rates have soared; voluntary childlessness rates have increased; fertility rates have declined; personal freedom and fulfillment have assumed greater emphasis in both public and private discourse; and a growing convergence toward egalitarianism has been evidenced in the gender role norms of men and women (Barich & Bielby, 1996; Bowen & Kilpatrick, 1995; Bumpass, 1990; Thornton, 1989; Yankelovich, 1981). Traditional assumptions about the homemaker wife and the breadwinner husband have been challenged as an increasing number of men and women negotiate new rules for work and marriage based on norms of fairness and shared responsibility (Barich & Bielby, 1996). Although men and women have made progress in achieving a fairer distribution of duties and rewards in the work and family realms, gender remains a defining source of stratification that constrains women's opportunities in paid employment and limits men's participation in family work. Despite the increasing labor force participation of women, especially married women with young children, at least one constancy remains from Whyte's day: the role strain felt by women as they attempt to juggle the demands from their multiple statuses in the context of existing "cultural mandates" about the roles of men and women (Coser & Rokoff, 1974).

Despite women's greater participation in the paid labor force, as a group, the career success and the psychological well-being of women in the labor force remain thwarted by traditional expectations for women and by a lack of support on both the work front and the home front, even in dual-career families in which both husband and wife occupy high-status jobs (Hertz, 1986; Hochschild, 1989). Neither front is "gender neutral" (Ferree, 1990; Geller & Hobfoll, 1994).

On the work front, men still occupy the top tier of jobs that are associated with high pay and prestige. Women remain concentrated in low-wage, female-dominated occupations and are like missing persons across a number of career fields (Mahony, 1995). Although women are closing the wage gap, they still earn only about 70 cents for every dollar that men earn (Dobosz, Mitchell, Papazian, Sepah, & Smith, 1997). Even more alarming, although still underrepresented, the proportion of women who graduate from college with science degrees has appeared to have peaked; in some majors, such as computer science and economics, the proportion of women who receive degrees has declined (Dembner, 1996).

Although the number of women-owned businesses has increased over the last decade and an increasing number of women are moving into the upper-management ranks of more progressive companies (Moskowitz, 1996; Schumuckler, 1996), women hold less than 5% of senior manager positions in large corporations (Brooks & Groves, 1996). In a recent survey by Catalyst of 1,251 female high-ranking executives at Fortune 1000 companies, the respondents described gender as a significant definer of their career experience, a barrier that they overcame by working hard and by consistently performing beyond expectations at work (cited in Crittenden, 1996). Many of these women felt limited in their career advancement by an unsupportive corporate culture that included male stereotyping and a lack of access to informal networks in the workplace.

On the home front, women continue to perform a disproportionate share of family work (Berk, 1985; Pittman, Solheim, & Blanchard, 1996; Spitze, 1988). The gap in the number of hours that men and women devote to family work has decreased, but the decrease is explained more by women's withdrawal than by men's participation. As a consequence, employed women continue to experience greater levels of role conflict and role strain than men in balancing work and family responsibilities (Berger, Cook, DelCampo, Herrera, & Weigel, 1994). Stress has become a defining characteristic of dual-earner households.

Although a greater number of workplaces are attempting to develop policies and programs that promote gender equity and that help employees balance work and family demands, such workplaces remain the exception rather than the rule. The workplace culture has lagged even further behind behavior shifts and has remained traditional in many respects for both men and women. As recently concluded by Hochschild (1997), "The workplace has changed women more than we have changed it" (p. 39).

This chapter provides an overview of workplace programs and policies relevant to work-family and gender issues in the United States, including those initiated by government and employers. Following a historical perspective on the respective roles of government and the private sector in responding to the needs of citizens and families, an update is provided of the current status of workplace programs and policies in the United States, including a discussion of selected structural forces that have encouraged an expanded interest and response. The "profit ethic" is discussed in the context of the sociology of motives as a cultural force that is restraining the development of more equitable and family-responsive workplaces. The chapter concludes by offering predictions for the future direction of workplace programs and policies in the United States.

THE HISTORICAL CONTEXT

The legislation and policies of the 1930s New Deal, in which the federal government assumed basic responsibility for public welfare, represented an early turning point in the history of workplace supports for employees (Kamerman & Kingston, 1982). An understanding of these sociohistorical forces and developments provides a context to understand trends in the development of workplace supports today.

Welfare Capitalism

During the 19th century, the United States shifted from an agrarian society to an industrial one. As workers migrated from farms to towns to fuel the engines of the industrial revolution, supports were needed to accommodate them. As described by Reid (1995), "The streets surely were not paved with gold for most individuals, and the realities of this new industrial order were harsh, indeed" (p. 2211). In response to this situation and encouraged by a unique American ideology rooted in the Constitution and the Bill of Rights that calls for minimal government involvement in private enterprise and in the personal lives of citizens and families (Googins, 1994), employers assumed an increasing role for the welfare of their employees and their employees' families during the late 1800s and early part of the 20th century (Brandes, 1976). This response, which Brandes (1976) termed "welfare capitalism," was encouraged by the government, in part, as a solution to labor troubles in the late 1880s and assumed by companies, in part, in an attempt to prevent the development of trade and labor unions (Kamerman & Kingston, 1982; Orthner, Bowen, & Beare, 1990). In this context, company paternalism reached its pinnacle during the 1920s, having evolved to exert considerable control and influence over almost every aspect of the worker's life—including provisions for housing, medical care, education, and social and recreational outlets (Kamerman & Kingston, 1982).

Trends and developments in the late 1920s and the early 1930s began to challenge the viability of welfare capitalism and the need for more leadership and involvement from the federal government (Kamerman & Kingston, 1982; Orthner et al., 1990). As factories incorporated new technology, like automation, production tasks required fewer workers, creating a surplus of labor. Developments in transportation, including the increasing availability of automobiles, meant that workers no longer needed to live in close proximity to the work site. Workers also began to resent the encompassing control that the workplace exercised over almost every aspect of their lives, as well as the lives of their families. An increasing number of public and voluntary social service agencies also appeared to assist individuals and families with difficulties (Brilliant, 1995; Reisch, 1995).

The weakening of the economy that culminated in the Great Depression struck a "final blow" to welfare capitalism and showed that neither the private nor the voluntary social service sector had the ability or resources to respond adequately to the needs of individuals and their families in such times (Kamerman & Kingston, 1982; Reisch, 1995). A more active government role was also consistent with Progressivism, a social and political movement in the late 19th and early 20th centuries that questioned the wisdom of unbridled capitalism, encouraged social responsibility for problems associated with rapid industrialization, advocated for child labor laws and women's suffrage, and encouraged collective responsibility for the general welfare (Reid, 1995).

A New Order

A "new order" in which the government assumed greater responsibility for public welfare arose from the ashes of the Depression. As concluded by Reid (1995),

> More than any specific piece of legislation, the New Deal brought to American life an unprecedented federal-level focus, a new progressive coalition, and a

permanent strengthening of the federal government that would place it at the center of responsibility for the character of American society and the welfare of its citizens. (p. 2215)

One product of this "new order" was a growing separation between work and family life in the workplace as employers adopted a more rational and bureaucratic management ethic (Orthner et al., 1990). Encouraged by such works as *Scientific Management* by Taylor (1947), a "masculine ethic" and a "separate worlds" orientation between work and family life developed in the workplace and in the larger society and fueled an increasing division of labor between men and women (Kanter, 1977a, 1977b). Men were defined as responsible primarily for paid work, while women were responsible primarily for family work. Based on this new organizational ethic, family demands were subordinated to organizational demands, and work organizations operated to minimize the potential inclusion of family life into the workplace (Aldous, 1969; Bowen, 1991; Kanter, 1977b; Sussman, 1977).

Despite the end of welfare capitalism in its most developed form, private industry never totally disengaged from responding to the private needs of employees and their families. For example, even during the Great Depression years, Ford Motor Company continued to teach English to new immigrant employees and provided financial assistance to help employees and their families who faced special hardships (Masi, 1982). As during World War I, many private and government employers provided child care during World War II so that women could move into jobs left vacant by men entering military service (Brown, 1984). In the years after World War II, trade and labor unions grew significantly in power and influence and successfully negotiated with employers to provide workers with a range of fringe benefits, including health care insurance and pension plans. Yet, the respective roles of government and industry in assuming responsibility for the general welfare had shifted. The role of the federal government in providing public social services grew exponentially in the years following the Depression, especially during the 1960s and 1970s, to create what has been described as the "modern welfare state" (Reisch, 1995). In addition, since the end of World War II, members of Congress have played an active role in sponsoring bills that protect the employment rights of women; 29 such laws were enacted from 1945 to 1990 (Burstein, Bricher, & Einwohner, 1995).

The Clarion Call

Faced with low economic growth, a mounting federal deficit, high welfare costs, and a burgeoning federal bureaucracy, the Reagan administration attempted to stimulate the economy during the 1980s through tax cuts, by reducing the federal role in and expenditures for public social services through block grants, and by encouraging employers to assume more responsibility for the private lives of employees and their families (Bowen, 1988; Jansson & Smith, 1996; Reisch, 1995). As described by Googins (1994), such policies are consistent with "the images of the original tenets of the founding fathers that a nation governs best which governs least" (p. 202). Conferences were sponsored by the federal government and partnerships were formed with employee unions to debate the respective roles of government, business, and labor in helping employees balance work and family demands and to encourage employers to broaden their role and scope in support of the nation's families (Bowen, 1988; Bureau of National Affairs, 1986).

Government and union efforts to address work-family and gender equity issues have intensified since the Reagan years. Bills sponsored in the U.S. Congress that address family and gender issues in the workplace have increased significantly during the last decade (Burstein et al., 1995). In 1993, shortly after taking office, President Clinton signed the Family and Medical Leave Act (FMLA), which requires employers with 50 employees or more to extend up to 12 weeks of unpaid, job-protected leave to employees who are facing serious health problems either themselves or in their families or who have responsibility for a newborn or adopted child (Commission on Leave, 1996). Although a relatively small proportion of employees who qualify for FMLA leave have actually taken advantage of the law so far, employer compliance with the law is high, and most employers report minimal costs associated with its implementation (Commission on Leave, 1996). The Clinton administration has been particularly responsive to women's voices for equal opportunity and the need for workplace policies and programs that help men and women meet responsibilities in both the workplace and family (Moskowitz, 1996).

THE CURRENT SITUATION

If paid work and family work were explained by choice alone, it would seem that men and women would be equally likely to perform these tasks and to experience similar levels of success and gratification from role performance. But paid work and family work are not explained by choice alone; they are influenced by larger contextual effects that constrain pure voluntarism (Bowen & Pittman, 1995). Among these contextual effects are government and workplace policies and supports.

Workplaces in the United States have become more responsive in recent years to the family needs of and demands on their employees. But there is a long way to go to accomplish the goal of work-family balance and gender equity, in which family and gender considerations become an integral variable in business planning, decision making, and job design. Although estimates vary depending on the workplace policies and programs that are the subject of review (Galinsky, Bond, & Friedman, 1994; MacDermid & Targ, 1995), probably no more than 5% of workplaces in the United States offer work-family strategies that are considered at the cutting edge. The United States continues to significantly lag in comparison with other industrial nations (Aldous, 1990; Pleck, 1992).

The Top 5%

Many large-scale corporations, such as Dupont, IBM, and Merck, have been trailblazers in developing an impressive array of personnel policies and support programs that promote gender equity in the workplace and help employees to balance work-family demands and responsibilities. Some of these corporations have received national recognition for their innovative policies and programs. For example, 10 companies were identified in a recent issue of *Business Week,* from among 37 publicly traded companies, on the basis of their work-family policies and benefits and the degree to which employees reported that they take advantage of these policies and benefits without jeopardizing their careers (Hammonds, 1996). The top-scoring companies represented a number of employment sectors.

Working Mother magazine conducts an annual survey to identify the 100 best companies for working women. In addition to workplace policies and programs that support employees in balancing work and family responsibilities, the criteria for selection include attention to pay and career-advancement opportunities for women. In its 1996 survey (Moskowitz, 1996), 17 companies made the list for the first time, including two Wall Street companies.

Many companies today offer an impressive array of family-friendly programs, including child care and elder care assistance, reimbursement accounts, alternative work schedules, information and referral services, paid personal days for child and family responsibilities, fitness centers, and stress-management and family-life education programs (see Pleck, 1992). A growing number of public and private employers have established policies that extend benefits to the partners of employees in cohabiting relationships (Wisensale & Heckart, 1993), including same-sex couples. In some cases, companies have expanded their human resources divisions to include new titles, such as work-family manager, that symbolize recognition and expanded attention to issues of gender equity and work-family balance (Hammonds, 1996). These benefits and supports play an important role in starting to level the corporate playing field for men and women and in promoting the ability of employees to integrate work-family demands and responsibilities.

Driving Forces

The expanded interest and response by such employers in addressing work-family and gender issues in the workplace have been stimulated by a number of demographic and social trends. First, women are in the paid workforce to stay (Commission on Leave, 1996). No trend in American society has perhaps received as much attention as the increase in women's labor force participation, especially among mothers with young children. The proportion of women with children under 3 in the labor force now exceeds 50% (Dortch, 1996), a proportion that Kamerman and Kahn (1981) consider a "tipping point" in the development of family-oriented policies and programs in the workplace. In part, this trend is driven by low birthrates and labor shortages that have opened up new opportunities for women. It is also fueled by new economic realities that have paralleled changes in the U.S. economy, including a stagnation in real wages (Bowen, Desimone, & McKay, 1995; Hewlett, 1990). In many two-parent households, two incomes are an economic necessity, not a luxury—an attempt to sustain rather than enhance family income (Mishel & Bernstein, 1994).

Second, gender politics in marriage are being redefined as men and women struggle to negotiate relationships based on norms of shared responsibility for paid work and family work. Economics is not the only motivating force that is propelling women into the labor force and sustaining their employment. Like their male counterparts, an increasing number of women are pursuing careers, not just jobs, and receive dividends from work beyond their paychecks (Commission on Leave, 1996; Yankelovich Partners, 1996). In addition, an increasing number of fathers want to be full participants in the care and rearing of their children (Bowen & Orthner, 1991; Levine & Pittinsky, 1997). Both men and women are beginning to demand that the workplace develop policies and programs that align with new politics in intimate relationships and break down the traditional division of family work and paid work by gender.

A third factor is that stress levels among men and women in U.S. society are at epidemic levels (Yankelovich Partners, 1996). In part, this increased level of stress results from the role conflict and role strain that men and women experience as they attempt to juggle the multiple and omnivorous demands from work and family spheres. An increasing number of baby boomers are facing situations of "life-cycle squeeze" (Oppenheimer, 1974) as they simultaneously balance demands from children on one end of the developmental curve and elder care responsibilities on the other.

Higher stress levels today are also related to turbulence in the workplace that has shattered the idea of job security and made change a normative state in the workplace. Downsizing, restructuring, declines in real wages, cuts in salary and traditional benefits, increases in involuntary part-time work, and layoffs have increased job displacements and feelings of economic vulnerability and distress (Bowen et al., 1995; MacDermid & Targ, 1995; Voydanoff, 1990). Often without the backup support from a second adult, single parents, especially single mothers, are particularly vulnerable to the vagaries of the employment sector. Many of these parents are also caught in the web of recent welfare reforms that neglect broader structural barriers to employment and economic self-sufficiency (Bowen et al., 1995; Wilson, 1987).

In part, employers have attempted to offset employment fears by expanding workplace supports to the survivors (Hammonds, 1996). Yet the employer's "bottom line" still dictates the priorities for most employees. In a survey of nearly 8,000 employees across 37 companies with family-friendly histories, which was conducted by *Business Week* and the Center on Work and Family at Boston University (Hammonds, 1996), three fifths of survey respondents described their employers as "not" or "only somewhat" entering "the people variable" into the corporate decision-making equation. In a recent national survey by Yankelovich Partners (1996) of 1,003 parents who had children under 16 living with them, nearly three fifths evaluated their jobs as "very stressful," and the majority (51%) described their job security as either "insecure" or only "fairly secure."

Finally, research suggests that the more employees perceive that their employers appreciate their contributions and show concern for their well-being as people, the greater the dividends for the employer, in the form of greater organizational commitment, job attendance, job performance, and organizational citizenship (Bowen, 1998; Eisenberger, Fasolo, & Davis-LaMastro, 1990; Shore & Wayne, 1993). These studies suggest that workplace policies and programs that address work-family and gender equity issues may contribute to the organization's "bottom line" to the extent that they increase the employee's sense of organizational support. However, evaluations that have addressed the economic merit of workplace policies and programs have produced equivocal results about their cost benefit and have been noted for their lack of methodological rigor (Beinecke, 1994). Still, anecdotal accounts and descriptive studies across a number of organizations suggest that family-friendly supports for employees do promote organizational outcomes by increasing employee productivity, reducing absenteeism and turnover, and increasing employee morale and organizational commitment (Hammonds, 1996). The effectiveness of these policies and programs depend in large part on the extent to which employees are engaged in a collaborative process with management in designing the programs and the extent to which they penetrate into the underlying organizational culture to shape the responses of work managers and front-line supervisors (Rapoport & Bailyn, 1996). Bowen and Orthner (1991) suggest that organizational behavior in support of families has evolved faster than the underlying organizational culture, especially for men.

The Other 95%

Despite notable examples of family-friendly corporations, the workplace has generally been slow to respond to the challenges faced by men and women on both the work front and the home front. Formal work-family initiatives have been confined mostly to larger companies, with relatively few companies offering a full range of work-family policies and benefits. In most cases, the programs and supports offered by companies are relatively superficial and cosmetic responses to the complex issues faced by employees in balancing work and family responsibilities (Hammonds, 1996). In addition, low-wage employees, including blue-collar, service-sector employees, and seasonal workers, who may most need work-family supports, are the least likely to have them available (Folbre, 1995; Galinsky et al., 1994; Pleck, 1992; Schwartz, 1994).

Overall, such initiatives have failed to penetrate into what Hammonds (1996) describes as the "yawning divide between family-friendliness in theory and in practice" (p. 75). The structure of work has remained very traditional in many respects, with employees still expected to get the job done. The underlying organizational culture has failed to keep pace with innovations in the workplace to support families (Bowen & Orthner, 1991; Orthner et al., 1990; Raabe & Gessner, 1988). Women with young children remain the primary users of policies and programs that are intended to assist employees with meeting family responsibilities. Traditional assumptions about gender and parenting responsibilities persist in many work settings (Schwartz, 1994), assumptions that are at odds with the way men and women are increasingly constructing gender role norms and responsibilities in the home.

Policies and programs in the workplace that promote the career success of women may be sabotaged by work-family policies and programs that are directed toward women, since they reinforce rather than deconstruct cultural mandates that constrain opportunities for both men and women (Coser & Rokoff, 1974; Galinsky, 1990; Levy, 1994; Spakes, 1991). Workplace programs and policies that address work-family and gender equity issues must work in concert.

EXCUSES AND JUSTIFICATIONS: THE PROFIT ETHIC

Although there are increasing societal expectations for workplaces to become more family responsive and gender sensitive, employers have been slow to create a work environment that improves the lot for women and supports employees in meeting family responsibilities. A rich tradition in sociology has invoked the concept of motive to help explain the discrepancy between norms and behavior (Keller, 1994, pp. 8-10).

A number of social structural motives could be discussed, including contrasting views by the political Right and the political Left about the role of women in society (Aldous, 1990); differences of opinion among advocacy groups, even among feminists, about the potential consequences of workplace policies and programs on the career advancement of women (Littleton, Friedan, Auerbach, Resnik, & Geller, 1994; Pleck, 1992); the respective roles and responsibilities of the federal and state government (Kamerman, 1989); and current patterns of mate selection in which women marry men who are older and who have higher social status than themselves (Mahony, 1995). This part discusses the "profit ethic," in the context of the sociology of motives, as a social structural motive or explanation for current trends in policies and programs that address work-family and gender equity.

The "profit ethic" operates as a higher-order cultural motive that frames and informs lower-tier values and points of view that are more manifest and explicit in governing the conduct of work and family life. Until such higher-order motives are identified and changed, efforts to create workplaces with more family-friendly and gender-neutral environments are likely to experience limited success. Such a macrosystem focus broadens our perspective beyond individual and dyadic dynamics to consider how work and family and gender are institutionalized in U.S. society. As concluded by Lopata (1993), it is inefficient to expect individuals to solve problems that lie at the social structural level.

The Sociology of Motives

Motives are socially constructed through interaction over time and are determined by both the actor and the observer as an "adequate" or the "correct" explanation for the actor's behavior (Mills, 1940; Weber, 1957, pp. 98-99). In *A Sociology of the Absurd,* Lyman and Scott (1970) refer to motives as "accounts," which they define as "a linguistic device employed whenever an action is subjected to valuative inquiry" (p. 112). By buffering the incongruity between action and expectation, Lyman and Scott consider accounts, when accepted by interactants, to reduce social conflict and to promote social stability.

When an actor's behavior is considered by others to have fallen short of expectations (to be incorrect or wrong), two types of accounts may be called on, based on whether actors acknowledge the incorrectness of their action or its consequences and whether they assume responsibility for it (Lyman & Scott, 1970). First, actors may deny the offensive nature of their action but accept full responsibility for it. Lyman and Scott refer to such accounts as "justifications." For example, a corporation may accept responsibility for not extending benefits to part-time employees, most of which are women, but defend this as a typical action among its competitors that protects jobs in the long run. Second, actors may acknowledge the wrongness of their behavior but deny responsibility for it. Such accounts are labeled "excuses" by Lyman and Scott. For example, a corporation may acknowledge that it is unfair that more women do not occupy senior management positions in the firm but claim that too few women have enough seniority and experience to qualify for these positions (see Crittenden, 1996, for actual data about such a claim). According to Lyman and Scott, "Vocabularies of accounts are likely to be routinized within cultures, subcultures, and groups, and some are likely to be exclusive to the circle in which they are employed" (p. 124).

Motives operate at both the individual and the societal level, which reciprocally inform one another over time. In addition, as negotiated realities, motives change and evolve as social conditions change and develop, including the rise and fall of social and behavioral science theories. As such, depending on the reference group, motives may or may not be accepted as valid accounts for one's behavior. For example, earlier in the 20th century, the gender imbalance of men and women in management positions was explained in part as a consequence of women's greater emotional instability, as compared with men, for this level of responsibility—what Lyman and Scott (1970) identify as a biological excuse. Today, a social structural motive rather than an individual perspective is more likely to be invoked to explain this situation; for example, that there is an availability of experienced women in the management pipeline.

The Profit Ethic

The development and implementation of family-friendly policies and programs in the workplace have most often been evaluated against the corporate "bottom line." How do these initiatives increase corporate profitability? This profit ethic is rooted in capitalism and rests on the rationality of neoclassical economics and utilitarian theory. From this perspective, "personal development programs" (Heuberger & Nash, 1994) are viewed as economic costs to be minimized. When this profit ethic in the United States is compared with the ethics of "solidarity," "social responsibility," "universalism," and "gender equality" that inform family policy in Sweden (Haas, 1996), it is not difficult to understand why companies in the United States have lagged behind those in most other industrialized nations in the development of workplace policies and programs that help employees better integrate work-family demands and responsibilities. This is especially the case in the context of historical traditions of limited government intrusion into the private lives of citizens and a free market for balancing the laws of supply and demand that are the cornerstone of American "laissez-faire" democracy.

Of course, there are exceptions to the dictating force of "bottom line" materialistic traditions in the United States. But, in many ways, behavioral and social scientists, even feminist researchers and advocates, are contributing to what Bellah (1990) labels as the "triumph of capitalism" (p. 228). From its roots in economics and anthropology, utilitarian theory has become a dominant theoretical perspective that frames our discussions of work-family and gender equity issues—explaining choices and exchanges on the basis of rewards, costs, and self-interests (Bellah, 1990). In a recent seminar that addressed challenges in the structure of work for men and women with family responsibilities (Littleton et al., 1994), Auerbach captured what Bellah (1990) describes as the "commodification of family life" (p. 231):

> Essentially, the way in which family responsive policies are discussed now is in efforts to prove that they are economically beneficial and threaten costs in their absence. The problem that I have is that feminists are participating in this. . . . There is no longer any language about why these policies might be good for people, children, or families. (Littleton et al., 1994, pp. 1078-1080)

As long as the profit ethic remains the defining criterion for our efforts on behalf of children and families, progress in addressing work-family and gender equity issues in the workplace is likely to be slow.

The self-interest ethic that is embedded in neoclassical economics is beginning to be challenged by a growing number of academicians and social and cultural commentators, including Adams (1996), Bell (1991), Etzioni (1988), Folbre (1994), Hochschild (1989), Lerner (1996), ul Haq (1995), and Wolfe (1989). The neoclassical paradigm is also under fire in the economic community (Etzioni, 1988; Shields, 1993). Perhaps, as suggested by Lerner (1996), it is time to reform the economy by repealing the existing bottom line and replacing it with a "caring ethos" in which success depends on the extent to which social arrangements and practices "nurture ethically, spiritually, ecologically sensitive human beings who are capable of sustaining long-term, loving relationships" (p. 226). From his perspective, the workplace would become a center for the development of human potential and social connection and caring. In this context, the profit ethic as a motive for explaining the gap between social expectation and response in the workplace will become unacceptable as an account for inaction.

CONCLUSION AND FUTURE DIRECTIONS

In supporting employees in meeting work-family responsibilities in these turbulent times, the public sector still functions more as a cheerleader to the private sector than as a model employer itself or a responsible team player with private employers and community leaders. Total taxes that are used to promote the common good constitute less than one third of the gross national product

(GNP) in the United States, as compared with approximately one half of the GNP in Sweden. In addition, trends in government suggest a desire to transfer even more of its responsibilities to the private sector (Kamerman, 1996).

The role of private industry in support of citizens and families can only go so far. Evidence does suggest that the workplace is responding to the growing tensions between work and family life and receives both tangible and intangible dividends for its response to these issues. However, Googins (1994) casts doubt about the ability of employers to bear the increasing costs of support programs in the context of global competition in which international competitors have the advantage of greater public involvement in providing for the common good. According to Folbre (1995),

> When considering whether corporations should play a part in this personal realm at all, bear in mind that nonparents who participate in Social Security and Medicare will be supported in their old age by other people's children. Concluding that parents and children deserve more support, however, doesn't imply that employers should pick up the whole tab. The cost of raising children should be shared by all who will benefit from their future labor: the taxpayers. (p. 16)

Too much reliance on employers for meeting the social and economic needs of families may also marginalize entire population groups, especially the unemployed and those with more tenuous relationships with the employment sector (Googins, 1994).

Googins (1994) suggests that, parallel to the period in the late 1920s and early 1930s when the "social contract" was redefined between the public and private sectors, today there is a need for greater government involvement and a reconsideration of the paradigm that informs the respective roles that the public and private sectors play in response to the needs of families. He argues that

> any new configuration of the social contract will not require so much a diminished role for government as a different role that would avoid the stigma of excessive incompetence and intrusiveness. Such a role would include a government willing to promote a partnership and collaboration in insuring a common level of supports. (p. 210)

The voluntary public social service sector, which has been a critical resource in the provision of social services in the United States since the beginning of the 20th century, must play a viable role in this partnership between government, employers, and families.

A "caring ethos" must be the cornerstone for this new partnership in support of families. From this perspective, the quality of life is determined by more than one's collections; it is determined by one's connections as well. It is time to break free from the tyranny of neoclassical assumptions and the "profit ethic" and incorporate an economic theory that recognizes the role of larger contextual effects in individual decision making and includes "normative-affective considerations" as components of choices and patterns of social interaction (Etzioni, 1988).

The future success of the partnership between the public and private sectors and our progress in support of families rests on incorporating a foundation of values that reinforces the ideals of collective responsibility and social action. From a social psychological perspective, a "value transformation" must parallel the "behavioral transformation" that drives the existing social contract. Our Scandinavian counterparts provide a role model for such a transformation, and Etzioni (1988) provides an alternative economic paradigm for reframing the social contract:

> Where the neoclassical assumption is that people seek to maximize one's utility, . . . we assume that people pursue at least two irreducible "utilities," and have two sources of valuation: pleasure and morality. . . . The neoclassical assumption that people render decisions rationally . . . is replaced by the assumption that people typically select means, not just goals, first and foremost on the basis of their values and emotions. . . . The neoclassical assumption that the individual is the decision-making unit, is changed here to assume that social collectivities . . . are the prime decision-making units. . . . The neoclassical assumption that the market economy can be treated as a separate system, a system that is basically self-containing, and whose distinct attributes can be studied by the use of a perfect competition model, is replaced here with the assumption that the economy is a subsystem of a more encompassing society, polity, and culture. (pp. 4-5)

Government leaders and proponents of workplace initiatives to support employees in responding to family demands must understand that the solution to balancing work and family demands requires more than attention to equal opportunity for men and women in the workplace and the development of family-friendly policies and programs; it requires attention to the fundamental ways in which work and family are institutionalized in the United States. As concluded by Schwartz (1994), "Basic beliefs about what is required to demonstrate career commitment and to make a valuable contribution in the workplace have not evolved in tandem with the introduction of family-friendly policies" (p. 38). Work and family life are inextricably connected, and policies and programs that address them must acknowledge this interface to support men and women in achieving their ambitions and negotiating relationships on the basis of an equal footing in both the home and the workplace.

REFERENCES

Adams, E. (1996, June 2). Life and work becoming more and more unconnected. *Chapel Hill News*, p. A5.

Aldous, J. (1969). Occupational characteristics and males' role performance in the family. *Journal of Marriage and the Family, 31,* 707-712.

Aldous, J. (1990). Specification and speculation concerning the politics of workplace family policies. *Journal of Family Issues, 11,* 355-367.

Barich, R., & Bielby, D. (1996). Rethinking marriage: Change and stability in expectations, 1967-1994. *Journal of Family Issues, 17,* 139-169.

Beinecke, R. (1994). Assessing the economic impact of personal development programs. In F. Heuberger & L. Nash (Eds.), *A fatal embrace? Assessing holistic trends in human resources programs* (pp. 65-109). New Brunswick, NJ: Transaction.

Bell, D. (1991, November). *The AMAE orientation: The logic of connection in family process.* Paper presented at the National Council on Family Relations Theory Construction and Research Methodology Preconference, Denver, CO.

Bellah, R. (1990). The invasion of the money world. In D. Blankenhorn, S. Bayme, & J. Elshtain (Eds.), *Rebuilding the nest: A new commitment to the American family* (pp. 227-236). Milwaukee, WI: Family Service America.

Berger, P., Cook, A., DelCampo, R., Herrera, R., & Weigel, R. (1994). Family/work roles' relation to perceived stress: Do gender and ethnicity matter? *Journal of Family and Economic Issues, 15,* 223-242.

Berk, S. (1985). *The gender factory: The apportionment of work in American households.* New York: Plenum.

Bowen, G. (1988). Corporate supports for the family lives of employees: A conceptual model for program planning and evaluation. *Family Relations, 37,* 183-188.

Bowen, G. (1991). *Navigating the marital journey. Map: A corporate support program for couples.* New York: Praeger.

Bowen, G. (1998). Effects of leader support in the work unit on the relationship between work spillover and family adaptation. *Journal of Family and Economic Issues, 19,* 25-52.

Bowen, G., Desimone, L., & McKay, J. (1995). Poverty and the single mother family: A macroeconomic perspective. *Marriage and Family Review, 20*(1/2), 115-142.

Bowen, G., & Kilpatrick, A. (1995). Marriage/partners. In R. Edwards (Ed.), *Encyclopedia of social work* (pp. 1663-1674). Washington, DC: National Association of Social Workers.

Bowen, G., & Orthner, D. (1991). Effects of organizational culture on fatherhood. In F. Bozett & S. Hanson (Eds.), *Fatherhood and families in cultural context* (pp. 187-217). New York: Springer.

Bowen, G., & Pittman, J. (Eds.). (1995). *The work and family interface: Toward a contextual effects perspective.* Minneapolis, MN: National Council on Family Relations.

Brandes, S. (1976). *American welfare capitalism 1880-1940.* Chicago: University of Chicago Press.

Brilliant, E. (1995). Voluntarism. In R. Edwards (Ed.), *Encyclopedia of social work* (pp. 2469-2482). Washington, DC: National Association of Social Workers.

Brooks, N., & Groves, M. (1996, August 25). New Mattel CEO joins tiny sorority. *News and Observer,* pp. 1F, 4F.

Brown, C. (1984). Employee assistance 1: Building an in-house service. *New England Journal of Human Services, 4*(4), 20-23.

Bumpass, L. (1990). What's happening to the family? Interactions between demographic and institutional change. *Demography, 27,* 483-498.

Bureau of National Affairs. (1986). *Work and family: A changing dynamic.* Washington, DC: Author.

Burstein, P., Bricher, R., & Einwohner, R. (1995). Policy alternatives and political change: Work, family, and gender on the congressional agenda, 1945-1990. *American Sociological Review, 60,* 67-83.

Commission on Leave. (1996). *A workable balance: Report to Congress on family and medical leave policies.* Washington, DC: U.S. Department of Labor, the Women's Bureau.

Coser, R., & Rokoff, G. (1974). Women in the occupational world: Social disruption and conflict. In R. Coser (Ed.), *The family: Its structures and functions* (pp. 490-511). New York: St. Martin's.

Crittenden, A. (1996, May). Up the corporate ladder: A progress report. *Working Woman,* p. 22.

Dembner, A. (1996, September 29). Fewer female students choosing science majors. *News and Observer,* p. 29A.

Dobosz, A., Mitchell, K., Papazian, E., Sepah, T., & Smith, S. (1997, September/October). How are we doing? *Ms.,* pp. 22-27.

Dortch, S. (1996, July). Moms on the line: The share of mothers in the labor force continue to grow. *American Demographics, 25,* p. 27.

Eisenberger, R., Fasolo, P., & Davis-LaMastro, V. (1990). Perceived organizational support and employee diligence, commitment, and innovation. *Journal of Applied Psychology, 75,* 51-59.

Etzioni, A. (1988). *The moral dimension: Toward a new economics.* New York: Free Press.

Ferree, M. (1990). Beyond separate spheres: Feminism and family research. *Journal of Marriage and the Family, 52,* 866-884.

Folbre, N. (1994). *Who pays for the kids? Gender and the structures of constraint.* London: Routledge.

Folbre, N. (1995, February). Should corporate America be in the baby-sitting business? *Working Woman,* p. 16.

Galinsky, E. (1990). *The relevance of British career break schemes for American companies.* New York: Families and Work Institute.

Galinsky, E., Bond, J., & Friedman, D. (1994). *Highlights: The national study of the changing workforce.* New York: Families and Work Institute.

Geller, P. A., & Hobfoll, S. E. (1994). Gender differences in job stress, tedium, and social support in the workplace. *Journal of Social and Personal Relationships, 11,* 555-572.

Googins, B. (1994). Redefining the social contract. In F. Heuberger & L. Nash (Eds.), *A fatal embrace? Assessing holistic trends in human resources programs* (pp. 199-211). New Brunswick, NJ: Transaction.

Haas, L. (1996). Family policy in Sweden. *Journal of Family and Economic Issues, 17,* 47-92.

Hammonds, K. (1996, September 16). Balancing work and family: Big returns for companies willing to give family strategies a chance. *Business Week,* pp. 74-80.

Hertz, R. (1986). *More equal than others: Women and men in dual-career marriages.* Berkeley: University of California Press.

Heuberger, F., & Nash, L. (Eds.). (1994). *A fatal embrace? Assessing holistic trends in human resources programs.* New Brunswick, NJ: Transaction.

Hewlett, S. (1990). Good news? The private sector and win-win scenarios. In D. Blankenhorn, S. Bayme, & J. Elshtain (Eds.), *Rebuilding the nest: A new commitment to the American family* (pp. 207-226). Milwaukee, WI: Family Service America.

Hochschild, A. (1989). *The second shift: Working parents and the revolution at home.* New York: Viking.

Hochschild, A. (1997, September/October). Time for change. *Ms.,* pp. 39-40.

Jansson, B., & Smith, S. (1996). Articulating a "new nationalism" in American social policy. *Social Work, 41,* 441-451.

Kamerman, S. (1989). Child care, women, work, and the family: An international overview of child care services and related policies. In J. Lande, S. Scarr, & N. Gunzenhauser (Eds.), *Caring for children: Challenge to America* (pp. 93-110). Hillsdale, NJ: Lawrence Erlbaum.

Kamerman, S. (1996). The new politics of child and family policies. *Social Work, 41,* 453-465.

Kamerman, S., & Kahn, A. (1981). *Child care, family benefits, and working parents.* New York: Columbia University Press.

Kamerman, S., & Kingston, P. (1982). Employer responses to the family responsibilities of employees. In S. Kamerman & C. Hayes (Eds.), *Families that work* (pp. 144-208). Washington, DC: National Academy Press.

Kanter, R. (1977a). *Men and women of the corporation.* New York: Basic Books.

Kanter, R. (1977b). *Work and family in the United States: A critical review and agenda for research and policy.* New York: Russell Sage Foundation.

Keller, K. (1994). *Mothers and work in popular American magazines.* Westport, CT: Greenwood.

Lerner, M. (1996). *The politics of meaning: Restoring hope and possibility in an age of cynicism.* Reading, MA: Addison-Wesley.

Levine, J., & Pittinsky, T. (1997). *Working fathers: New strategies for balancing work and family.* Reading, MA: Addison-Wesley.

Levy, S. (1994, November). *In search of family friendliness: A theoretically based model for workplace evaluation.* Paper presented at the annual meeting of the National Council on Family Relations, Minneapolis, MN.

Littleton, C., Friedan, B., Auerbach, J., Resnik, J., & Geller, L. (1994). Rethinking the values of work and economic measures of costs and benefits: What realities of family and work for women and men must now be taken into account in the workplace. *American Behavioral Scientist, 37,* 1074-1089.

Lopata, H. (1993). The interweave of public and private: Women's challenge to American society. *Journal of Marriage and the Family, 55,* 176-190.

Lyman, S., & Scott, M. (1970). *A sociology of the absurd.* New York: Appleton-Century-Crofts.

MacDermid, S., & Targ, D. (1995). A call for greater attention to the role of employers in developing, transforming, and implementing family policies. *Journal of Family and Economic Issues, 16,* 145-170.

Mahony, R. (1995). *Kidding ourselves: Breadwinning, babies, and bargaining power.* New York: Basic Books.

Masi, D. (1982). *Human services in industry.* Lexington, MA: D. C. Heath.

Mills, C. (1940). Situated actions and vocabularies of motive. *American Sociological Review, 5,* 904-913.

Mishel, L., & Bernstein, J. (1994). *The state of working America: 1994-95.* Armonk, NY: M. E. Sharpe.

Moskowitz, M. (1996, October). 100 best companies for working mothers. *Working Mother,* 10-70.

Oppenheimer, V. (1974). The life-cycle squeeze: The interaction of men's occupational and family life cycles. *Demography, 11,* 227-245.

Orthner, D., Bowen, G., & Beare, V. (1990). The organization family: A question of work and family boundaries. *Marriage and Family Review, 15*(3/4), 15-36.

Pittman, J., Solheim, C., & Blanchard, D. (1996). Stress as a driver of the allocation of housework. *Journal of Marriage and the Family, 58,* 456-468.

Pleck, J. (1992). *Work-family policies in the United States.* In H. Kahne & J. Giele (Eds.), *Women's work and women's lives: The continuing struggle worldwide* (pp. 248-275). Boulder, CO: Westview.

Raabe, P., & Gessner, J. (1988). Employer family-supportive policies: Diverse variations on the theme. *Family Relations, 37,* 196-202.

Rapoport, R., & Bailyn, L. (1996). *Relinking life and work: Toward a better future.* New York: Ford Foundation.

Reid, P. (1995). Social welfare history. In R. Edwards (Ed.), *Encyclopedia of social work* (pp. 2206-2225). Washington, DC: National Association of Social Workers.

Reisch, M. (1995). Public social services. In R. Edwards (Ed.), *Encyclopedia of social work* (pp. 1982-1992). Washington, DC: National Association of Social Workers.

Schumuckler, E. (1996, May). The top 50 women business owners. *Working Woman,* pp. 31-52.

Schwartz, D. (1994). *An examination of the impact of family-friendly policies on the glass ceiling.* New York: Families and Work Institute.

Shields, P. (1993). A new paradigm for military policy: Socioeconomics. *Armed Forces and Society, 19,* 511-531.

Shore, L., & Wayne, S. (1993). Commitment and employee behavior: Comparison of affective commitment and continuance commitment with perceived organizational support. *Journal of Applied Psychology, 78,* 774-780.

Spakes, P. (1991). A feminist approach to national family policy. In E. Anderson & R. Hula (Eds.), *The reconstruction of family policy* (pp. 23-42). Westport, CT: Greenwood.

Spitze, G. (1988). Women's employment and family relations: A review. *Journal of Marriage and the Family, 50,* 595-618.

Sussman, M. (1977). Family, bureaucracy, and the elderly individual: An organizational/ linkage perspective. In E. Shanas & M. Sussman (Eds.), *Family, bureaucracy, and the elderly* (pp. 2-20). Durham, NC: Duke University Press.

Taylor, F. (1947). *Scientific management.* New York: Harper & Row.

Thornton, A. (1989). Changing attitudes toward family issues in the United States. *Journal of Marriage and the Family, 51,* 873-893.

ul Haq, M. (1995). *Reflections on human development.* New York: Oxford University Press.

Voydanoff, P. (1990). Economic distress and family relations: A review of the eighties. *Journal of Marriage and the Family, 52,* 1099-1115.

Weber, M. (1957). *Max Weber: The theory of social and economic organization* (A. Henderson & T. Parsons, Trans.). Glencoe, IL: Free Press.

Whyte, W., Jr. (1956). *The organization man.* New York: Simon & Schuster.

Wilson, W. (1987). *The truly disadvantaged: The inner city, the underclass, and public policy.* Chicago: University of Chicago Press.

Wisensale, S., & Heckart, K. (1993). Domestic partnerships: A concept paper and policy discussion. *Family Relations, 42,* 199-204.

Wolfe, A. (1989). *Whose keeper?* Berkeley: University of California Press.

Yankelovich, D. (1981). *New rules: Searching for self-fulfillment in a world turned upside down.* New York: Random House.

Yankelovich Partners. (1996, June). *The impact of workplace changes on families and children.* Paper presented at Family Re-Union V: Family and Work, Nashville, TN.

7

Workplace Programmes and Policies in the United Kingdom

JULIA BRANNEN

SUZAN LEWIS

The boundaries between employment and family lives have always been fluid and subject to changes taking place, both in the organisation of employment and in social relationships outside the workplace. The management of different spheres of obligations also depends on the role of public policy. In this chapter, we discuss the U.K. context in which the management of work and other personal obligations is being identified as an issue for employers. We follow this with a discussion of the research that has examined the extent and effects of workplace policies and programmes. We end with a discussion of some indicators of good practice among companies.

THE U.K. CONTEXT

Public Policy

As Chapter 3 suggested, in the United Kingdom, policies and programmes that cater to the needs of employees with family and other personal obligations, henceforth referred to as "family-friendly" policies, have historically been

---

EDITORS' NOTE: The authors' use of British spellings has been retained.

firmly *outside* the reach of public policy. In part, this is because the U.K. Conservative government of 1979 to 1997 prioritised unfettered, or free-market, forces throughout its period in power. Starting in the 1980s, it sought to create a workforce that was more exploitable from employers' point of view by reducing the scope and extent of statutory employment protection and welfare benefits, abolishing minimum-wage-setting mechanisms, and eroding legal support for collective bargaining (Walsh, 1997). This process was labelled "flexibilisation," and it constituted a departure from a system of employer-employee relations that limited the demands employers could make on employees; it also undermined the notion of citizenship developed in the postwar creation of the welfare state. In this context, workforce flexibility largely implied responsiveness to the needs and demands of employers; employees were expected to take care of their own interests and needs and to negotiate individually with their employers if and when they required help in fulfilling family and other obligations.

Child care throughout the early years of childhood and out-of-school care have never been a focus for U.K. public policy, with the exception of some efforts to provide day care during the Second World War. In the 1980s, and especially in the 1990s, the U.K. government adopted a consistently oppositional stance with respect to any involvement in child care provision. From the government's perspective, helping to develop child care constituted unwarranted intervention in the private lives of individuals, as the following not atypical comment made by the U.K. minister for competition and consumer affairs suggests:

> I recognise that individuals may have to make difficult choices to balance the responsibilities of bringing up children with paid employment, but unlike the Labour Party, the Government believes that such matters are best decided by parents, not Brussels or Westminster. What suits one family will be unacceptable to another. (*Hansard,* 1995, p. 943)

Toward the end of the Conservative administration, a number of factors, including the growing number of mothers of young children in the workforce and pressure from the European Union (EU), combined to persuade the government to consider the need for a national child care strategy. In 1996, the Department for Education and Employment published a proposed strategy on child care, which served as a basis for discussion with community and employer groups. However, it was reiterated in this document that child care was (still) considered a private responsibility and that mothers should have a choice about whether to work outside the home (overlooking the financial necessity in most families). Discussions of a child care strategy focused mainly on out-of-school care for school-age children. The report noted the considerable contribution of private child care providers, including employers, who were encouraged to continue to develop such services (Department for Education and Employment, 1996).

EU directives that address the work-family interface, notably advocating parental leave and leave for family reasons, were met with much Conservative government opposition, which resulted in the delay of the development of such laws throughout the European Union. However, British employers will soon be required to offer (unpaid) parental leave, like their counterparts elsewhere in the European Union, because the new Labour government has agreed to sign the social chapter of the European Union's Maastricht Treaty, which calls for countries to provide these benefits.

The lack of government policies concerning day care and parental leave is only one factor that has forced employers to consider finding a role for themselves in the provision of policies and programmes that address the work-family interface. A number of other factors have propelled the issue on to the public agenda, both among employers themselves and among organisations that lobby for solutions to the problem of reconciling employment with family life and other obligations.

The Demographic Time Bomb

The first factor concerns the recognition of a "demographic time bomb" (National Economic Development Organisation, 1988). This recognition occurred in Britain in the 1980s, heralding an imminent shortage of young males, the traditional source of labour force recruits. The anticipated skills shortage created a need for employers to recruit and retain nontraditional sources of workers—that is, women, and even mothers with young children, whose labour force participation in the United Kingdom has historically been very low (Berry-Lound, 1990; Hansard Society, 1990; Metcalfe, 1990). Within the public discourse, the emphasis shifted from seeing women workers as a problem to discussing the untapped potential of the large number of women who were not employed or who were underemployed because of child care or other caring responsibilities.

Examples of significant organisations that took the demographic-time-bomb issue seriously and the ways in which they sought to address it are worth mentioning. In 1990, the Institute of Management Studies published a document titled *Retaining Women Employees: Measures to Counteract Labour Shortages,* which surveyed the availability, reasons for introduction, and take-up of practices designed to improve women's retention (Metcalfe, 1990). These practices included offering women the chance to choose their arrival and departure times within a narrow framework (flextime), maternity and career break provision, assistance with child care, and various forms of equal opportunity policies for women. In the same year (1990), the Institute of Personnel Management published *Work and the Family: Carer-Friendly Employment Practices,* which used the demographic argument and business case to argue for workplace policies to enable those with family commitments to combine work and family (Berry-Lound, 1990). The discussion of child care within the second document was broadened to include all forms of dependent care, emphasising another demographic trend, the aging of the population. This publication also introduced the term *family friendly,* drawing on policies then being developed in U.S. corporations, and linked this notion with that of "forward looking" employers, pointing not only to the policies' advantages of recruitment and retention but also to the public relations benefits for employers.

Mothers' Employment

The demographic time bomb was followed by a second demographic trend, a major upturn in the number of mothers of young children in the labour market. The level of labour market participation among mothers of young children historically has been remarkably low in comparison with other countries in Scandinavia and North America (Martin & Roberts, 1984). In the mid-1980s, the participation level of mothers of small children began to climb steeply (McCrae, 1991). It continued to increase in the early 1990s even during a downturn in the U.K. economy, and it was still continuing upward in 1998. Between 1984 and 1994, the proportion of mothers in the labour force with children under 5 years old rose from 27% to 45%, while the proportion of employed mothers with children ages 5 to 10 increased from 57% to 65% (Brannen, Moss, Owen, & Wale, 1997). In 1994, the overall employment rate for mothers with dependent children was twice that for other women. In contrast, fathers' employment fell slightly over the same period (Brannen et al., 1997).

Labour Market Flexibility

By the early 1990s, the economy was not as strong as it had been, and this brought with it a different set of problems. The recession brought in its wake increased unemployment and redundancy, and the argument for recruiting and retaining female employees was seriously weakened. Companies sought not only to survive in the recession but also to adopt policies that would give them the flexibility they felt they needed to deal with the poor economy and the global context of economic change. They developed and implemented a variety of strategies, such as downsizing the labour force, "delayering" (reducing the layers of middle management), and even outsourcing business functions to other companies. All these efforts involve major organisational restructuring (Woodall, Edwards, & Welchman, 1997).

Eight out of ten organisations had undergone major restructuring or a change in business methods in the past 12 months, according to the results of a survey of 300 companies employing up to 250 employees each conducted by a large U.K. employment agency and the central government in 1995. Around one half had substantially revised their methods of doing business in the past year (*New Ways to Work,* 1995). The likelihood of change increased with organisational size; public-sector governmental organisations were more likely to restructure than were private-sector manufacturing organisations (although more than half of the latter had still done so). While most respondents acknowledged that restructuring was related to changes in technology, 60% said it was also prompted by competitive pressures and a new demand for skills.

As others have suggested (Green, 1992), restructuring efforts designed to create a more flexible labour supply are not all the same. A distinction has been made between defensive flexibility and offensive flexibility. Defensive flexibility is apparent in strategies that involve shifts from a reliance on a stable, full-time labour force to a reliance on a labour force involving temporary employee contracts, part-time employment, and casual employment. The survey of 300 work organisations described above found that 85% of organisations used temporary or fixed-term contracts, and 63% employed subcontracted labour. About one third had reduced work hours for senior staff (35%) and used home-based staff (35%). A small but significant minority (14%) employed "teleworkers," that is, workers in a noncentral location linked by information technology (*New Ways to Work,* 1995). In contrast, offensive flexibility may be secured by using leading-edge technologies and by making the work process itself more flexible through the greater involvement of workers, the upgrading of skills, and the flattening of management structures.

The distinction between the two different types of employer flexibility has provided a useful starting point for cross-national labour market comparisons (Walsh, 1997). Defensive flexibility has been associated with the rise of a neoliberal philosophy in the United Kingdom, while offensive flexibility is associated with a neocorporatist approach, which is more common in other countries, such as Australia (Walsh, 1997). Certainly, in the United Kingdom, the growth of temporary work is particularly remarkable in the public sector, aligned to budgetary constraints and privatisation such as compulsory "competitive tendering," which obligates authorities to obtain competitive bidders for jobs such as cleaning or catering, which had previously been undertaken internally (Casey, 1991).

Although companies are increasingly likely to develop strategies to create for themselves a more "flexible" workforce, U.K. employment statistics indicate only a slight increase in the actual numbers of individuals officially recorded as being in temporary employment. (Temporary employment rates for mothers of dependent children, in fact, fell slightly between 1984 and 1994; Brannen et al., 1997.) However, as Rubery (1987) comments, "The relative muted growth of temporary work in Britain may highlight the fact that the protection afforded by the standard employment contract has continuously been eroded for all workers" (p. 297).

In the United Kingdom, one of the symptoms of employers' attempts to make the labour market more flexible for their own purposes is the growing trend by which those who are in employment work ever longer hours. Instead of hiring new workers and committing to them with benefits and so on, it is easier for employers to request or require existing employees to work overtime when the needs of the company require more labour power. Between 1984 and 1994, full-time and longer-hours part-time employment rose among mothers of dependent children, while shorter part-time hours fell. Meanwhile, fathers' working hours have been continuously high over the past decade, with 57% of fathers working more than 40 hours a week. In fact, British fathers work the longest hours in Europe (Brannen et al., 1997).

The lengthening of working hours has a major impact at the household level and is a crucial aspect of the work-family interface. Indeed, those who work long hours are likely to be in households in which their partners also work long hours. This is strikingly the case among families with dependent children. The single-breadwinner family with father at work and mother non-employed is in decline, whereas dual-breadwinner households, together with households with no parent in employment, have become the norm (Brannen et al., 1997).

Employees are developing different ways of working for themselves. Working from home has become much easier with new telecommunications systems; self-employment is high among fathers, compared with other men. Moreover, self-employed fathers and self-employed mothers have very high levels of overtime work hours (more than 40 hours per week; Brannen et al., 1997). With many of these changes comes the very real sense for individuals of never being "off the job."

All these labour market changes, which can lead to substantial changes in the world of work and even to increased unemployment, have increased levels of anxiety and stress among workers. In this, some leading-edge employers have recognised the need for organisational practices to maintain productivity and morale among their surviving workforces.

THE INTRODUCTION OF FRIENDLY POLICIES INTO THE WORKPLACE

In the second part of this chapter, we examine the different strategies employers have used to introduce and develop so-called family-friendly policies. First, it is necessary to discuss what family friendliness is.

In its U.K. usage, *family friendliness* has been coined to cover the recognition that employers may have a significant part to play in enabling their employees to "reconcile" their employment and family life obligations. However, as family-friendly policies have been discussed and introduced, there has developed a need for a more inclusive terminology. Regarding the term *family,* the case is being made to find new terms that recognise ties and obligations that do not fit easily with the term *family* but that come up in the context of household and other changes in individuals' lives (Lewis, 1996). The terms *friendly* and *reconciliation* (the latter drawn from the language of the European Union's charter) are increasingly recognised as problematic because they obscure inherent conflicts of interests and the different needs of various parties and groups, both inside and outside organisations (Moss, 1996).

Communication problems also come up because many employers use the terms *family friendliness* and *flexibility* interchangeably. Although family-friendly practices may offer employees some flexibility in how to combine work and family roles, not all flexible policies developed by employers to help them exploit workers more profitably can be considered family friendly (Simkin & Hillage, 1992). For example, offering flexibility by allowing employees to work from home is not necessarily family friendly if the practice does not take into account who provides care for the children. "Flexible" work in the form of temporary and fixed-term contracts, subcontracting, and self-employment, all patterns that are increasing in the United Kingdom, is not necessarily family friendly because it does not guarantee the provision of a secure income. Flexible working needs to be conceptualised as a two-way process involving a consideration of the needs of employees as well as those of business.

The first strategy employers have used to develop family-friendly policies has been to extend companies' commitment to equal opportunities policy and practice, in both the unreconstructed sense of easing women's double burden and the subsequent enlightened version that involves changing the rules by which men pursue employment to the exclusion of sharing family responsibilities. Second, family friendliness has been introduced into companies as part of the business case to achieve greater efficiency and to retain and provide incentives for a highly trained workforce. Third, family friendliness is part of a challenge to the new corporate cultures, which have been the hallmark of the 1990s. For example, family-friendly policies may soften some of the negative aspects of radical organisational change, which often have a disproportionately negative effect on women (Woodall et al., 1997). New corporate values place employment or the company first, as manifest in the tendency of companies to institutionalise overtime work (also called the "long-hours culture"). The challenge of family-friendly policy is to suggest that the practice of working long hours is not necessarily synonymous with productivity and efficiency and that it may cause, rather than cure, absenteeism if it is detrimental to health and well-being.

Equal Opportunities and Gender Equality

Equal opportunities legislation in the United Kingdom has governed the opportunities of men and women to employment, in particular with respect to the Equal Pay and Sex Discrimination Acts that went into the statute book in 1976. The United Kingdom was the first and remains one of the few countries to set up an Equal Opportunities Commission. Equal opportunities policies have been particularly common in the public sector, where ideological commitment has been strong; they are also popular in banking, where recruitment and retention of women have been significant motivating forces.

Concern about equal opportunities developed from the dominant liberal rights discourse in which there was a requirement for "likes to be treated as alike" and from the idea that women are not fundamentally different from men (Webb, 1991). These ideas assume that inequalities arise from the interference of individual biases and prejudices in otherwise rational organisational processes. Within organisations, equal opportunities policy constitutes a set of top-down bureaucratic controls and procedures targeted primarily at recruitment and assessment procedures (Rubin, 1997).

In the United Kingdom, equal opportunities have largely revolved around *women's* access to employment and to promotion. These ideas have been slow to encompass broader notions of gender equity that span both the private (family) and public (employment) spheres. The private sphere has thus far been largely constructed as an issue of responsibility for children and has been extended more recently to issues concerning elder care and its relation to employment obligations. Only recently has there developed a recognition that other types of personal obligations employees have may need to be taken into account. Equal opportunities ideology in the United Kingdom has been slow to embrace the notion that men as well as women participate in family life and take on family obligations, which may affect fulfillment of employment obligations and vice versa. Opportunities for part-time work and career breaks have largely been constructed as addressing the assumed needs of women, enabling them to carry out domestic duties while continuing to be employed. As studies of flexible employment have shown, women occupy about half the flexible jobs, although these jobs are disproportionately part-time (Dex & McCulloch, 1995).

Equal opportunities policies have yet to challenge the prevailing male model of work in which full-time work is the norm and ideal for men.

A more developed objective of equal opportunities is to create equal representation of men and women at all levels of the organisation. With this goal, some supposedly family-friendly policies, such as career breaks and part-time work, serve to perpetuate gender inequalities in the workplace (Lewis, 1996). Moreover, policies and practices designed to remove the "glass ceiling" preventing women's promotion to top management positions underestimate the influence of informal cultures and practices that impede women's access to higher occupational statuses.

The "diversity approach" (Herriot & Pemberton, 1995) goes a step further by emphasising the contributions made by diverse groups, thereby changing the unilinear system of values that assumes only "male" patterns of work are valuable. This approach has the advantage of providing individuals with needed flexibility; at the same time, this new flexibility helps make the company more economically productive. However, policies that transgress judgmental positions are likely to be deflected from their intended course. For example, attempts by the British Broadcasting Corporation to treat gay couples in the same way as married couples caused a furor in the press, resulting in benefits being withdrawn for married couples rather than being extended to others (Cooper & Lewis, 1995).

Economic Competitiveness, Efficiency, and Flexibility

Family-friendly policies are attractive to employers only if they yield benefits to organisations. Benefits that make up the "business case" include recruitment and retention of women (it is assumed men do not leave work to have children so policies are not directed toward them), maximising and enhancing the productivity and potential of the whole workforce, minimising stress, and hence reducing absenteeism. The House of Commons Select Committee on Mothers in Employment examined the business case for the introduction of family-friendly policies. Quoting the chairman of a large supermarket chain (Sainsburys), the case for cost effectiveness and retention of highly trained workers is clearly put:

> We . . . believe it makes commercial sense to encourage women to progress to higher management positions. . . . It is very costly to lose valuable staff and to replace them with new recruits. For every woman at senior manager level who leaves because her wish for development is frustrated, we estimate it costs us £5000 to find and train a new recruit to the same standard. For store managers and their deputies the figure is nearer £10,000. No business can afford this level of waste. (*New Ways to Work,* 1995, p. 1)

The "cost effectiveness" of such policies is seen as crucial. The figure from the Institute of Management Studies of the cost of every "lost" employee as the equivalent of the full annual costs of the leaver is widely quoted by those endeavouring to develop family-friendly policies within organisations (Forbes & McGill, 1988). The arrival in the United Kingdom of annual awards to employers for family friendliness is also a sign of the strength of business arguments, reflecting a similar practice in the United States, Australia, and the European Union.

Changing Corporate Cultures:
The Problem of Long Hours

While companies are busy developing programmes to be more family friendly, they tend to ignore other aspects of corporate culture that have particularly negative consequences for family life and other personal obligations. Key issues for employees concern control within the workplace, because feelings of control are critical determinants of individuals' levels of stress and well-being, which in turn spill over into relationships outside work (Barling, 1994). Work time is another important factor that may have implications for the well-being of others, notably children and partners. There is some evidence of greater satisfaction in households when workplace time is reduced through a flextime policy (Cunningham, 1989).

Time is not only quantitative; it has other dimensions. The practice of "presenteeism" (Cooper & Lewis, 1995), that is, the physical presence in the workplace of employees who are psychologically preoccupied with nonwork matters and therefore underperform, suggests one way in which time has meaning in the workplace (Lewis, 1997b). Similarly, many so-called family-friendly policies in the workplace depend on "legitimate" reasons for absence from work. Policies must address the meanings given to presence in or absence from the workplace if they are to be successful. When working long hours is seen as synonymous with commitment to the job, productivity, and interest in the pursuit of a career, then family-friendly policies are likely to be exclusionary; that is, they are directed to and are likely to be taken up by "noncareerist" workers, typically women in lower-level jobs. When leave from work, though legitimate, is not deemed compatible with the values that underpin promotion, for example, then it is likely to perpetuate gender inequity.

The Impact of Family-Friendly Policies:
The Research Evidence

There are a number of problems in the so far limited available evidence on family-friendly policies and practices. First, most of the research has focused on the perspective of the employer rather than the employee. Second, when evidence is available from both employers and employees, there is a problem of incompatibility of responses, with higher reporting of family-friendly policies by employers than by employees (McCrae & Daniel, 1991). One possible explanation for this is the possibility that some programmes are available only to selected members of the workforce and often at managerial discretion (Metcalfe, 1990). A third problem is that it is difficult to estimate whether employee-centred flexible working practices are growing, because these practices include a wide range of programmes. Moreover, some of these practices are new, so their incidence cannot be measured over time. A final problem concerns the assessment of the financial gains or losses of implementing family-friendly policies, which, as we have indicated, is one of the principal concerns of employers. Holterman (1995) suggests that it is almost impossible to prove or disprove financial gains because they can be attributed to a number of possible causes.

Despite these caveats, some conclusions can be drawn. First, family-friendly practices are increasing, but they are still not widespread (Berry-Lound, 1990; Forth, Lissenburgh, Callendar, & Millward, 1997; Metcalfe, 1990). If part-time working is included, the picture is, of course, different. Part-time work has continued to increase among women and is now practiced among men, though the proportion is still very low (Brannen et al., 1997). Three practices appear to be becoming relatively common: leave to care for a sick child (or for other family reasons), extended maternity leave, and paternity leave. Estimates of how widespread these practices are vary, but it appears that at least one fourth of employers offer leave to care for a sick child and extended maternity leave, and at least two thirds offer men some opportunity to take paternity leave (*Equal Opportunities Review*, 1995; Metcalfe, 1990). However, in most cases, leaves are provided by employers only on a discretionary basis. Less common employer practices designed to help workers combine family and work include career breaks, reported by 12% of organisations (McCrae & Daniel, 1991), and child care, with less than 10% of employers giving any help (Berry-Lound, 1990; Metcalfe, 1990).

Even at companies where programmes formally exist, employees seem unlikely to take advantage of them. A study in Wales found that the number of employees who used flexible working hours and job sharing was small (Chwarae Teg, 1996). National data from employees' perspectives on child care also bear this out; only a small proportion of families (1%) used a workplace facility, and not many more received other types of child care assistance from their employer (Bridgewood & Savage, 1993).

A second conclusion that can be drawn from the research to date is that family-friendly policies are not spread evenly throughout the labour market; they are more common in the public sector and in large organisations (*Equal*

Opportunities Review, 1995). Small and medium-size employers have lower levels of provision. Local government authorities have national agreements that cover enhanced maternity leave. When employer-provided child care is available, it has been concentrated in the public sector and in business and finance sectors (see Brannen, Meszaros, Moss, & Poland, 1994). There is evidence that employer-provided child care is, to some extent, regionally specific, with a concentration in Greater London and the southeast of Britain (Berry-Lound, 1990; Working for Childcare, 1990). Family-friendly practices are also more likely to be concentrated in organisations with a higher proportion of women workers (Metcalfe, 1990).

Some possible benefits to organisations have been documented. For example, Network South East claimed a 20% return on its investment in family-friendly programmes, rising to 55% in the fifth year; its gains included greater workforce retention, less absenteeism, and increased productivity. A study of 243 large companies showed that women returned to work after maternity leave sooner in nine of ten companies that offered between five and seven family-friendly benefits (*Equal Opportunities Review,* 1995).

PRINCIPLES OF GOOD PRACTICE

The notion of good practice is inevitably subjective and difficult to define. It can best be understood within the context of public policy and economic conditions and the specific driving and restraining factors in any country (Lewis, 1997a). In the U.K. context, there is poor child care provision and services for other dependents; managers have discretion over which individuals are allowed to take advantage of the family-friendly forms of work; long hours at work are commonplace; and work-family is constructed as only a woman's issue. Good practice can be understood in terms of the extent to which these issues are addressed.

Dependent Care

Public-sector employers, particularly in local government, have often taken the lead in the provision of child care and other dependent care as part of their commitment to equal opportunities and because they often have a predominantly female workforce. The reliance on an internal market of women employees has also motivated a number of hospitals, banks, and financial institutions to develop child care facilities, including nurseries, holiday play schemes, and child care coordinators. Examples of employers that have implemented such provisions include the Royal Borough of Kingston, the Oxfordshire County Council, Midland Bank, and Allied Dunbar.

Initially introduced in the finance sector, career breaks for child care provide an example of the difficulty of designating policies as good practice. A career break of up to 5 years with either a guarantee or a possibility of returning to the same job at the same level was initially hailed as providing parents (in practice, mothers) with increased options. However, the career break has proved problematic in many ways. It is a low-cost option for organisations, but in the context of downsizing and restructuring, it has not always been possible to guarantee jobs for career breakers (or indeed for continuous employees) after 5 years. Many companies are now playing down the option of career breaks or are removing the guarantee of a job at the end. From the employees' point of view, there are a number of disadvantages, often including financial hardship, because career breakers are not usually allowed to take up other employment during the break without their original employer's permission.

Flexibility and Management Discretion

A volatile labour market, perceived and actual job insecurity, and the erosion of employment rights have made many employees reluctant to take up family-friendly provisions such as reduced-hours employment, flexibility in work hours, or leaves to care for children, especially if these are dependent on management discretion and are constructed as favours rather than rights, as is generally the case in Britain. Any policy or practice that enhances employee autonomy or normalises ways of working can therefore be regarded as an example of good practice. Policies can contribute toward a "win-win" solution for employees and employers. For example, Asda Stores, a supermarket chain, operates a shift system to adapt to long opening hours and has developed policies that will allow employees flexibility in adapting to this system, to the benefit of both workers and the organisation. Policies include a shift-swapping scheme under which any worker can arrange (via notices on staff boards or other means) to swap any shift with another worker from any department without requiring management permission. In high-growth areas such as the private caring sector, employers offer every variety of shift and flexible- and reduced-hours working to attract both clients and employees.

Work-Family Integration as a Women's Issue

Although sex discrimination legislation does not permit companies to offer provisions other than maternity leave to only women, most employers regard work-family concerns as primarily a women's issue. There are nevertheless some exceptions. For example, Oxfordshire County Council emphasises that its flexible working options and child care provisions are not just for women, nor are they solely for parents or those in certain occupations or levels. The council argues that all employees, and hence the organisation itself, can benefit from a healthy balance between work and other areas of life.

IKEA, the Swedish home-furnishing multinational, has also addressed work and family issues in a way that is gender equitable. A project to make the company more family friendly was initiated by a voluntary-sector organisation, Exploring Parenthood. It was motivated by concern about the stress associated with the transition to parenthood, the lack of equal involvement in parenting by fathers (despite the growing employment rates of women with children), and the lack of employer support for fathers to be more involved in parenting. The project resulted in a number of innovations that challenge the notion that family has no place in the workplace and recognise that men as well as women have work-family integration concerns. The innovations include a new parents' programme for all pregnant staff and their partners, which offers support and follow-up to enable staff to resume and sustain employment after childbirth. There is also information about and help with child care, to aid staff retention, and an information and advice service, designed to ensure that problems experienced by staff, however minor, can be resolved before they escalate and disrupt work, family, or both. This counselling can be provided on- or off-site and is seen as integral to the company's human resources and quality processes. A consultation service for managers and supervisors has also been developed; it includes management training on work and family issues and advice to management on issues relating to parenthood, child care and other dependent care, family relationship problems, stress management, and gender issues in the workplace (Burnell & Goodchild, 1996).

Addressing the Long-Hours Culture

In 1995, another voluntary organisation, Parents at Work, ran a high-profile national campaign on the "long-hours culture," including sponsoring a national Go Home on Time Day. Campaign packs sent to employers and individuals and media coverage drew attention to the negative impact that long hours have on workers and their families, as well as the negative impact they can have on productivity. The campaign contributed to an awareness of the issue of "face time," which often causes parents and others to work longer than is really necessary.

Barclays Technology Services (BTS), a male-dominated division of the Barclays Group, took this campaign seriously and continues to confront the issue. Barclays has a long-established equal opportunities programme that includes, for example, opportunities for job sharing, career breaks, responsibility breaks, and part-time work; it also recognises that workplace culture can limit the effectiveness of formal policies. To combat the culture of long hours, BTS is currently running a campaign that directly challenges the belief that working long hours demonstrates commitment. A number of Go Home on Time

Days were held, all supported by posters, handouts, and articles in the company newsletter, to raise awareness of the benefits of balancing work and nonwork time and to promote examples of good work practices. Employees, including managers, are urged to work "smarter not harder" and are given tips about how to achieve this. For example, they are encouraged to think of the amount of time spent on travel or in meetings and to consider alternatives such as phoning, video conferencing, or combining visits to cut down on travel time. Other tips include the importance of considering whether meetings are really necessary and if they are deemed essential, to ensure that meetings are well prepared and have clear goals. The need to prioritise, delegate, and empower others to act is also emphasised. These and other strategies aim to save time and increase effectiveness so that work can be accomplished within a normal working day. The effectiveness of the BTS campaign has yet to be evaluated, but in the United Kingdom's long hours' context, a company's willingness to confront the issue may be an essential first step toward becoming a more family-friendly organisation.

CONCLUSION

Workplace policies and practices must be understood within their national sociopolitical, public policy, and economic contexts. The reconciliation of work and family has long been considered a private responsibility in Britain, one associated with women rather than men. This may change somewhat with the influence of the European Union and with the recent change to a Labour government. The government's endorsement of the EU social chapter, which includes provisions for parental leave and forthcoming legislation on equal treatment of part-time and full-time workers, constitutes a beginning, but many issues remain. We have argued that "employer good practice" should address the most pressing work-family issues in the United Kingdom: (a) the shortage of affordable and reliable child care, (b) the lack of job autonomy and job insecurity and the emphasis on management discretion in allowing individuals to use benefits, (c) the construction of work and family as a woman's issue, and (d) a long working hours culture. When employers address these issues, there is recognition that this is mutually beneficial to employees and the organisation.

References

Barling, J. (1994). Work and family: In search of more effective workplace interventions. In C. Cooper & D. Rousseau (Eds.), *Trends in organisational behaviour* (pp. 63-74). Chichester, UK: Wiley.

Berry-Lound, D. (1990). *Work and the family: Carer-friendly employment practices.* London: Institute of Personnel Management.

Brannen, J., Meszaros, G., Moss, P., & Poland, G. (1994). *Employment and family life: A review of research in the U.K. (1980-1994)*. Sheffield, UK: Employment Department.

Brannen, J., Moss, P., Owen, C., & Wale, C. (1997). *Mothers, fathers, and employment: Parents and the labour market 1984-1994*. Sheffield, UK: Department for Education and Employment.

Bridgewood, A., & Savage, P. (1993). *General household survey*. London: Her Majesty's Stationery Office.

Burnell, A., & Goodchild, J. (1996). *Developing work and family services*. London: Exploring Parenthood.

Casey, B. (1991). Survey evidence on trends in "non-standard" employment. In A. Pollert (Ed.), *Farewell to flexibility*. Oxford, UK: Basil Blackwell.

Chwarae Teg [Fair Play]. (1996). *Flexible working practices*. Cardiff, Wales: Author.

Cooper, C., & Lewis, S. (1995). *Beyond family friendly organisations*. London: Demos.

Cunningham, J. (1989). A compressed shift schedule: Dealing with some of the problems of shiftwork. *Journal of Organizational Behavior, 10*, 231-245.

Department for Education and Employment. (1996). *Work and family: Ideas and options for child care. A consultation document*. London: Author.

Dex, S., & McCulloch, A. (1995). *Flexible employment in Britain: A statistical analysis*. Manchester, UK: Equal Opportunities Commission.

Equal Opportunities Review [Newsletter]. (1995).

Forbes, A., & McGill, D. (1988). *Understanding wastage* (Report No. 105). Brighton, UK: Institute of Management Studies.

Forth, J., Lissenburgh, S., Callendar, C., & Millward, N. (1997). *Family friendly working arrangements in Britain* (Research Report No. 16). London: Department for Education and Employment.

Green, F. (1992). On the political economy of skill in the advanced industrial relations. *Review of Political Economy, 4*, 413-435.

Hansard [Report of the proceedings in the House of Parliament]. (1995, December). Vol. 268, no. 20. London: Her Majesty's Stationery Office.

Hansard Society. (1990). *The report of the Hansard Society Commission on Women at the Top*. London: Author.

Herriot, P., & Pemberton, C. (1995). *Competitive advantage through diversity*. London: Sage.

Holterman, S. (1995). The costs and benefits to British employers of measures to promote equality of opportunity. *Gender, Work, and Organization, 2* 102-112.

Lewis, S. (1996). Rethinking employment: An organisational culture change framework. In S. Lewis & J. Lewis (Eds.), *The work-family challenge: Rethinking employment* (pp. 1-19). London: Sage.

Lewis, S. (1997a). *European perspectives on work and family issues*. Boston: Boston College, Center for Work and Family.

Lewis, S. (1997b). Family friendly policies. A route to changing organisational change or playing around at the margins. *Gender, Work, and Organization, 4*, 13-23.

Martin, J., & Roberts, C. (1984). *Women and employment: A lifetime perspective*. London: Her Majesty's Stationery Office.

McCrae, S. (1991). *Maternity rights in Britain: The PSI report on the experiences of women.* London: Policy Studies Institute.

McCrae, S., & Daniel, W. (1991). *Maternity rights in Britain: First findings.* London: Policy Studies Centre.

Metcalfe, H. (1990). *Retaining women employees: Measures to counteract labour shortages.* Brighton, UK: Institute of Management Studies.

Moss, P. (1996). Reconciling employment and family responsibilities: A European perspective. In S. Lewis & J. Lewis (Eds.), *The work-family challenge: Rethinking employment* (pp. 20-33). London: Sage.

National Economic Development Organisation. (1988). *The demographic time bomb.* London: Author.

New Ways to Work [Newsletter]. (1995, April).

Rubery, J. (1987). Employers and the labour market. In D. Gallie (Ed.), *Employment in Britain* (pp. 251-280). Oxford, UK: Basil Blackwell.

Rubin, J. (1997). Gender equality and the culture of organizational assessment. *Gender, Work, and Organization, 4,* 24-34.

Simkin, C., & Hillage, J. (1992). *Family friendly working: New hope or old hype?* (Report No. 224). Brighton, UK: Institute of Management Studies.

Walsh, J. (1997). Employment systems in transition? A comparative analysis of Britain and Australia. *Work, Employment, and Society, 11,* 1-25.

Webb, J. (1991). The gender relations of assessment. In J. Firth-Cozens & M. West (Eds.), *Women and work: Psychological and organizational perspectives* (pp. 13-25). Milton Keynes, UK: Open University Press.

Woodall, J., Edwards, C., & Welchman, R. (1997). Organisational restructuring and the achievement of an equal opportunity structure. *Gender, Work, and Organization, 4,* 2-12.

Working for Childcare. (1990). *Meeting the child care challenge: Can the market provide?* London: Author.

8

From Equal Employment Opportunity to Family-Friendly Policies and Beyond

Gender Equity in Australia

ROHAN SQUIRCHUK

JULIET BOURKE

Since the turn of the century, and particularly in the last 30 years, fundamental changes have occurred in women's patterns of childbearing, child rearing, education, partnering, and employment. The experiences of Australian women employed at the end of the 20th century, particularly those with children, are markedly different from those of women employed before World War I. Although the same could be said of women in the United States, the United Kingdom, and Scandinavia, the path to gender equity in Australia is unique.

In Australia, that path is marked by three major peaks, each progressively higher than the last. First, in the early 1900s, women gained significant citizenship rights, including the rights to own property, vote, and hold public office. Second, World War II facilitated women's greater participation in the paid workforce, particularly of women who were married and to a lesser extent those with children. Third, the late 1960s witnessed the broad-based appeal of the

---

EDITORS' NOTE: The authors' use of British spellings has been retained.

women's liberation movement, which precipitated a strong demand for public acknowledgment of women's different experiences and needs.

In the 1970s, the demand for gender equity was channelled into a politicised campaign introducing a diverse range of social and economic reforms. These included the establishment of health, housing, and domestic violence services; the prioritisation of women's issues in election platforms; and the introduction of antidiscrimination legislation, equal pay, and industrial reforms. Consequently, by the late 1990s, notwithstanding continued occupational and hierarchical segregation, women had gained access to most (if not all) industries and many senior positions, and the gendered pay gap had narrowed.

This chapter highlights key policy and legal developments since the 1970s to promote gender equity in the Australian workplace. The focus will be on legal developments for three reasons: first, because law is a concrete manifestation of policy decisions; second, because international instruments have been progressively incorporated into Australia's domestic law; and third, because most Australian organisations have been more concerned about legal compliance than about strategically managing demographic changes.

An emerging trend in legal developments, and in leading government agencies and business organisations, has been the facilitation of gender equity through a recognition of family responsibilities. These developments have been stimulated by women's heightened participation in the labour market and by a more sophisticated intellectual understanding of what gender equity means. Gender equity no longer means just access to employment (which is formal equality); it also means access to the labour market on equitable terms and the provision of a supportive infrastructure (which is substantive equality). This conceptual development has prompted closer consideration of systemic structural and cultural barriers to gender equity, and, consequently, initiatives to promote gender equity have been broadened to include "family-friendly" policies.

HISTORICAL OVERVIEW OF
WORKPLACE POLICIES AND PROGRAMS

Although it may be said that Australian women have always "worked" since the beginning of the 20th century, major changes have recently occurred in employment patterns. Women now participate in a wider range of occupations and at more senior levels, and there has been a significant growth in part-time work. More and more women are entering the workforce before childbearing and returning to work after child rearing, and many are maintaining an attachment to the labour market during the very early years of child rearing.

Women's access to employment significantly changed in response to major world events. This started with an increased demand for women's labour force participation during World War I, which gave way to restrictions against their employment during the 1930s depression, and was followed by a resurgence of participation during World War II and thereafter. The most recent changes to women's employment have reflected a changing economy (particularly a growth in the service sector after World War II) and women's use of the political process to effect change.

To demonstrate just how far women have come along the path toward equality, this section provides a historical overview of significant workplace developments affecting gender equity since World War II. The focus is on national developments and reforms in New South Wales, Australia's most populous state within its federal system of government. It addresses women's central concerns, including access to employment, child care, and workplace conditions (including pay equity).

World War II presented a window of opportunity for women to challenge long-standing formal and cultural barriers to the accessing of employment, as well as workplace conditions. Because of the scarcity of labour, women were conscripted into heavy industry, manufacturing, the transport industry, and large-scale farming. Consequently, job opportunities were created for a wider range of women than ever before, including those who were married, those who had children, and those from the middle class.

Moreover, the scarcity of labour prompted the introduction of better working conditions for women, including better pay and, for the first time, employment-related child care. During the war, the female basic wage was raised to 75% of the male wage under the 1943 National Security Regulation, and the government provided some funding for community-based child care. A brief digression into Australia's history of substantial pay inequity and its failure to provide a supportive infrastructure for women's employment highlights the significance of these two initiatives.

Until World War II, wages were fixed mostly by tribunals within the industrial relations system, and the tribunals and trade unions colluded in the protection of male employees' wages. In 1907, in the *Harvester* case (*Ex parte H v. McKay*), the Australian Conciliation and Arbitration Commission established a basic wage for males on the basis of their breadwinner status (i.e., having the responsibility of supporting a wife and three children). In 1912, in the *Fruit-pickers* case (*Rural Workers' Union v. Mildura Branch of the Australian Dried Fruits Association*), the commission specifically rejected an argument that female and male basic wages should be the same. In 1918, the commission declared that a female employee's wages should be half of a comparable male employee's wages (which was extended to 54% in 1919) because "a boy knows from birth he will be a breadwinner; that is his lot in life. A girl learns that in all probability she will marry. Her work will only be an episode in her life" (Ryan & Conlon, 1975, p. 83).

Similar attitudinal barriers faced those who advocated government-funded child care during World War II to facilitate the employment of women. This represented a significant attitudinal shift, because formal child care was originally conceived as a means of providing philanthropic care to underprivileged and malnourished children during the 1930s depression. In 1942, the Commonwealth Department of Labour and National Service formally sanctioned the employment of married women in a broad range of war service occupations, and with this sanction the availability of affordable and quality child care for preschool-age and school-age children became a public issue for working mothers (Brennan, 1998, p. 44).

Notwithstanding the pressing need for women's labour, trade unions, the Catholic Church, and the Australian Labor Party were particularly "sensitive to any possible undermining of the privileged status of male labour . . . and opposed any policy which might undermine the sexual division of labour within the family" (Davis, 1988, pp. 236-237). Consequently, the federal government offered only nominal funding to child care centres to extend their hours of operation to enable the employment of married women in "essential war work" (Brennan, 1998, p. 47). In marked contrast, Kessler-Harris (1981) reports that, during wartime, U.S. industry and government offered women an extensive range of child care supports (including funding for community child care and the construction of on-site nurseries) as well as conducive workplace conditions, including shorter hours, "shopping facilities, hot lunches, convenient banking arrangements, and sometimes even laundry services" (pp. 141-142).

The window of opportunity for women's employment closed with the cessation of World War II. Government funding for child care ceased, and women were expected to embrace domesticity and leave their employment positions vacant for returning service men. Nevertheless, the 1947 Census revealed that some gains for gender equity persisted. Married women continued to participate in the labour market at a higher rate than previous generations (i.e., more than 10%) and to reenter the workforce after a long child-rearing period (i.e., around age 45; Hugo & Wood, 1983).

In the late 1960s, the women's liberation movement attracted a groundswell of approval among Australian women. This did not result in the introduction of improved workplace policies and programs until the window of opportunity reopened in the early 1970s. In 1972, after 23 years of conservative government, the Australian Labor Party was elected to the federal Parliament. The Labor Party's campaign slogan captured community discontent—"It's time"—and they entered power with a promise to introduce a broad range of social reforms.

The Labor Party's election platform dovetailed with women's interests, and, during the campaign, the newly formed Women's Electoral Lobby (WEL) established itself as the primary political channel for the women's movement. More than that, WEL provided the new federal government with clearly articulated and concrete policy demands: "equal pay, equal employment opportunity (EEO), equal access to education, free contraceptive services, abortion on demand and free 24-hour child care" (Sawer, 1990, p. 2).

The impact of women's lobbying was reflected in the federal (Labor) government's subsequent implementation of policies and bureaucratic machinery to promote gender equity during its short period of power (1972-1975) and in the adoption of similar reforms in state governments in the late 1970s and early 1980s. In 1972, the federal government authorised the reopening of the *Equal Pay* case (*Commonwealth Public Service Association v. Public Service Board*); in 1973, the prime minister appointed Elizabeth Reid as a ministerial adviser on women's issues; and the government sanctioned funding for training programs and support services for women. Most important, in 1974, the prime minister gave his personal support to International Women's Year and asked his ministers, as well as state and territory premiers, to prepare programs to improve women's status (Sawer, 1990).

To weather a change of government, and thus to keep the window of opportunity open, women sought to entrench their political influence within the bureaucratic structure itself. Consequently, in 1975, WEL lobbied for the establishment of a central coordinating agency with a formal network of departmental contacts—an agency that would focus on the development and monitoring of government policies but that left the day-to-day implementation to the departments themselves. This innovative model was subsequently adopted by the federal government and state governments (Sawer, 1990), and its success can be measured by the raft of progressive policies that have been introduced in the private and public sectors since the 1970s, as well as by women's penetration of government agencies.

In particular, women have been encouraged to expand their educational horizons—to remain at secondary school longer, to select more diverse subjects, to obtain tertiary and trade qualifications, and to participate in job-training programs. As a result, women now make up more than 50% of secondary students and university graduates (Australian Bureau of Statistics and Office of the Status of Women, 1997) and are more highly represented in nontraditional fields of study. By 1994, women university students dominated the arts, humanities, social sciences, health, and education; they equaled male participation in the previously male-dominated area of law and were almost equally represented in the previously male-dominated areas of business administration and economics (Poole & Langan-Fox, 1997). The changes in educational qualifications have facilitated greater opportunities for women to participate in the labour market, both in new sectors and at senior levels.

During this period, the most significant source of growth in the labour market has been from the reentry of women after the early years of child rearing. Hence, greater attention has focused on the provision of long-day care, after-school care, and vacation care. Since 1972, successive governments have gradually improved the quality of community-based child care and expanded its availability. In 1973/1974, the total expenditure on children's services programs, to support the establishment of child care places and to provide some fee relief to parents, was $10 million. By 1995/1996, this had increased to more than $1 billion (Bryce, 1997).

Although it is difficult to compartmentalise the effect of governmental reforms on women's employment, changes to the big picture are graphic. Women have substantially increased their overall participation in the labour force. In 1966, 84% of men and 36% of women participated in the labour force (Australian Bureau of Statistics, 1986), whereas by 1996 those figures converged to 73% and 53%, respectively (Australian Bureau of Statistics, 1997). Furthermore, women have made significant inroads into occupational and hierarchical segregation, particularly in the public sector. In the (federal) Australian Public Service in 1973, women made up 29% of employees, less than 2% of senior officers, and 0.3% of managers (the "Senior Executive Service"). By 1993, women made up 46% of employees, almost 26% of senior officers, and almost 15% of the Senior Executive Service (Sedgwick, 1994). By 1996, the latter percentage had further increased to 19% (Auditor-General, 1997). Finally, equal pay initiatives in the early 1970s have led to the narrowing of the gendered pay gap to 20% for all employees and 10% for full-time workers (Hughes, 1998).

TRENDS AND EXPLANATIONS FOR TRENDS

The 1970s and 1980s were characterised by the introduction of industrial and legislative reforms to assist women to better participate in the workforce. Because of Australia's lack of a constitutional Bill of Rights, state and federal governments have created a mosaic of discrimination, affirmative action, and industrial laws to foster human rights (including protection from sex discrimination in employment). These legislative initiatives have been stimulated by both domestic pressure and international trends. The first wave of legal reforms removed overt discrimination against women, especially in relation to recruitment, and thus facilitated "formal" equality. The next wave of reforms responded to the identification of covert structural and attitudinal barriers to women's full participation in the workforce and a growing awareness of the need to address women's different working patterns to achieve "substantive" equality. This section will outline legislative initiatives to enhance women's status in the workforce, the merging of social justice and business arguments for gender equity, and the recent development of family-friendly legislation and policies.

Since the 1970s, each Australian jurisdiction has introduced, and subsequently expanded, legislation to prohibit discrimination on the basis of sex,
marital status, and pregnancy in employment, and to prohibit sexual harassment.
The most important pieces of discrimination legislation, in terms of impact and
innovation, have been the New South Wales Anti-Discrimination Act 1977
(ADA) and the federal Sex Discrimination Act 1984 (SDA). Both acts provide
a confidential conciliation process for the resolution of complaints (arbitrated
by an independent agency—namely, the Anti-Discrimination Board and the
Human Rights and Equal Opportunity Commission, respectively) and lead to a
public legal hearing only as a last resort.

Complaints under discrimination legislation can be brought to redress only
past discrimination or harassment; nevertheless, key cases have generated
considerable publicity and stimulated widespread changes to employment practices. Women effectively challenged their exclusion from certain male-
dominated occupations (e.g., as pilots in the 1979 *Wardley v. Ansett Transport
Industries* case); from studies (e.g., from technical subjects in the 1986 *Leves
v. Haines* case); and from promotional opportunities (e.g., as senior flight
attendants in the 1985 *Squires v. Qantas Airways Limited* case and as foreign
correspondents in the 1988 *Styles v. The Secretary of the Department of Foreign
Affairs and Trade* case). Women asserted their right to work in an environment free from sexual harassment and called to account the harasser and
their employer (e.g., in the 1985 *Hill v. Water Resources Commission* case)
and even unsupportive trade unions (e.g., in the 1994 *Horne and McIntosh v.
Press Cloth Joint Venture and the Metal and Engineering Workers' Trade
Union* case).

Furthermore, both federal and state governments have introduced legislation
to encourage employers to proactively identify and eliminate gender discrimination. In 1980, New South Wales amended the ADA to compel public-sector
employers to implement EEO management plans; this was followed federally
by amendments to the Public Service Act 1922 (in 1984) and the introduction
of the Equal Employment Opportunities (Commonwealth Authorities) Act in
1987. However, to date, only the federal government has introduced similar
legislation to compel large private-sector employers to counter systemic sex
discrimination. Under the Affirmative Action (Equal Opportunity for Women)
Act of 1986 (AAA), private businesses, community organisations, nongovern-
ment schools, and trade unions with more than 100 employees, as well as
higher-education institutions, are required to develop, implement, and report on
their affirmative action programs. The AAA does not provide a system of quotas
but does require employers to set forward estimates each year and to evaluate
demonstrable change. When it was first introduced, the only sanction for
noncompliance with the AAA was "naming in Parliament" (a way of publicly
announcing an organisation's breach of the law). However, the act was strength-

ened in 1993 by providing that noncompliance rendered an employer ineligible for specified forms of industry assistance and government contracts.

These reforms have been complemented by industrial developments in federal and state jurisdictions. Industrial tribunals have played a significant role in improving wages and working conditions for women, especially since the 1972 federal *Equal Pay* case established the principle of equal pay for work of equal value (*Commonwealth Public Service Association*). Because most employees are covered by federal or state awards and agreements (Morehead, Steele, Alexander, Stephen, & Duffin, 1997), some important systemic reforms have been achieved by the centrally regulating industrial tribunals. Important decisions include the introduction of unpaid parental leave to enable working parents to care for a child for up to 12 months after birth or adoption (*Maternity Leave* case, 1979; *Paternity Leave* case, 1990) and paid "family caregiver's" leave to allow employees to provide short-term care for an ill family or household member by accessing their sick leave or bereavement leave entitlements (*Family Leave* test case, 1994; *Personal/Carer's Leave* test case, 1995). Some jurisdictions have now incorporated these entitlements into industrial legislation, and all provide paid parental leave for government employees.

UN initiatives, such as the International Women's Year in 1975 and the Year of the Family in 1994, have also played an important role in increasing and maintaining Australia's interest in gender equity. Furthermore, the federal government has demonstrated its sensitivity to international approval by progressively introducing international instruments into domestic legislation (and thereby providing Australians with litigable human rights). The Convention on the Elimination of All Forms of Discrimination Against Women was adopted in 1979 and came into force in 1981, and the International Labour Organisation's (ILO) Convention 156, Workers with Family Responsibilities, was ratified in 1990 and came into force in 1991. Both conventions have resulted in legislative reforms—namely, the introduction of the previously mentioned Sex Discrimination Act 1984 and its amendment in 1994 to prohibit dismissal from employment on the basis of family responsibilities.

UN initiatives have also affected the industrial arena. In 1993, the federal government introduced the Industrial Relations Reform Act to empower the Australian Industrial Relations Commission to make equal remuneration orders, thus partially implementing ILO Convention 111, Equal Remuneration. Despite a change of government from labour to conservative in 1996, the equal remuneration provisions were continued in the new federal Workplace Relations Act 1996. Similarly, in 1996, New South Wales introduced its own Industrial Relations Act, which updated the previous state statutory definition of *equal pay* to "equal remuneration for men and women doing work of equal or comparable value."

In 1998, the New South Wales Industrial Relations Commission conducted an official inquiry into pay equity. The commission selected six case studies for a comparison between female-dominated industries and occupations and male-dominated industries and occupations. The commission concluded that, although a centralised wage-fixing system is a more effective means of rectifying pay inequity than a decentralised system, undervaluation of women's work may still arise (because of gendered assumptions about work value, occupational segregation, and the poor bargaining position of women in female-dominated occupations). The commission suggested that pay inequity may be actively ameliorated by the development of a new equal remuneration principle that would allow the commission to more intensively supervise industrial instruments.

These important legal reforms have positively affected recruitment and promotion practices and have led to the extensive implementation of training programs to eliminate sexual harassment in the workplace. Correspondingly, women's participation in the workforce has accelerated, particularly among women with children. Nevertheless, it has been observed that some sectors and positions have remained virtually impervious to gender equity; these could be called "the last frontiers." In 1995, only 16% of federal and state parliamentarians were women, and very few women held ministerial and cabinet positions, let alone led governments (Office of the Status of Women, 1997). Similarly, in 1991, only 25% of judicial posts were held by women; very few had been appointed to superior courts (Office of the Status of Women, 1997); and only one woman, Justice Mary Gaudron, had been appointed to Australia's most superior court, the High Court. With respect to business, only a handful of women head large private organisations or sit on boards of management (Korn/Ferry International, 1994). Finally, women from non-English-speaking backgrounds, aboriginal women, and women with disabilities continue to be extremely marginalised.

The failure of discrimination, affirmative action, and industrial laws to fully enhance women's status in the workplace has prompted consideration of the limitations inherent in the legislation itself, of bias among those who administer law, and of underlying systemic discrimination against women's different patterns of work. Consequently, in the 1990s, a number of national task forces were established to identify the more covert and indirect barriers to women's equitable workforce participation and to give wider consideration to women's social, economic, and political status.

Some of the most influential national reports have included the 1992 federal government report *Half Way to Equal: Report of the Inquiry Into Equal Opportunity and Equal Status for Women* (House of Representatives Standing Committee, 1992); the Law Reform Commission's 1994 report *Equality Before the Law: Women's Equality;* and the 1995 Industry Task Force on Leadership and Management Skills report *Enterprising Nation: Renewing Australia's Managers to Meet the Challenges of the Asia-Pacific Century* (also known as *The Karpin Report*).

In addition, industry-specific studies have considered the position of women in the legal profession, management, and the finance sector. These include the 1994 New South Wales report titled *Research on Gender Bias and Women Working in the Legal System* (Keyes Young, 1995) and the federal reports *Barriers to Women Working in Corporate Management* (Women's Employment, Education, and Training Advisory Group, 1994) and *Glass Ceilings and Sticky Floors: Barriers to the Careers of Women in the Australian Finance Industry* (Still, 1997).

Each of these reports has contributed to a more sophisticated understanding of the need for cultural change to achieve substantive equality for women. Special attention has been given to the persistence of outdated management practices and workplace conditions and to career structures that favour full-time employees with minimal family responsibilities. Because women continue to shoulder the primary share of caring responsibilities, often by working part-time, these normative and structural workplace practices favour men and thus constitute indirect sex discrimination in employment. Indeed, the federal government has acknowledged that

> Community, employer and union attitudes about the equitable sharing of family responsibilities, which strongly influence the way we organise our working and family lives, are often out of step with the facts about the broadening roles of men and women. (Work and Family Unit, 1992, p. 9)

Given women's substantial numeric presence in the workforce, these reports have also highlighted the strong business case for promoting gender equity at every organisational level (including through the development of family-friendly policies). The 1995 Industry Task Force on Leadership and Management Skills clearly linked the best management practices with the use of family-friendly workplace policies. The task force observed that work and family arrangements are an issue for men and women; however,

> despite obvious trends in society to greater flexibility of work arrangements, many Australian enterprises continue to act on the assumption that women's commitment to the family, real or potential, is cumbersome, time consuming and costly. Until enterprises begin to view work and family issues strategically and ensure that the talents of the *total* enterprise is most productively and efficiently utilised, women will continue to be penalised. (p. 241)

Consequently, the most recent legal and business developments have demonstrated a greater sensitivity to promoting gender equity by accommodating family responsibilities in the workplace. The focus has been twofold: first, on a formal acknowledgment of women's (current) greater assumption of the caregiving role and, second, on an encouragement of men's deeper involvement in the family. Thus, legal tribunals have questioned the "reasonableness" of employers' limiting women's access to part-time work and job-share arrangements at more senior levels (namely, as a law firm partner in *Hickie v. Hunt and Hunt Solicitors,* 1998, and as a local council finance officer in *FMSCEU(NSW) v. Nambucca Shire Council,* 1998); most jurisdictions have introduced gender-neutral legislation to prohibit discrimination in employment on the basis of family responsibilities. The following section will identify practical initiatives in leading organisations to implement family-friendly policies beyond legal minima.

GENDER EQUITY THROUGH FAMILY-FRIENDLY INITIATIVES IN PRACTICE

Over the past decade, Australian organisations have moved toward enterprise bargaining (i.e., a system in which employment agreements are negotiated between workers in an industry or workplace and management) and away from the former system of more centralised wage setting (which was usually negotiated by unions across several industries). This has been done to provide a safety net of minimum workplace conditions and pay. Leading organisations have capitalised on the enterprise bargaining process to introduce a range of work and family initiatives to attract and retain men and women with family responsibilities. This has been done by providing access to paid parental leave, part-time work after parental leave, flexible work hours, and child care facilities. Generally, these initiatives have been embedded in an organisation's more comprehensive management strategy to enhance gender equity.

Because family-friendly initiatives are relatively new to Australia and evaluative research is in its infancy (Russell, Savage, & Durkin, 1992), this section of the chapter highlights workplace policies that have received public approval through the annual national Corporate Work and Family Awards. These awards are jointly sponsored by government and business organisations—the *Australian Financial Review* newspaper, the Council for Equal Opportunity in Employment, the Australian Chamber of Commerce and Industry, and the Work and Family Unit in the federal Department of Workplace Relations and Small Business. In 1998, the highest award was presented to AMP Limited, which provides financial and business services. (See Russell & Edgar, this volume, which highlights another award-winning company in the mining industry.)

AMP Limited employs more than 5,600 staff across 44 locations in Australia. The average age of staff members is 34 years old, and women make up nearly 60% of all employees. In preparation for AMP's *1995 Employees Enterprise*

Agreement, AMP surveyed its staff and found that 34% had children under the age of 18 and that many wanted to be able to work from home (46%) and have improved access to part-time work (31%). Accordingly, during 1996/1997, AMP introduced a range of family-friendly leave policies, including 6 weeks' paid parental leave for the primary caregiver and expanded opportunities for part-time work, job sharing, and working from home.

AMP's decision to introduce these policies was business generated:

> We want to be an Employer of Choice and recognise that to attract and retain the people we want working at AMP, we need to adopt policies that support employees with family responsibilities. To make this change sustainable, we needed to change our culture and integrate the new family practices into our approach to managing our people. (AMP Limited, 1998b, p. 7)

AMP staff have responded very positively, and business objectives have been met. More than 70 men and 350 women have taken paid parental leave between 1996 and 1998, and "75% of men and 74% of women agreed that their manager is considerate of their life outside work" (in comparison with the international performance norm of 57% and Australia's norm of 60%; AMP, 1998b, pp. 8-9). In addition, the retention rate after maternity leave has increased from 52% in 1992 to 90% in 1997, and the resignation rate has dropped for all employees (from 18% for women and 15% for men in 1993 to 11% for women and 12% for men in 1997; AMP, 1998b, p. 11). AMP explicitly attributed much of this improvement to the introduction of family-friendly policies.

AMP's adoption of work and family policies is, however, just one of a set of strategies that has been adopted to enhance gender equity. Encouraged by the appointment of George Trumball as head of the board in 1994, as well as by a supportive senior executive, and stimulated by affirmative action legislation, AMP has reduced hierarchical and occupational segregation and improved pay equity. AMP has obtained remarkable results through an intense and comprehensive program designed to raise awareness, formalise harassment and affirmative action policies, educate employees, and integrate affirmative action principles into training programs and selection processes.

In 1990, women were unrepresented among senior management ("the Executive"; i.e., the top 65 employees) and constituted fewer than 105 of the 800 employees in middle levels ("the Management"). However, by 1998, women made up nearly 20% of the Executive and 25% of the Management (AMP Limited, 1998a). In addition, more women have moved into the traditionally male sales and service area (44% in 1997, up from 34% in 1996), into paraprofessional positions (62% in 1997, up from 55% in 1996), and into professional occupations (62% in 1997; AMP, 1998a). Part-time positions had increased from 2% in 1992 to 6% (AMP, 1998a). It is important to note that, by 1998, 27 of these positions had been taken up by managers (21 women and 6 men).

Consequently, the 1997 climate survey indicated that "overall there is no difference between men and women in their perceptions of AMP as a place to work. In fact, in categories relating to the management environment and opportunities for career advancement, women actually responded more favourably" (AMP, 1998b, p. 3).

Unfortunately, most organisations have not promoted gender equity as well as AMP has, not even when engaged in the enterprise bargaining process. In 1996, the Human Rights and Equal Opportunity Commission (HREOC) investigated the impact on women of industrial "demands to work increasingly flexible hours" (p. 5). The commission observed that management often initiated enterprise bargaining negotiations to achieve numeric or functional (company) flexibility but that few workplaces gave consideration to employee-oriented flexibility. This is of particular concern, given the correlation between enterprise agreements with flexibility conditions and female-dominated industries and workplaces (HREOC, 1996, p. 32). The commission recommended continued monitoring of the impact of flexible working time arrangements on women, particularly by the Australian Council of Trade Unions.

CONCLUSION: THE WAY FORWARD

In Australia, the path to gender equity has been staggered. Until relatively recently, women's attention focused on obtaining equal opportunities in employment—better access to employment and better working conditions for a more diverse group of women. This chapter has highlighted the central role that law has played in meeting some of those goals. It has also highlighted the persistence of structural and cultural barriers to women's working at senior levels and in traditionally male occupations, as well as the marginalisation of workers with family responsibilities—all of which have undermined the full attainment of gender equity.

In the 1990s, women have been numerically positioned to "reveal and challenge the male-centred attitudes that structure the workplace" (Abrams, 1989, p. 1185), including the normative separation of work and family. However, for cultural change to occur, numeric equality needs to be linked to a better understanding of substantive equality. In 1998, High Court Justice Mary Gaudron (1998) commented,

[Thirty years ago] women did not really dare to be different from their male colleagues . . . [because] to assert that women were different, with different needs, would have been construed as an acknowledgment of incompetence: to question the bias of the law would have been to invite judgement as to one's competence to be a member of the profession. And thus very many of us became honorary men. We thought that was equality . . . [but equality] involves the recognition of genuine difference and where it exists, different treatment adapted to that difference. (pp. 122-123)

The most recent developments in law and best business practice reflect a greater appreciation of the need to accommodate (and capitalise on) diversity in employment. Many organisations lag behind these changes. It is predicted that, in the following decade, family-friendly policies will be given more comprehensive attention as a result of the aging of the population and women's increased workforce participation, especially among those in their primary years of childbearing (25-34) and child rearing (35-44; see Glezer & Wolcott, this volume). Predictions are that by the year 2011, 79% of women ages 25 to 34 will be employed (up from 66% in 1993), and 84% of those in the 35-44 age group will be in the labour force (up from 70% in 1993; Australian Bureau of Statistics, 1995).

We suggest that the most immediate concerns will be about the pace of reforms, whether they will be systemic or the privilege of the minority elite, and how wider economic and industrial changes can affect them. Moreover, some key institutions and policies are under attack. These include Australia's highly centralised and regulated wage bargaining system (the linchpin of pay equity); the establishment and maintenance of independent and government-sponsored watchdogs (such as the Human Rights and Equal Opportunity Commission); the provision of formal, affordable, and quality child care; and the supply of public-sector positions (a major employer of women). In 1998, the conservative federal government and some state governments appeared to be giving greater credence to policies that they considered to favour economic rationalism than to those that favour social justice.

In the 21st century, the challenge for women and men who wish to achieve gender equity will be to demonstrate the interdependency of economic and social policies, to entrench work and family initiatives in standard government and business employment practices, and to encourage the equal valuing of work in the home and in the labour market.

REFERENCES

Abrams, K. (1989). Gender discrimination and the transformation of workplace norms. *Vanderbilt Law Review, 42,* 1183-1248.
AMP Limited. (1998a). *AMP Affirmative Action Agency report 1997.* Sydney: Affirmative Action Agency.
AMP Limited. (1998b). *AMP Corporate Work and Family Award application.* Submitted to the Corporate Work and Family Awards competition, held by the Council for Equal Opportunity in Employment, Australia.

Auditor-General. (1997). *Equity in employment in the Australian Public Service: PSMC and other agencies.* Canberra: Australian National Audit Office. Available: http://www.anao.gov.au.

Australian Bureau of Statistics. (1986). *The labour force, Australia: Historical summary, 1966-84* (Catalogue No. 6204.0). Canberra: Author.

Australian Bureau of Statistics. (1995). *Australian social trends 1995* (Catalogue No. 4102). Canberra: Australian Government Printing Services.

Australian Bureau of Statistics and the Office of the Status of Women. (1997). *Australian women's yearbook 1997.* Canberra: Australian Government Printing Services.

Brennan, D. (1998). *The politics of Australian child-care: Philanthropy to feminism and beyond* (Rev. ed.). Cambridge, UK: Cambridge University Press.

Bryce, Q. (1997). Advocating quality child-care. In E. Davis & V. Pratt (Eds.), *Making the link: Affirmative action and industrial relations* (pp. 25-28). Canberra: Australian Government Printing Services.

Commonwealth Public Service Association v. Public Service Board ("Equal Pay case"), 147 CAR 172 (1972).

Davis, L. (1988). *Minding children or minding machines: Women's labour and child-care in Australia during World War II and the post-war reconstruction.* Unpublished PhD dissertation, Macquarie University, Sydney.

Ex parte H v. McKay ("Harvester case"), 2 CAR 1 (1907).

Family Leave test case, 57 IR 121 (1994).

FMSCEU(NSW) v. Nambucca Shire Council (Unreported), Cambridge C, IRC 97/6771, 26 (1998).

Gaudron, M. (1998). Speech to launch Australian women lawyers. *Australian Law Journal, 72,* 119-124.

Hickie v. Hunt & Hunt Solicitors (Unreported), Human Rights and Equal Opportunity Commission, H96/185 (1998, March 7).

Hill v. Water Resources Commission, EOC 92-127 (1985).

Horne and McIntosh v. Press Cloth Joint Venture and the Metal and Engineering Workers' Trade Union, EOC 92-556 (1994).

House of Representatives Standing Committee on Legal and Constitutional Affairs. (1992). *Half way to equal: Report of the inquiry into equal opportunity and equal status for women.* Canberra: Australian Government Printing Services.

Hughes, H. (1998, June). Equal pay for work of equal value: Moving toward, or away from, wage justice for women? *Issue Analysis, 2,* 1-13. Available: http://www.cis.org.au/Issues/1A2.htm.

Hugo, G., & Wood, D. (1983). *Recent fertility trends and differentials in Australia* (Working Paper Series No. 57). South Australia: Flinders University of South Australia, National Institute of Labour Studies.

Human Rights and Equal Opportunity Commission. (1996). *Stretching flexibility: Enterprise bargaining, women workers, and changes to working hours* [Report of the Flexible Working Hours and Women Project]. Sydney: Author.

Industry Task Force on Leadership and Management Skills. (1995). *Enterprising nation: Renewing Australia's managers to meet the challenges of the Asia-Pacific century.* Canberra: Australian Government Printing Services.

Kessler-Harris, A. (1981). *Women have always worked: An historical overview.* New York: Feminist Press.

Keyes Young. (1995). *Research on gender bias and women working in the legal system.* Sydney: New South Wales Government Printer.

Korn/Ferry International. (1994). *Towards 2000: Women executives in Australia.* Sydney: Korn/Ferry International World Wide Executive Search.

Law Reform Commission. (1994). *Equality before the law: Women's equality* (Report No. 69, Part 2). Canberra, Australia: Alken Press.

Leves v. Haines, EOC 92-192 (1986).

Maternity Leave case, 218 CAR 120 (1979).

Morehead, A., Steele, M., Alexander, M., Stephen, K., & Duffin, L. (1997). *Changes at work: The 1995 Australian Workplace Industrial Relations Survey.* Sydney: Addison Wesley-Longman.

Office of the Status of Women. (1997). *Fourth UN World Conference on Women: Platform for action. Australia's implementation report.* Canberra: Australian Government Printing Services.

Paternity Leave case, 36 IR 1 (1990).

Personal/Carer's Leave test case—stage 2, 62 IR 48 (1995, November).

Poole, M., & Langan-Fox, J. (1997). *Australian women and careers: Psychological and contextual influences over the life course.* Cambridge, UK: Cambridge University Press.

Rural Workers' Union v. Mildura Branch of the Australian Dried Fruits Association ("Fruit-pickers case"), 6 CAR 62 (1912).

Russell, G., Savage, G., & Durkin, K. (1992). *Balancing work and family: An emerging issue for private and public sector.* Unpublished paper, Macquarie University, Sydney, and University of Western Australia, Brisbane.

Ryan, E., & Conlon, A. (1975). *Gentle invaders: Australian women at work 1788-1974.* Sydney: New Century Press.

Sawer, M. (1990). *Sisters in suits: Women and public policy in Australia.* Sydney: Allen and Unwin.

Sedgwick, S. (1994, May). *EEO and the resource management framework.* Paper presented at the national EEO conference "Building and Equity Culture: The Agenda for the 1990s," Canberra, Australia.

Squires v. Qantas Airways Limited, EOC 92-135 (1985).

Still, L. (1997). *Glass ceilings and sticky floors: Barriers to the careers of women in the Australian finance industry.* Sydney: Human Rights and Equal Opportunity Commission.

Styles v. The Secretary of the Department of Foreign Affairs and Trade, EOC 92-239 (1988).

Wardley v. Ansett Transport Industries, EOC 92-002 (1984).

Women's Employment, Education, and Training Advisory Group. (1994). *Barriers to women working in corporate management.* Canberra: Australian Government Printing Services.

Work and Family Unit. (1992). *Strategy for implementing International Labour Organisation Convention 156 across Commonwealth policies and programs.* Canberra, Australia: Department of Industrial Relations.

9

Programs and Policies Promoting Women's Economic Equality and Men's Sharing of Child Care in Sweden

LINDA L. HAAS

PHILIP HWANG

In Sweden, the government has been the major force involved in helping parents combine paid employment with raising children. This involvement began in the 1960s, when a growing economy and expansion of public-sector services led to a demand for women's labor power. To facilitate women's entry into the labor force, the Swedish government decided to provide more institutional supports, including ensuring equal employment opportunity for women, subsidizing child care, and mandating paid parental leave for both fathers and mothers. Government efforts to support working mothers were not just motivated by economic concerns, however. Two specific ideological goals have also strongly influenced the development of work-family programs: gender equality and children's well-being. Sweden is unusual in that these two goals are not seen as being in serious conflict with each other. In many societies, people regard promotion of

AUTHORS' NOTE: The research reported here has been financially supported by the Ford Foundation, the Swedish Council for Research in the Humanities and Social Sciences, and Indiana University.

dual-earner families as harmful to children's well-being (Hantrais & Letablier, 1996). In Sweden, the majority of people do not feel small children suffer if mothers work outside the home (Sundström, 1997a).

Anticipating that the widespread entrance of mothers into the labor market would lead to women's holding a burdensome double role, women activists pressed the government to advocate a model of equality that would change men's roles as well as women's. In 1968, the Swedish government endorsed a model of gender relations called *jämställdhet* (gender equality), which declares that women and men should have equal rights, responsibilities, and opportunities in the areas of breadwinning, child care, household work, and participation in public life (Haas, 1992).

Equality is well institutionalized in the Swedish government, partly because of the high number of women who have been elected to public office. Women have made up more than one third of members of parliament since the 1980s; after the 1998 election, they made up 43%. A cabinet minister and equality council are responsible for promoting gender equality in general, while an equal employment opportunities ombudsman and commission monitor progress toward equality in work life and education. Many government commissions and working groups have been appointed over the years to take up issues related to gender, representing all major segments of society, including companies and unions (which represent 87% of all workers). All government agencies and departments, including schools, must consider gender issues in their personnel policies as well as in their operations; all proposed legislation and policy changes must be reviewed for their impact on gender (Anderson, 1998; Hedman, Johansson, Sundström, & Thermaenius, 1998).

The well-being of children preceded gender equality as a goal of Swedish social policy, dating from the 1930s. Children's rights are protected by a government ombudsman and influential nongovernmental organizations. Children's economic security has received the highest priority. Although the government helps parents meet children's basic needs through universal and means-tested benefits (e.g., child allowances and free health care), it promotes children's economic security mostly by facilitating parents' employment. Swedes' strong interest in children's cognitive and social development has encouraged the government to develop an extensive network of heavily subsidized, high-quality day care and after-school care services, for the benefit of children as well as working parents (see Björnberg, this volume). Children's emotional security is also seen as very important; this includes children's right to have a relationship with both parents, which justifies governmental mandates that require employers to allow men time off for child care (Haas, 1992).

Of the targeted policy areas, the Swedish government has been most successful at providing day care (Björnberg, this volume; Björnberg & Gardberg, 1998; Broberg & Hwang, 1991; Gornick, Meyers, & Ross, 1997; Kärrby, 1995; Lamb,

1998; Pringle, 1998). Government initiatives promoting women's economic equality and fathers' sharing of early child care have been less successful in achieving *jämställdhet*. Such a dramatic change in social structure requires support from all sectors of society. In Sweden, this especially includes employers and unions, who historically have played "a major role in the administration . . . and implementation of government social and economic policies" (Gould, 1996, p. 75). This chapter analyzes the progress Sweden has made in achieving women's economic equality and men's sharing of early child care, and it discusses how work organizations and unions have helped or hindered government efforts. It ends with a discussion of the potential for the creation of work conditions that would help men and women share breadwinning and child care roles.

WOMEN'S ECONOMIC EQUALITY

When gender equality first became a political goal in Sweden, the first subject to be addressed was women's ability to be economically independent and family breadwinners through their own wage work (Nyberg, 1997). Government officials and researchers are concerned about four dimensions of women's employment: participation and work hours, relative wages, labor market integration, and access to economic power.

Women's Labor Force Participation and Work Hours

The government has long held a general policy of full employment that has included women; this is backed up by the National Labor Market Board, which monitors labor supply and demand and provides labor market training. One policy that made a dramatic difference in women's labor force participation was the 1971 change in tax policy that lowered dual-earner couples' tax bills by levying taxes on individuals instead. This change encouraged many women to abandon full-time housewifery and enter the paid labor market (Sundström, 1997b).

Companies and unions both have supported government efforts to involve more women in the labor force, although not particularly because of a commitment to gender equality. Before the 1980s, companies and the public-service sector needed women's labor power to expand; since then, employers have realized that taking advantage of women's competence increases effectivity (Svenska Arbetsgivareföreningen [SAF], 1993). Unions decided as early as the late 1940s that they would support women's working because they were concerned that labor shortages would threaten economic stability (Mahon, 1997; Qvist, Acker, & Lorwin, 1984).

Sweden has the highest women's labor force participation rate in the world, especially among mothers of children under school-age (Svensson, 1995). In 1995, 76% of all women ages 16 to 64 were in the labor force, compared with 80% of men. A high percentage (79%) of mothers of preschool-age children were also employed (Statistiska Centralbyrån, 1997). The average number of paid work hours for employed women with children under 3 years old was 36 hours a week, while employed fathers' average was 47.5 hours. Both groups' average work hours had increased from 1984 (when it was 31.2 for mothers of children under 3 and 44.5 for fathers with children under 3; Flood & Gråsjö, 1997).

A high proportion (40%) of women worked part-time in 1995, compared with only 9% of men (Nyberg, 1997). Since the recession that began in the early 1990s, a growing number of women work part-time involuntarily, including at least 15% of those who are blue-collar workers (Björnberg, this volume; Lundgren, 1993). Most part-time work, however, is voluntary, and most part-time jobs average around 30 hours a week. Parents are entitled to reduce their workday to 6 hours until their children are 8, and many mothers take advantage of this (without 8 hours' pay). Public-sector (governmental) work organizations, where most women work, are especially likely to accommodate parents who want to work part-time (Sundström & Duvander, 1998). The availability of part-time jobs has helped women remain attached to the labor market during the early childbearing years (Sundström, 1997b). Unions have improved the status of part-time work by negotiating job security, pro-rated benefits, and good pay (Qvist et al., 1984). The availability of secure part-time jobs for mothers, however, reinforces the pattern in which women are more family oriented than men, and it blocks women's chances of being promoted in some companies where the norm is for career-oriented people to work full-time (Roman, 1994; Wahl, 1992).

To overcome this disadvantage, female activists in the Social Democratic Party have, for more than 20 years, advocated a 6-hour workday for all employees (Karlsson, 1996). They believe this change would further gender equality by increasing women's job opportunities outside the public sector and making men's jobs less of a barrier to their involvement in child care. Parents would not face job discrimination if all workers worked the same workweek (Haas, 1992). Periodically, the proposal for a 6-hour day reemerges as an issue for political debate. In the late 1990s, the debate focused not on gender equality but on the 6-hour day's potential for reducing unemployment and increasing employee productivity (Crofts, 1998; "De nya jobben," 1996; Rembe, 1997; Roos, 1998).

Some work organizations have experimented with a 6-hour day on their own. A few local governments have introduced the 6-hour day (with full pay) to reduce stress among parents of small children with difficult caregiving jobs

("Först ut med sextimmarsdag," 1995). In one experiment in Stockholm, the implementation of a 6-hour day for a limited number of workers in the public sector significantly improved their attendance and energy at work ("Sjufrån-varon sjunker," 1997). These benefits were associated with parents' spending more time with children and with stress-reducing activities, such as exercise and gardening. Men with 6-hour days also increased their time spent in housework (Olsson, 1998; "Tre milj för sex timmar," 1996). Most local governments, however, perceive a 6-hour day as too expensive to implement on a large scale (Asker, 1998; "Sextimmarsdag blir för dyrt," 1998).

Some private-sector employers have also implemented a 6-hour day (paying workers for 7 or 8 hours). With the time they have had off each week, employees have spent more time with their families and in relaxing activities, leading to improved worker morale and productivity ("De nya jobben," 1996). According to one survey, many private employers are interested in experimenting with the 6-hour day ("Nya bud om kortad arbetstid," 1996).

The Social Democratic–led government in the late 1990s announced that a reduced workweek was a political goal but one that should be instituted gradually, through collective bargaining agreements between local unions and employers. (Parliament has never legislated work hours.) So far, such agreements have typically involved small reductions in work time (e.g., 12 minutes a week), so a universal 6-hour day is still far off ("Fackliga arbetstidskrav," 1995). Most unions, employers, and policymakers are not yet comfortable with the idea of replacing the societal male norm of an 8-hour day with mothers' traditional norm of 6 hours (Mahon, 1997; Sörestedt, 1997).

Relative Wages

Women's ability to be equal breadwinners and economically independent relies not only on their ability to participate in the labor market to the same extent as men but on their ability to hold jobs with good earnings. Swedish women's earned wages are high in comparison with women's wages in other countries (Blau, 1998; Lommerud, 1997; Sainesbury & Nordgren, 1997).

Women's wages are comparatively high because most women are unionized, and unions have worked to reduce overall income differences between occupations. In the 1960s and 1970s, unions negotiated contracts with employers to raise the wages of the lowest-paid workers at the expense of higher-paid workers. The goal was not to promote gender equality; however, because women were the majority of low-income workers, they benefited even more than men from this "wage solidarity" policy. Although women's wages were climbing anyway because of increased education, the wage solidarity policy is credited with lessening a good portion of the gender-based wage gap (Blomqvist, 1994). In 1960, full-time working women's wages averaged only

50% of men's; by the 1980s, their pay averaged 80% of men's, where progress stalled (Edin & Richardson, 1997; Meyerson & Peterson, 1997b; Nyberg, 1997).

The gender gap in earned wages in Sweden is not generally the result of gender differences in human capital (e.g., education, work experience) or family responsibilities (e.g., time spent in child care; Hemström, 1998; Mueller, Kuruvilla, & Iverson, 1994; Persson & Wadensjö, 1997; Wadensjö, 1997). Societal-level factors have emerged as more significant, reflecting what Nordic researchers call the "gender contract." The gender contract is a set of unspoken rules and widely accepted expectations that society has for the rights and obligations that define the relations between women and men; this contract also includes normative conceptions about the circumstances under which these rules and expectations can be negotiated (Pettersson, 1996; Rantalaiho, 1997). The three most essential elements of the gender contract that have prevailed over time are (a) men have more power than women, (b) the roles of the sexes are different, and (c) men's roles and ways of thinking and doing are more valuable than women's. All three elements are reflected in explanations for the gender wage gap.

One main reason for the wage gap is "statistical discrimination"; women tend to be paid less than men regardless of job type because they are likely to have male supervisors who systematically undervalue all women's educational qualifications and work experience (Hemström, 1998; Hultin & Szulkin, 1997a, 1997b). Another reason is that the jobs men do are regarded as socially more important (Berggren, 1997; Jonung, 1998). If women and men held the same types of jobs, the gender wage gap would lessen from 20% to 13% (LeGrand, 1997).

In 1994, the government amended the 1980 equality law to require all employers with 10 or more employees to investigate (and "make visible") wage differences between men and women in their organizations, including situations in which women are paid less for jobs in which the skills and effort required are similar to men's (Sundberg, 1996, p. 90). Unions are supposed to be given access to this information, but as of 1998, this has not happened on a large scale ("Vill ge facket mer makt," 1998). Unexplained wage differences are supposed to be corrected by companies and unions working together to develop concrete plans for gradually equalizing wages (Sundberg, 1996). The government can hold employers legally accountable if they continue to engage in wage discrimination, but few charges have been filed so far (Frisk, 1995; Nikell, 1996a).

Although threatening to take more direct control over wages, the government still prefers to place responsibility for reducing gender-based wage differences on companies and unions, because these "labor market partners" have traditionally determined wages. To help, unions can apply for government funds to prepare bargaining proposals for equal pay for jobs of comparable worth

(Jansson, 1997). In some areas of the labor market, companies and unions have made some progress in reducing gender-based wage gaps. The decentralization of wage negotiations (initiated by employers) has unexpectedly led to opportunities to build cases for raising women's pay in local situations in which the skills and effort required of women's jobs have been similar to those of men's. The largest Swedish union, Kommunal, used this approach in the 1990s to raise women's average pay from 85% to 95% of men's (Fürst, 1997; Thörn, 1997). Raising the wages of traditional women's occupations through comparable-worth efforts can improve women's ability to be economically independent. However, widespread reliance on this strategy seems likely to reinforce occupational segregation, because women might be discouraged from crossing over gender borders to seek better-paying jobs (Jonung, 1998).

Sex Segregation

Sex segregation of occupations has always existed in Sweden, but government efforts to facilitate housewives' large-scale entry into the labor market exacerbated this pattern. Women seeking to enter the labor market received training mostly in "women's" areas (e.g., clerical, caregiving), and with the large growth in these occupations, sex segregation became more pronounced (Blomqvist, 1994; Jonung, 1998).

In the 1990s, although Swedish women and men had similar levels of education, they held quite different jobs. Women's jobs more often involved office work, bank telling, retail sales, health care, child care, elder care, restaurant work, and cleaning. Men's jobs usually involved technical work, heavy manufacturing, farming, logging, and truck driving (Jakobsen & Karlsson, 1993). In 1996, only 10% of employed women and 8% of employed men worked in gender-neutral jobs (i.e., neither sex was represented less than 40% or more than 60%; Nyberg, 1997). Experts disagree whether the Swedish level of sex segregation is similar to or higher than levels in other industrialized societies (Blomqvist, 1994; Boje & Nielsen, 1993; Gönas & Spånt, 1997; Nermo, 1997).

To reduce segregation, the government has sponsored several projects since the 1980s, including having schools take up the issue, giving girls experiences in technology, granting preferential access to the underrepresented sex in educational majors, subsidizing employers who hire the underrepresented sex, and sponsoring regional efforts to desegregate particular occupations (Blomqvist, 1994; Hagberg, Nyberg, & Sundin, 1996; Pettersson, 1996, 1997; Ulmanen, 1995). However, these initiatives, along with the government's 1980 legal prohibition of discrimination in recruitment and promotion, have been mainly unsuccessful in reducing sex segregation, because of the force of the gender contract. At the workplace, male managers collectively get to decide what type of work women ought to do (Blomqvist, 1994; Johansson, 1998; Rantalaiho, 1997; Roman, 1994). When recruiting, most employers assume women will work less than men to be with their children, which gives employers an economic incentive to place women in less valuable jobs, for which they can easily find replacements (Hemström, 1998).

This process has locked many women into jobs that involve caregiving work that women once did at home (e.g., elder care), jobs that directly benefit men (e.g., office work), or jobs that fit notions about what men think women are especially good at (e.g., customer relations). When women seek jobs outside categories men consider appropriate, they face hostility and harassment from male coworkers and customers (Roman, 1994). They must reconcile conflicting norms for their behavior (e.g., how to be aggressive without being considered unladylike). Women are also often shut out of informal social networks that provide valuable information and contacts essential to do jobs well or to get ahead (Blomqvist, 1994; Pettersson, 1997; Roman, 1994; Wahl, 1997).

One proposed solution to ending sex segregation in the labor market is to increase the number of women in management, where they could work to establish new norms for recruitment and promotion and create working conditions that facilitate success for both sexes. In the meantime, some companies are critically examining their recruitment processes and training men to understand that there are productivity gains from mixed-sex work groups (Högberg, 1997; Johansson, 1997; Jonung, 1998; Pettersson, 1997; Roman, 1994; Sundberg, 1996; Wahl, 1997).

The gender contract also operates to reinforce sex segregation in the family. Partners negotiate employment decisions based on the assumption that women's choices must be combinable with child care, whereas men's need not be. Men tend to dominate this decision-making process in subtle ways (Johansson, 1997). Because many jobs are not easily combinable with responsibility for children, occupational segregation results from women and men "freely" choosing the jobs they will take. A necessary condition for occupational integration then would be women and men's sharing power within the family as well as responsibility for children.

The 1994 amendment to the equality law, which strengthened the government's right to eliminate pay discrimination, also requires companies to take "active measures" to develop an integrated workforce, in which no sex is underrepresented (less than 40%) in any occupation. Although the Equality Ombudsman's Office recommends that such measures could include targeted recruitment of the underrepresented sex, suggestions focus more on offering individuals already employed within a company the opportunity to try nontraditional occupations. Such opportunities include customary routes such as promotion and special training opportunities and noncustomary ones such as mentoring programs and job rotation plans (Sundberg, 1996).

Companies are likely to include measures to desegregate their workforces in written equality plans that the government requires them to file every year. Plans should be developed by workplace-based equality committees representing employers and unions (Bergh, 1998). However, despite the government's power to fine companies for noncompliance, most companies have been slow to take equality plans seriously. Unions have also not been as active in plan development as the government expected (B. Andersson, 1997; Haas & Hwang, 1996; Nikell, 1996b; Pincus, 1997).

Economic Power

Increasing the numbers of women in management is another area that the government would like to see included in company equality plans because women's share of economic power has historically been small. Attention to the touchy issue of the persistence of male power is a relatively new development in Sweden, even among feminists. Up till now, efforts to bring about gender equality have not required men's relinquishment of anything; the focus has been on what men have to *gain* by sharing breadwinning and child care.

Swedish women's chances of holding top management positions are greatest in the public (governmental) sector, in which they made up 43% of top managers in 1995. Women were more likely to be high-level managers in extremely female-dominated occupations, which are common in the public sector (Ohlsson & Öhman, 1997). Women made up 72% of the public-sector labor force, however, so they are still not equally represented at top organizational levels.

Women's likelihood of being in a top management position in private-sector companies is quite small, partly because they make up only 37% of private-sector workers (Nyberg & Sundin, 1997; Statistiska Centralbyrån, 1992). In 1995, in companies traded on the Swedish stock exchange, only *one* chief executive officer (CEO) was a woman; of all private companies, only 10% of CEOs were women (Hultbom, 1997; Ohlsson & Öhman, 1997). Considering the members of top management beneath the level of CEO, women made up only 5% of these positions in the 200 largest private companies in our study (Haas & Hwang, 1993). Looking at all private-sector businesses regardless of size, women's share of top positions in 1995 was larger, 20%, up from 10% in 1990 (Hedman et al., 1998). This increase may be related to women's achieving better representation in smaller organizations based on companies' deliberate efforts to recruit or promote women (see below). It might also be related to the fact that the percentage of women who own their own business is increasing, while the percentage of men who own their own business is decreasing (Nyberg, 1997). The government has encouraged women to become self-employed by offering them 12-month start-up grants (whereas men are offered only 6-month grants).

Women's access to power in work organizations is substantially less than their access to power in national politics. Recruitment processes in private-sector organizations tend to reproduce male dominance. Manager selection has been a secretive process, dominated by a few people holding traditional gender role attitudes. Suitable candidates have emerged from men's personal networks or from similar companies also headed by men. Women's formal educational or work-related credentials are weighed heavily, while other skills or personality traits that might make them good managers (e.g., good communication skills) are not respected (Blomqvist, 1994; Frisk, 1995; Holgersson & Höök, 1997; Hultbom, 1997; Meyerson & Peterson, 1997a; Roman, 1994; Wahl, 1997).

In the 1990s, Swedish employers became more concerned about getting women into management positions, as they began to regard women's under-representation as a misuse of resources. Women employees also pressured employers to act, as part of equality plan work (Blomqvist, 1994; SAF, 1993). Companies still blame the underrepresentation of women in management mostly on women's lack of competence, ambition, and self-confidence (Holgersson & Höök, 1997). To remedy this, companies have stepped up efforts to help individual women succeed—for example, through women-focused leadership training courses, mentor programs, and leadership networks (Holgersson & Höök, 1997; Roman, 1994). The government has assisted companies by financing the first year of a Leadership Academy, oriented to improving women's leadership potential (Nikell, 1996c). Although these efforts have been successful in helping individual women achieve promotion to higher-level positions in management, further progress requires companies to reconsider recruitment criteria as well as how leadership and gender are socially constructed within organizations (G. Andersson, 1997; Berggren, 1997; Edin, 1997; Holgersson & Höök, 1997; Hultbom, 1997; Nyberg & Sundin, 1997; Rantalaiho, 1997; Wahl, 1997).

Another reason companies give for the small number of women in management is that women find a management career difficult to combine with parenthood. Women who are hired as managers can expect to be held to the same norms as men, regarding extreme loyalty to the company, long hours at work, and willingness to travel and relocate often (Edlund, Ahltorp, Andersson, & Kleppestø, 1990; Gustafsson, 1997; Meyerson & Peterson, 1997a; Wahl, 1997). It is often said that it is nearly impossible for two managers to live together and have children without the children suffering (Gustafsson, 1997; Wahl, 1992). To follow management careers, women have been more likely than men to adjust work to family needs, in accordance with the gender contract.

Female managers spend less time at work than male managers in order to take responsibility for children and housework. Male managers, on the other hand, depend on their wives who stay at home, work part-time, or decide not to pursue careers (G. Andersson, 1997).

Rather than urge men to participate more in housework (another touchy issue in Sweden in which little progress has been noted; Flood & Gråsjö, 1997), some companies have offered allowances to managers to purchase cleaning, laundry, and ironing assistance (Frisk, 1995; Högberg, 1997). It is very expensive for Swedish dual-career couples to legally hire private household workers to help them manage family and home responsibilities. Even if couples can find people willing to do this type of work, they must pay high taxes on their wages as well as make contributions to domestic workers' vacation, sick leave, disability, and retirement benefits (Blomqvist, 1994). Proposals have been made to give couples tax breaks if they hire domestic help, but most Swedes oppose legislation that would grant government resources to privileged groups or would facilitate the emergence of a new servant class (Fransson, 1998).

Swedish women have been increasing their representation in union leadership posts at a faster pace than they have entered company management, although they are still underrepresented, considering that they make up half of all union members. In 1996, women made up 27% of the leadership of the mostly blue-collar federation Landsorganisationen (LO), up from only 7% in 1985. In 1996, women held 39% of top positions in the white-collar federation Tjänstemannens Centralorganisationen (TCO), up from 18% in 1985 (Ahlross, 1997; Bergqvist, 1997; Nyberg & Sundin, 1997).

These increases are the result of deliberate efforts some unions have made to interest more women in active union work. In the 1990s, some unions began to recognize how much they depended on women as members; women are more likely to join unions than are men, and the number of women belonging to unions has increased dramatically over time (Bergqvist, 1997). Unions have also been motivated to act by the growing militancy of union women, who have formed their own organizations to push for gender equality. An example is Tjejligan (the Gal's Gang), made up of 14,000 mostly blue-collar women workers from LO.

To successfully recruit more women into management positions, many unions have discovered that they need to change members' underlying assumptions about gender and leadership. Leadership is being redefined to be more inclusive of women's language, values, experiences, and roles so that women who want to move up do not have to fit the traditional image of the tough, masculine union boss (Svenska Industritjänstemannaförbundet [SIF], 1993). In addition, there have been efforts to redefine meeting formats and union jobs to be more flexible and less bureaucratic. Because unions are powerful agents of change in Swedish workplaces, women's greater involvement in union leadership positions could lead to work organizations becoming much more accommodative of workers' family responsibilities in the future.

PARENTAL INSURANCE

Most efforts to bring about gender equality in Sweden, at the governmental, corporate, and union levels, have focused on women's economic independence rather than on changing men's roles (Haas & Hwang, 1995, 1996; Widerberg, 1993). However, there is one government program that aims to do both—parental leave.

Swedish women had the right to paid maternity leave as early as 1955; by the 1970s, discussion about gender equality had progressed to the point that responsibility for reproduction was considered men's as well as women's. In response to recommendations of a government-appointed commission that included representatives from employers and unions, the Swedish parliament in 1974 replaced maternity leave with a program of "parental insurance," funded by employers' payroll taxes. The Swedish system of parental insurance is widely regarded as the most generous in the world (Haas, 1992; Rubery, Smith, Fagan, & Grimshaw, 1998).

Parental insurance involves mainly two types of leave. "Regular" parental leave includes (in 1998) 12 months of leave from work with pay compensated at 80%. Parents taking regular parental leave must be in charge of children's care and in direct contact with them during the biggest part of the day, except for time spent in errands and housework; they can take the 12 months' leave in whole or part days until the child reaches the age of 8 (Riksförsäkringsverket, 1997). From the beginning, the intention was that fathers should share this leave with mothers, so 1 month was reserved for each parent; the remaining highly compensated 10 months of leave could be taken by either parent. Men's "reserved" month, however, was easily signed over to mothers. In 1994, to encourage more fathers to take parental leave, these months became impossible to allocate to the other parent; if fathers do not use their "pappa" month, couples lose it.

The second type of parental insurance, "temporary" parental leave, compensates working parents when they stay home with sick children, care for children when their caretakers are sick, accompany children to receive health care, or visit day care centers or schools. Parents may take up to 60 days of temporary leave per child per year until children reach age 12; in 1998, they received 80% of their wages in compensation. Included in "temporary" parental leave are 10 "daddy" days fathers can take within 2 months of childbirth.

Parental-leave regulations have been successful in encouraging women to develop a permanent attachment to the labor force. To be eligible for parental insurance, individuals must have been employed at least 6 months before childbirth or 12 months during the previous 2 years. This has led to a high employment rate among young women and to delayed childbearing. Parental-leave time counts toward vacation and retirement benefits, so parents who use it are not penalized (Riksförsäkringsverket, 1997). To encourage women to remain attached to the labor force between children, parental-leave rules maintain the same level of compensation for parental leave for a later child, if no more than 30 months has elapsed since the birth of the first child (Försäkringskassan, 1997; Sundström & Duvander, 1998). Three out of four mothers return to active employment before their children are 3 (R. Andersson, 1997). Mothers of preschool-age children identify themselves with occupations as much as other women do and report paid employment as important to their identity, even more than men do (Ahrne & Roman, 1997; Eriksson, 1998).

Men's Use of Parental Leave

Parental leave has been specially designed to develop men's interest in child rearing, by offering men the same opportunities to stay home for children that women receive. Since the leave was first offered to men in 1974, the government has engaged in periodic campaigns, through various departments and advisory groups, to increase men's interest in parental leave (Bekkengen, 1996b; Haas, 1992). Local social insurance offices that come into direct contact with prospective parents have received increased funding to move beyond informing couples of men's right to take parental leave to actively encouraging couples to share it (Bekkengen, 1996b).

Government efforts to encourage men to take parental leave have been somewhat successful. Hoem (1995) has estimated that one fifth of children born in Sweden since 1974 have had their fathers take regular parental leave to care for them. Sweden's rate of fathers' taking parental leave is much higher than any country that offers men this option (Rubery et al., 1998). But not all fathers take leave, and there are some signs that progress has stalled. Until recently, the percentage of fathers who took regular parental leave rose with each passing year, starting at 3% in 1974 and reaching 55% for children born in 1990 (Sundström & Duvander, 1998). For children born in 1994, this figure dropped to 51%. Suggested reasons for this decline include reduced compensation levels (from 90% to 75%), closer attention being paid to whether men requesting leave were in fact the primary caregiving parent (e.g., during the summer months), and men's fears that taking leave during a recession might jeopardize their employment opportunities (Bekkengen, 1996b; Riksförsäkringsverket [RKV], 1996, 1997).

Another sign that equality has not been reached is that fathers take a relatively small proportion of the regular leave all parents take. The highest percentage came in 1994, when fathers took 11.4% of all days; in 1995, this figure lowered to 9.7%, rebounding slightly in 1996 to 10.6% (RKV, 1996; Sundström & Duvander, 1998).

Fathers take a much higher proportion of temporary parental leave than they do regular parental leave, typically to care for sick children. However, this percentage has also declined recently. In 1990, men took 44% of all temporary leave days taken by parents; by 1996, this had dropped to 34%. For children born in 1995, 79% of fathers took an average of 7.9 special "daddy" days available within the first 2 months of childbirth or adoption; this is down from 1990, when 90% of fathers took all 10 days. These declines have been attributed to declining levels of compensation brought on by budget cuts (Berlin, 1997; Sundström & Duvander, 1998).

In examining why Swedish men do not take parental leave more often, given the government's considerable encouragement for them to do so, it is important to look at how the gender contract governs social relations in two spheres, family and work. Within the family, negotiations surrounding who takes parental leave tend to be subtly male dominated and to take place against a background in which women's greater family orientation and men's greater employment orientation are taken for granted. There is often little discussion of sharing leave; when women earn less and men are seen as indispensable at the workplace, it seems inevitable that the couple will "choose" the traditional alternative of mothers' taking all or most of the leave (Bekkengen, 1996a, 1996b, 1997). Fathers who take leave tend to have partners whose education and occupational status is similar to theirs (Ahrne & Roman, 1997; Bekkengen, 1996b; Haas, 1992; Hoem, 1995; Sundström & Duvander, 1998).

The gender contract controlling social relations at work also influences men's interest in taking parental leave and their expectations of themselves as fathers (Bekkengen, 1996a; Näsman, 1997). According to the head of the federation of Swedish companies (SAF), all companies understand that they should not deny men the legal right to take parental leave (Helte, 1998). Moreover, the equality law insists that employers must develop "active measures" to encourage men to take parental leave (Jämställdhetsombudsmannen, 1992). In Wahl's 1993 study of Swedish companies with more than 200 employees, only 14% reported trying to make it easier for fathers to take parental leave (Wahl, 1995).

Although most unions have made some efforts to inform men of their legal rights, they seem to have done little to actively encourage men to take parental leave (Bekkengen, 1996b; Widerberg, 1993). Our 1995 study of the largest unions in 136 corporations found only 15 (11%) had done anything to help men take leave. Efforts focused more on resolving individuals' problems (e.g., arranging a substitute) than on developing institutional supports (e.g., bargaining for extra compensation; Haas & Hwang, 1996).

Variations in Companies' Response to
Men's Interest in Parental Leave

Despite a lack of support from the workplace, Swedish men's interest and involvement in active parenthood has grown, in response to partner pressure and government encouragement (see Björnberg, this volume). The vast majority (80%) of men in 1996 agreed that fathers should have as much responsibility as mothers for practical chores related to children, and half of all fathers wished they could spend more time with their children (Ahrne & Roman, 1997). Over 10 years' time, middle-level white-collar fathers have become less interested in promotion if it means more time away from home (Nilsson, 1992). Only one third of top male managers prioritize work over family, and the majority say they spend too little time with their children (G. Andersson, 1997). Men's absolute time spent in child care has increased, although mothers remain small children's primary caregivers (G. Andersson, 1997; Axel & Flood, 1998; Flood & Gråsjö, 1997; Haas, 1992; Lamb et al., 1988; Nyberg, 1997; Wahl, 1992).

Changes in men's orientation toward parenthood are helping to make visible the underlying conflict between reproduction (families) and production (companies) in Sweden (Bekkengen, 1996a; Näsman, 1997). Our survey of the largest 200 Swedish companies, along with 48 interviews with personnel officers and fathers from nine of these companies, revealed that men's growing interest in fatherhood is an important force slowly transforming company culture. Fathers' growing interest in children, women's growing commitment to employment, and governmental campaigns and legislation supporting men's taking parental leave have all led to changes in companies' response to men as fathers. Some companies are changing faster than others, however (G. Andersson, 1997; Bekkengen, 1997; Haas & Hwang, 1995, 1997; Näsman, 1997; Pincus, 1997).

The analysis of our survey and interview data led us to develop three heuristic categories, called stages, that distinguish Swedish companies' response to men's interest in taking parental leave. Companies do not perfectly fit within these stages, but the stages help make sense of the variation in company attitudes toward fathers and reasons for organizational change. (See Haas & Hwang, 1995, for details on how companies were classified.)

Stage 1: Passive Opposition

Just under one third (31%) of the large private-sector companies in our study fell into a category we label Stage 1, *passive opposition* (a term borrowed from Pincus, 1997). Stage 1 companies were not negative toward men's participation in family, but they expected men's involvement with children to be limited mostly to the weekends. They were willing to cope with a temporary crisis in family arrangements (e.g., a sick child) but frowned on men's taking extended parental leave or working reduced work hours. No special programs or policies helped employees manage family responsibilities, because the companies took for granted that employees' wives would be primarily responsible for children, based on "the natural order of things."

Because employers cannot legally deny men's right to take parental leave, they used a strategy of silence that men had to interpret for themselves. According to a production manager,

> It might make a difference if the company would come out and formally say that we don't disapprove of those who take parental leave. . . . Then it is up to you how you want to be involved in the family. Now, we just assume that it would negatively affect your career.

Companies' passive opposition to active fatherhood was also evident in their expectations for worker loyalty. A midlevel manager confided,

> There is the unspoken understanding that there is complete commitment to the job. For this, I get a salary, power, and privileges. And if I choose to have another outlook on life, for example, to prioritize family, it would be very difficult to keep this job.

Personnel officers acknowledged that there were some key positions in their company that required men's families to endure substantial sacrifice (e.g., jobs in which men were regularly required to be away from home 3 nights of the week). Companies did not question why jobs had to be structured in this way. They often blamed outsiders, as in one personnel officer's statement, "The Swedish export industry is becoming more international and we are obligated to adjust ourselves to other cultures."

Despite Stage 1 companies' passive opposition to men's taking parental leave, we found that at least some fathers dared to take leave in every company. These men were resolute (as one coworker said, "He would have to be strong and believe wholeheartedly that he has chosen right") and self-confident ("You have to believe in yourself"). These pioneers were seen as role models by younger men in the organization, who were concerned about how they would someday reconcile their interest in fathering with their loyalty toward the company. The higher up the leave-taker was in the organization, the more likely other men were to regard his ability to negotiate leave as a sign that company policy was becoming less oppositional.

Stage 2: Conditional Support

Most of the companies in our study (two thirds) fell into a category we call Stage 2. In this stage, companies accepted men's interest in being together with their children and had developed some concrete father-friendly policies, including having someone in higher management assuming responsibility for work-family balance. The companies claimed they "didn't mind" if men took leave, and men throughout the organizations could cite several examples of men who had done so. Companies' support for men's taking parental leave, however, was almost always "conditional."

The first condition for men's taking parental leave was that no other arrangements for children's care could reasonably be made. Men could take leave if their wives' jobs were inflexible or if the couple had negotiated a shared parenting pattern that was to persist after leave. As one personnel director said, "If we demand that all men should stay here, then there will certainly be an increase in divorce and then you don't know what will happen."

Another condition for men's leave-taking was that they were valuable employees, worth going to the trouble for. As one personnel officer said, "If this is a person you don't want to lose, you work something out." On the other hand, it was difficult to allow employees who were "indispensable" to go on parental leave. Indispensable men tended to be involved in long-term project work, to have a specialized competence that was difficult to replace, or to supervise other workers. (See also Bekkengen, 1997; Odabas, 1998.) Under these circumstances, a determined father and a sympathetic personnel manager could try to negotiate conditions for the father to stay home. These conditions could involve working overtime beforehand to complete important long-term projects, agreeing to be always accessible by phone or fax when knowledge was needed, and coming in periodically for important meetings and training.

Men at lower levels of the organization could find that their leave-taking was conditional on supervisors' or coworkers' support, since these were the employees who would have to do the leave-taker's work or train substitutes. (See also Bekkengen, 1996a; Haas, 1992; Hwang, Eldén, & Fransson, 1984; Näsman, 1997.) Men whose jobs were organized into semiautonomous work teams made up of fathers or younger men found support easier to come by than did men who worked under more direct supervision or with men who were older or not oriented toward active fatherhood.

When fathers took leave, they told others how enjoyable it was, which raised the number of leave applicants even more. One personnel officer said, "We have had a number of men take parental leave in the company, so we are rather accustomed to it." After many experiences with fathers' taking parental leave, some companies discovered unexpected advantages to fathers' leave-taking.

Fathers often returned with increased work-related competence, including enhanced abilities to balance multiple tasks, deal with the unknown and unexpected, tolerate interruptions, develop social relations, handle stress, and learn
something new. (These outcomes are also mentioned by Bekkengen, 1996a;
Björnberg, 1994; Högberg, 1997; Näsman, 1997; Nilsson, 1992.) Even arrangements made to cover men's jobs while they were gone often yielded unexpected
benefits by facilitating the development of other workers' skills and giving the
company a chance to try out new, more flexible work arrangements. Over time,
the accumulation of positive experiences could lead companies to reconsider
more thoroughly the values and norms on which work was based.

Stage 3: Active Support

Very few companies (3%) in our study of large private companies had made
the transition to what we call Stage 3. In this stage, the corporate culture was
actively supportive of men in their fathering roles. The company, and not the
individual father, took responsibility for working out ways for men to take
parental leave. Research on public-sector companies in Sweden suggests that
some of them probably fall in this category, because several offer financial
incentives for men to take parental leave, and men who work in the public sector
have been found to have parental-leave rates that are significantly higher than
men in the private sector (Bekkengen, 1997; Haas, 1992; Hoem, 1995). Stage
3 companies had typically developed written policies and formal programs to
facilitate men's involvement in parental leave.

In Stage 3 companies, leadership on this issue came from the top, often from
young managers who were fathers themselves or from older men who wanted
young men to have more chances to be together with their children than they
had had. One older CEO at one of the companies in our survey decided in 1994
to pay an extra month's pay to fathers who stayed home with their children for
at least 3 months. He explained this decision in a newspaper interview: "I am
54 years old and know now that I ought to have been at home with my own
children. If there was one thing I could change in my life, that would be it"
(Sönne, 1994, p. A7).

The active support shown toward fathers typically had an ideological and an
economic base. Ideologically, companies were concerned about the welfare of
children, already an important value in Swedish culture. For example, one
economist said, "It is the children we must prioritize, and we must not fail them
or there will be a lost generation." A personnel officer said men should take
leave to "see the child develop, and you don't want to miss this chance; you
have only one chance once to be together like this with your child."

Economically, companies recognized that there were productivity gains in
having men take parental leave. To realize these gains, however, companies

needed to have a long-term perspective on employee development. As one personnel officer said, "You have a long life, and the time with children is only a small part." Men returning from parental leave expressed loyalty to their companies, because they realized that their company supported their achieving a good balance between work and family; this loyalty would encourage retention and high productivity. Fathers' leave-taking was also labeled a "merit," an experience that helped men develop skills and self-confidence that in turn enhanced their work productivity (Bekkengen, 1996a; Björnberg, 1994; Nilsson, 1992; Sundberg, 1996). One personnel officer said, "The dad who has been at home is a much more mature person, and he has a little more depth than what the others have." Another said, "Really, it is a step in manager development that a person is at home and takes care of children, for it means a new situation, and every new situation a person handles is development."

Stage 3 companies' experience with leave-taking fathers had led them to understand that many aspects of traditional organizational culture hindered men's and women's opportunities to be equal breadwinners and caregivers, so they were willing to reexamine work practices more broadly. Examples of changes that had been made in these companies (or that others have discovered since in other Swedish companies) include instituting regular cross-training and job rotation, giving worker teams more autonomy and responsibility for their own work, measuring productivity by performance rather than by work hours, regularly phasing in new people into long-term projects, developing alternative career paths for specialists and managers, allowing careerists with small children to take "responsibility breaks" while still working, allowing more flexibility in terms of where work is performed (e.g., home), and facilitating part-time work and job sharing, including management positions (Högberg, 1997; Näsman, 1997).

CONCLUSION

The Swedish government has engaged itself in an ambitious effort to bring about gender equality in society through initiatives designed to develop women's economic independence and facilitate men's involvement in early child care. Policy efforts have been somewhat successful in challenging traditional women's and men's roles. Swedish women have advanced perhaps further than women in other countries when it comes to achieving the goal of economic independence, because most have a permanent position in the labor force at a decent pay level. The combination of institutional supports for working parents and the success of women's own adaptive strategies for combining multiple roles has resulted in a situation that many women in the world find enviable. More than 90% of Swedish mothers of small children report no problems with role conflict. The sum of women's total work hours (including paid and unpaid work) is nearly identical to that of men, at around 63 to 64 hours a week for parents with children ages 3 and under; working mothers also have as much leisure time as working fathers (Ahrne & Roman, 1997; Axel & Flood, 1998; Eriksson, 1998; Flood, 1995; Flood & Gråsjö, 1997; Nyberg, 1997). Men's interest and involvement in child care have increased to a level at which more than half take advantage of paid parental-leave benefits and express the desire to alter their work situations to be accommodative to family responsibilities. In general, Swedish women's and men's chances of combining reproductive and productive roles have improved to the point that Sweden appears to be "an oasis in a desert of inequality" (Rantalaiho, Heiskanen, Korvajärvi, & Vehviläinen, 1997, p. 4).

Companies and unions have helped the Swedish government develop policies regarding equal employment opportunities and parental leave. However, companies and unions have been slow to take on gender equality as an important goal and to initiate their own programs.

Consequently, Swedish women are more likely to work part-time and hold occupations clustered in service areas on the middle and lower rungs of the organizational ladder, a result of the hegemony of male norms for recruitment and promotion, assumptions about women being primarily responsible for child care, and the persistence of male power. Despite men's interest in being together with their children, some men encounter difficult barriers to taking parental leave, especially if they are interested in having a career in a private company. Women's and men's ability to equally share breadwinning and child care roles, which lies at the heart of the Swedish model for gender equality, is limited by the extent to which companies and unions still base their policies on the traditional gender contract, which reinforces male dominance and a gender-based division of labor in the home and at the workplace.

It is widely expected that the government's consistently strong advocacy of gender equality and children's well-being, along with women's increasing commitment to employment and men's growing interest in active fathering, will eventually influence the private sector at an ideological level. It is often said, even by the most conservative top managers, that this is "a generation issue." As the older generation retires, everyone expects younger workers to have different priorities and interests that will shape a new, more family-friendly organizational culture.

In the meantime, Sweden is concentrating on reducing unemployment and a budget deficit; consequently, the needs of the private sector have taken center stage in political life (Bergqvist, 1997; Gould, 1996). In the 1998 election, no political party promised any new initiatives to promote gender equality. If gender equality is to be advanced under Sweden's present set of financial circumstances and political priorities, programs and policies must come from companies and unions and be clearly cost-effective.

There are reasons for optimism. Although it is too soon to know for sure that equality plans will become an effective mechanism for bringing about organizational change, the government requirement that companies create plans has meant that "there is a platform for equal opportunities issues at practically every workplace throughout Sweden" (Åström, 1995, p. 13). Several important changes in work life have been piloted by companies and unions; if extended, these could dramatically undermine the traditional gender contract. These include a 6-hour day, equal pay for comparable work, and more women in management. Agents for change include women inside and outside government, who are recognized as "a powerful force in Swedish society" (Gould, 1996, p. 88), especially since they have begun to form alliances across political and social class lines. There is also a growing group of men interested in active fatherhood who are likely to press companies to change until Sweden reaches its goal of *jämställdhet*.

REFERENCES

Ahlross, M. (1997). It takes two to tango! In A. Edam (Ed.), *Mot lika villkor?* [Toward equal conditions?] (pp. 192-210). Stockholm: Raben/Prisma.

Ahrne, G., & Roman, C. (1997). *Hemmet, barnen och makten* [Home, children, and power] (Statens Offentliga Utredningar [SOU; Government official reports] Report No. 13). Stockholm: Gotab.

Anderson, B. (1998). *En socialförsäkring för kvinnor och män: En kartläggning ur ett gender perspektiv* [Social insurance for women and men: A survey from a gender perspective] (Research Report No. 1). Stockholm: Riksförsäkringsverket [National Social Insurance Office].

Andersson, B. (1997, September 18). Jämställdhetsarbetet går dåligt: Arbetsgivare och fack sviker [Equality work goes badly: Employers and unions disappoint]. *Arbetet Nyheterna*, p. 28.

Andersson, G. (1997). Karriär, kön, familj [Career, gender, family]. In A. Nyberg & E. Sundin (Eds.), *Ledare, makt och kön* [Leadership, power, and gender] (SOU Report No. 135, pp. 68-108). Stockholm: Gotab.

Andersson, R. (1997). Attityder är problemet [Attitudes are the problem]. *Clara* [LO union women's magazine], *1* pp. 72-73.

Asker, A. (1998, June 19). Stopp för kortad arbetstid [Stop for shortened work time]. *Svenska Dagbladet*, p. 5.

Åström, G. (1995). Society in a gender perspective. In A. Wahl (Ed.), *Men's perception of women and management* (pp. 9-13). Stockholm: Ministry of Health and Social Affairs.

Axel, D., & Flood, R. (1998). Patterns of time use in France and Sweden. In I. Persson & C. Jonung (Eds.), *Women's work and wages* (pp. 91-121). London: Routledge.

Bekkengen, L. (1996a). *Föräldraledighet om man så vill* [Parental leave as one wants it] (Research Report No. 15). Karlstad, Sweden: Högskolan i Karlstad [Karlstad College].

Bekkengen, L. (1996b). *Mäns föräldraledighet: En kunskapsöversikt* [Men's parental leave: An overview of knowledge] (Working Paper No. 12). Karlstad, Sweden: Högskolan i Karlstad.

Bekkengen, L (1997). *Flexibel och förhandlingsbar eller ett faktum: Ett genusperspektiv på föräldraledighet inom arbetsorganisationer* [Flexible and negotiable or a fact: A gender perspective on parental leave with work organizations] (Research Report No. 6). Karlstad, Sweden: Högskolan i Karlstad.

Berggren, A. (1997). Marknaden i ett historiskt genus-perspektiv [The labor market from a historical gender perspective]. In A. Löfström (Ed.), *Lönepolitik och kvinnors löner* [Wage policy and women's wages] (pp. 109-125). Stockholm: Gotab.

Bergh, L. (1998). Jämställdhetslagen [The equality law]. In B. Westerberg (Ed.), *Han, hon, den, det: Om genus och kön* [He, she, and it: On gender and sex] (pp. 121-146). Stockholm: Ekerlids Förlag.

Bergqvist, C. (1997). Korporatismens nedgång: Kvinnornas framgång? [Corporatism's decline: Women's success?]. In A. Nyberg & E. Sundin (Eds.), *Ledare, makt och kön* (SOU Report No. 135, pp. 212-244). Stockholm: Gotab.

Berlin, E. (1997, November). Män tar allt mindre ansvar för sjuka barn [Men take less responsibility for sick children]. *Arbetsmiljö*, pp. 3-4.

Björnberg, U. (1994). Mäns familjeorientering i förändring [Men's family orientation in change]. In U. Björnberg, A. Kollind, & A. Nilsson (Eds.), *Janus och genus* [Opposites and gender] (pp. 49-71). Stockholm: Brombergs.

Björnberg, U., & Gardberg, C. (1998). Issues concerning the family in Sweden. In J. Ditch, H. Barnes, & J. Bradshaw (Eds.), *Developments in national family policies in 1996* (pp. 267-282). York, UK: University of York, European Observatory on National Family Policies.

Blau, F. (1998). The gender pay gap. In I. Persson & C. Jonung (Eds.), *Women's work and wages* (pp. 15-35). London: Routledge.

Blomqvist, M. (1994). *Könshierarkier i gungning: Kvinnor i kunskapsföretag* [Gender hierarchies on a see-saw: Women in knowledge-intensive companies]. Uppsala, Sweden: Acta Universitatis Upsaliensis.

Boje, T., & Nielsen, L. (1993). Flexible production, employment, and gender. In T. Boje & S. Hort (Eds.), *Scandinavia in a new Europe* (pp. 145-168). Oslo, Norway: Scandinavian University Press.

Broberg, A., & Hwang, P. (1991). Day care for young children in Sweden. In P. Moss & E. Melhuish (Eds.), *Day care for young children* (pp. 75-120). London: Routledge.

Crofts, M. (1998, September 22). . . .Och Schyman har fem krav för samarbete [And Left party head Schyman has five demands for working together with the Social Democratic Party in a coalition]. *Aftonbladet*, p. 13.

De nya jobben: Sex timmar genom avtal, inte ny lag [The new jobs: 6-hour day through collective bargaining, no new law]. (1996, February 8). *Aftonbladet*, pp. 16-17.

Edin, K. (1997, September 24). Viktigast att våga satsa många råd till kvinnliga chefer [Most important to dare to offer advice to female managers]. *Nerikes Allehande,* p. 11.

Edin, P., & Richardson, K. (1997). Lönepolitik, lönespridning och löneskillnader mellan män och kvinnor [Wage policy, wage spread, and wage differences between men and women]. In I. Persson & E. Wadensjö (Eds.), *Kvinnors och mäns löner: Varför så olika?* [Women's and men's wages: Why so different?] (SOU Report No. 136, pp. 87-103). Stockholm: Gotab.

Edlund, C., Ahltorp, B., Andersson, G., & Kleppestø, S. (1990). *Karriärer i kläm: Om chefen, familjen och företaget* [Careers in a squeeze: On managers, families, and companies]. Stockholm: Norstedts.

Eriksson, B. (1998). *Arbetet i människors liv* [Work in people's lives] (Monograph No. 66). Göteborg, Sweden: Göteborg University, Department of Sociology.

Fackliga arbetstidskrav förnyas [Union work time demands are being renewed]. (1995, November 18). *Svenska Dagbladet,* p. 22.

Flood, L. (1995). Division of labour in Swedish households: The Swedish experience 1984-1993. In T. Willemsen, G. Frinking, & R. Vogels (Eds.), *Work and family in Europe: The role of politics* (pp. 181-207). Tilburg, The Netherlands: Tilburg University Press.

Flood, L., & Gråsjö, U. (1997). Tid för barn, tid för arbete [Time for children, time for work]. In G. Ahrne & I. Persson (Eds.), *Familj, makt och jämställdhet* [Family, power, and gender equality] (SOU Report No. 138, pp. 159-184). Stockholm: Gotab.

Försäkringskassan [Social Insurance Office]. (1997). *Mamma, pappa & barn: Frågor och svar om föräldraförsäkringen* [Mommy, daddy, child: Questions and answers about parental insurance]. Stockholm: Försäkringskasseförbundet [Social Insurance Office Union].

Först ut med sextimmarsdag [First out with 6-hour workday]. (1995, March 30). *Göteborgs Posten,* p. 1.

Fransson, S. (1998, February 18). Pigdebatten också jämställdhetsfrågan? [Debate about the maid allowance—also an equality question?] *Göteborgs Posten,* p. 4.

Frisk, C. (1995, December 17). Hög kompetens hjälper inte: Få kvinnor lyckas nå toppen. *Göteborgs Posten,* p. 41.

Fürst, G. (1997). När kvinnor utvecklar nya lönemodeller [When women develop new wage models]. In A. Nyberg & E. Sundin (Eds.), *Ledare, makt och kön* (SOU Report No. 135, pp. 327-345). Stockholm: Gotab.

Gönas, L., & Spånt, A. (1997). *Trends and prospects for women's employment in the 1990s* (Report No. 4). Stockholm: Arbetslivcentrum [Center for Working Life].

Gornick, J., Meyers, M., & Ross, K. (1997). Supporting the employment of mothers: Policy variation across fourteen welfare states. *Journal of European Social Policy, 7,* 45-70.

Gould, A. (1996). Sweden: The last bastion of social democracy. In V. George & P. Taylor-Goodby (Eds.), *European welfare policy* (pp. 72-94). London: Macmillan.

Gustafsson, S. (1997). Feministisk politik and ekonomisk effektivitet [Feminist politics and economic effectivity]. In A. Löfström (Ed.), *Lönepolitisk och kvinnors* (pp. 89-108). Stockholm: Gotab.

Haas, L. (1992). *Equal parenthood and social policy: A study of parental leave in Sweden.* Albany: State University of New York Press.

Haas, L., & Hwang, P. (1993, November). *Fathers and company culture in Sweden.* Paper presented at the 30th seminar of the Committee on Family Research, International Sociological Association, Annapolis, MD.

Haas, L., & Hwang, P. (1995). Company culture and men's usage of family leave benefits in Sweden. *Family Relations, 44,* 28-36.

Haas, L., & Hwang, P. (1996, November). *Father-friendliness in Swedish unions.* Paper presented at the annual meeting of the National Council on Family Relations, Kansas City, MO.

Haas, L., & Hwang, P. (1997, November). *Changing roles of fathers in the private sector in Sweden.* Paper presented at the annual meeting of the National Council on Family Relations, Washington, DC.

Hagberg, J., Nyberg, A., & Sundin, E. (1996). *Att göra landet jämställdt* [To make the country gender equal]. Stockholm: Nerenius & Santerus.

Hantrais, L., & Letablier, M. (1996). *Families and family policies in Europe.* London: Longman.

Hedman, B., Johansson, L., Sundström, P., & Thermaenius, A. (1998). Vad har hänt? [What has happened?]. In B. Westerberg (Ed.), *Han, hon, den, det: Om genus och kön* (pp. 25-53). Stockholm: Ekerlids Förlag.

Helte, S. (1998, January 19). Messing will ha mer pappaledighet [Messing wants to have more fathers taking leave]. *Nerikes Allehanda,* p. 6.

Hemström, M. (1998). Gender differences in pay among young professionals. In I. Persson & C. Jonung (Eds.), *Women's work and wages* (pp. 145-169). London: Routledge.

Hoem, B. (1995). *Kvinnors och mäns liv: Del 1. Sysselsättning från 17 års ålder* [Women's and men's lives: Part 1. Occupations from 17 years of age]. Stockholm: Statistiska Centralbyrån [Central Bureau of Statistics].

Högberg, C. (1997, November). Framsynta företag främjar familjen? [Forward-looking companies promote the family?]. *Arbetsmiljö,* pp. 5-6.

Holgersson, C., & Höök, P. (1997). Chefsrekrytering och ledarutveckling [Top manager recruitment and leadership development]. In A. Nyberg & E. Sundin (Eds.), *Ledare, makt och kön* (SOU Report No. 135, pp. 17-45). Stockholm: Gotab.

Hultbom, C. (1997). Makt och ledarskap i börsbolagen [Power and leadership in the stock market]. In A. Nyberg & E. Sundin (Eds.), *Ledare, makt och kön* (SOU Report No. 135, pp. 46-67). Stockholm: Gotab.

Hultin, M., & Szulkin, R. (1997a). Chefernas kön och de anställdas lön: En studie av könsdiskriminering på svenska arbetsplatser [Managers' pay and employees' pay: A study of gender discrimination at Swedish workplaces]. In I. Persson & E. Wadensjö (Eds.), *Kvinnors och mäns löner: Varför så olika?* (SOU Report No. 136, pp. 151-172). Stockholm: Gotab.

Hultin, M., & Szulkin, R. (1997b). De låglönande på arbetsmarknaden: En analys av kvinnor och män under två decennier [The lowly paid in the labor market: An analysis of women and men during two decades]. In I. Persson & E. Wadensjö (Eds.),

Kvinnors och mäns löner: Varför så olika? (SOU Report No. 136, pp. 269-293). Stockholm: Gotab.

Hwang, C. P., Eldén, G., & Fransson, C. (1984). *Arbetsgivares och arbetskamraters attityder till pappaledighet* [Employers' and coworkers' attitudes toward fathers' taking parental leave] (Report No. 31). Göteborg, Sweden: Göteborg University, Department of Psychology.

Jakobsen, L., & Karlsson, J. (1993). Inledning [Introduction]. In L. Jakobsen & J. Karlsson (Eds.), *Jämställdhetsforskning* [Research on gender equality] (Research Report No. 5, pp. 1-19). Karlstad, Sweden: Högskolan i Karlstad.

Jämställdhetsombudsmannen [Equality ombudsman]. (1992). *Jämställdhetslag* [The equality law; brochure]. Stockholm: Author.

Jansson, N. (1997). Bekämpa lönediskrimineringen! [Fight wage discrimination!]. In A. Edam (Ed.), *Mot lika villkor?* (pp. 101-122). Stockholm: Raben/Prisma.

Johansson, U. (1998). The transformation of gendered work. *Gender, Work, and Organization, 5,* 42-58.

Johansson, V. (1997). Omsorgens organisering och jämlikheten mellan könen. In A. Jonasdottir (Ed.), *Styrssystem och jämställdhet: Institutioner i förändring och könmaktens framtid* [The ruling system and equality: Institutions in change and the future of gendered power] (SOU Report No. 114, pp. 86-106). Stockholm: Gotab.

Jonung, C. (1998). Occupational segregation by sex and change over time. In I. Persson & C. Jonung (Eds.), *Women's work and wages* (pp. 36-71). London: Routledge.

Karlsson, G. (1996). *Från broderskap till systerskap: Det socialdemokratiska kvinnoförndets kamp för inflytande och makt i SAP* [From brotherhood to sisterhood: The Social Democratic Party's Women's Association's struggle for influence and power in the party]. Stockholm: Arkiv Förlag.

Kärrby, G. (1995). Föräldrars uppfattningen om kvalitet i daghem [Parents' perspectives on day care quality]. *Socialvetenskaplig Tidskrift* [Social Science Journal], *2,* 208-226.

Lamb, M. (1998). Nonparental child care. In I. Sigel & K. Renninger (Eds.), *Child psychology in practice* (pp. 73-134). New York: John Wiley.

Lamb, M., Hwang, P., Broberg, A., Bookstein, F., Hult, F., & Frodi, M. (1988). The determinants of paternal involvement in primiparous Swedish families. *International Journal of Behavioural Development, 11,* 433-449.

LeGrand, C. (1997). Kön, lön och yrke: Yrkessegregering och lönediskrimering mot kvinnor i Sverige [Gender, pay, and occupation: Occupational segregation and wage discrimination against women in Sweden]. In I. Persson & E. Wadensjö (Eds.), *Kvinnors och mäns löner: Varför så olika?* (SOU Report No. 136, pp. 45-86). Stockholm: Gotab.

Lommerud, K. (1997). Lönebildning, löneskillnader och kvinnolöner [Wage building, wage differences, and women's wages]. In A. Löfström (Ed.), *Lönepolitik och kvinnors löner* (pp. 60-88). Stockholm: Gotab.

Lundgren, H. (1993, September 23). Kvinnorna försvinner från jobben [Women are disappearing from the job]. *Arbetsmiljö,* p. 13.

Mahon, R. (1997). Child care in Canada and Sweden: Policy and politics. *Social Politics, 4,* 382-418.

Meyerson, B., & Peterson, T. (1997a). Finns det ett glastak för kvinnor? En studie av svenska arbetsplater i näringsliv 1970-1990 [Is there a glass ceiling for women? A study of Swedish workplaces in the private sector 1970-1990]. In I. Persson & E. Wadensjö (Eds.), *Glastak och glasväggar: Den könssegregerade arbetsmarknaden* [Glass ceiling and glass walls: The sex-segregated labor market] (SOU Report No. 137, pp. 109-135). Stockholm: Gotab.

Meyerson, B., & Peterson, T. (1997b). Lika lön för lika arbete [Equal pay for comparable work]. In I. Persson & E. Wadensjö (Eds.), *Kvinnors och mäns löner: Varför så olika?* (SOU Report No. 136). Stockholm: Gotab.

Mueller, C., Kuruvilla, S., & Iverson, R. (1994). Swedish professionals and gender inequalities. *Social Forces, 73,* 553-573.

Näsman, E. (1997). Föräldraskapets synlighet i arbetskulturer [Parenthood's visibility in workplace culture]. In J. Bonke (Ed.), *Dilemmaet arbejdsliv-familjeliv i Norden* [Family-work dilemmas in the Nordic countries] (Report No. 5, pp. 55-101). Copenhagen, Denmark: Socialforskningsinstituttet [Social Research Institute].

Nermo, M. (1997). Yrkessegregering efter kön: Ett internationellt perspektiv [Occupational segregation by sex: An international perspective]. In I. Persson & E. Wadensjö (Eds.), *Glastak och glasväggar: Den könssegregerade*(SOU Report No. 137, pp. 82-108). Stockholm: Gotab.

Nikell, E. (1996a). JämO har vunnit sitt första lönemål [Equality ombudsman has won its first wage case]. *Jämsides* [Publication from the Equality Ombudsman's Office], *1,* 24-26.

Nikell, E. (1996b). Jämställdhetsplanerna måste bli bättre [Equality plans must become better]. *Jämsides, 1,* 10-11.

Nikell, E. (1996c). Ledarskapsakademin ska förändra näringslivets strucktur [Leadership academy will change the structure of the private sector]. *Jämsides, 1,* 8-10.

Nilsson, A. (1992). Den nye mannen: Finns han redan? [The new man: Does he exist yet?]. In J. Acker, A. Baude, U. Björnberg, E. Dahlström, G. Forsberg, L. Gönas, & H. Holter (Eds.), *Kvinnors och mäns liv och arbete* [Women's and men's lives and work] (pp. 219-243). Stockholm: SNS Förlag.

Nya bud om kortad arbetstid [New offers of shortened work time]. (1996, January 29). *Svenska Dagbladet,* p. 36.

Nyberg, A. (1997). *Kvinnor, män och inkomster* [Women, men, and incomes] (SOU Report No. 87). Stockholm: Gotab.

Nyberg, A., & Sundin, E. (1997). Inledning [Introduction]. In A. Nyberg & E. Sundin (Eds.), *Ledare, makt och kön* (SOU Report No. 135, pp. 1-16). Stockholm: Gotab.

Odabas, M. (1998, June 11). I längden löner det sig att vara ledig [In the long run it pays to take leave]. *Svenska Dagbladet,* p. 1.

Ohlsson, J., & Öhman, J. (1997). Kvinnliga och manliga chefer: Finns det ett glastak? [Female and male managers: Is there a glass ceiling?]. In I. Persson & E. Wadensjö (Eds.), *Glastak och glasväggar: Den könssegregerade arbetsmarknaden* (SOU Report No. 137, pp. 136-168). Stockholm: Gotab.

Olsson, L. (1998, August 27). S lovar anställda kortare arbetsdag [Social Democrats promise workers shorter workday]. *Svenska Dagbladet,* p. 10.

Persson, I., & Wadensjö, E. (1997). Vad vet vi: Vad behöver vi veta mer om? [What do we know: What do we need to know more about?]. In I. Persson & E. Wadensjö (Eds.), *Kvinnors och mäns löner: Varför så olika?* (SOU Report No. 136, pp. 1-13). Stockholm: Gotab.

Pettersson, L. (1996). *Ny organisation, ny teknik: Nya genus relationer?* [New organization, new technology: New gender relations?]. Linköping, Sweden: Linköping University, Tema Teknik [Interdisciplinary Program for Studies on Technology].

Pettersson, L. (1997). Kvinna och chef i ett tekniskt arbetsområde [Woman and manager in a technical work area]. In A. Nyberg & E. Sundin (Eds.), *Ledare, makt och kön* (SOU Report No. 135, pp. 301-326). Stockholm: Gotab.

Pincus, I. (1997). Män som hindrar och män som främjar jämställdhetsarbete [Men who hinder and men who promote equality work]. In A. Jonasdottir (Ed.), *Styrstem och jämställdhet* [The ruling system and equality] (SOU Report No. 114). Stockholm: Gotab.

Pringle, K. (1998). *Children and social welfare in Europe.* Buckingham, UK: Open University Press.

Qvist, G., Acker, J., & Lorwin, V. (1984). Sweden. In A. Cook, V. Lorwin, & A. Daniels (Eds.), *Women and trade unions in eleven industrialized countries* (pp. 261-285). Philadelphia: Temple University Press.

Rantalaiho, L. (1997). Contextualising gender. In L. Rantalaiho & T. Heiskanen (Eds.), *Gendered practices in working life* (pp. 16-30). London: Macmillan.

Rantalaiho, L., Heiskanen, T., Korvajärvi, P., & Vehviläinen, M. (1997). Studying gendered practices. In L. Rantalaiho & T. Heiskanen (Eds.), *Gendered practices in working life* (pp. 3-15). London: Macmillan.

Rembe, R. (1997, July 9). Börja med att sänka till sjutimmarsdag: Att sänka arbetstiden med en åttondel motsvarar väl arbetslöshetens storlek [Begin with the 7-hour day: To lower work time by an eighth to fight against the size of unemployment]. *Arbetet Nyheterna,* p. 3.

Riksförsäkringsverket [National Social Insurance Office]. (1996). *Pappaledighet från norr till söder* [Daddy leave from north to south] (Report No. 5). Stockholm: Author.

Riksförsäkringsverket. (1997). *Föräldrapenning förmåner* [Parental-leave privileges] (Report No. 10). Stockholm: Author.

Roman, C. (1994). *Lika på olika villkor: Könsegregering i kunskapsföretag* [Equal on unequal conditions: Sex segregation in a technology firm]. Stockholm: Symposium.

Roos, J. (1998, September). Schyman försvarade förslag om sextimmarsdag [Schyman defends proposal for a 6-hour day]. *Göteborgs Posten,* p. 31.

Rubery, J., Smith, M., Fagan, C., & Grimshaw, D. (1998). *Women and European employment.* London: Routledge.

Sainesbury, D., & Nordgren, M. (1997). I nedskärningarnas tecken: Välfärdsstaten och jämställdhet [Signs of reduction: The welfare state and gender equality]. In A. Stark (Ed.), *Lysnande framtid eller ett långt färväl? Den svenska välfärdsstaten i jämförande belysning* [Bright future or a long farewell? The Swedish welfare state as a comparative illustration] (SOU Report No. 115, pp. 5-36). Stockholm: Gotab.

Sextimmarsdag blir för dyrt i Askersund? [Six-hour workday becomes too expensive in Askersund?]. (1998, February 26). *Nerikes Allehanda,* p. 29.

Sjufrånvaron sjunker med kortare arbetstid [Sick leave sinks with shorter work time]. (1997, October 19). *Svenska Dagbladet*, p. 1.

Sönne, M. (1994, March 3). Anton lyfter pappas lön: Pappaledig får extra peng [Anton lifts his dad's wages: Daddy leave yields extra money]. *Östgöta Correspondenten*, pp. A2, A7.

Sörestedt, B. (1997, February 12). LO utan åsikter om kortare arbetstid? [LO without opinions on shorter work time?]. *Arbetet Nyheterna*, p. 3.

Statistiska Centralbyrån [Central Bureau of Statistics]. (1992). *Man är chef: En studie av kvinnor och män i ledande ställning i privat och offentlig sektor* [Men are the bosses: A study of women and men in leading positions in private and public sectors]. Stockholm: Author.

Statistiska Centralbyrån. (1997). *Statistisk årsbok* [Annual statistical report]. Stockholm: Author.

Sundberg, M. (1996). *JämOs bok om aktiva åtgärder* [The equality ombudsman's book on active measures]. Stockholm: JämO.

Sundström, M. (1997a). Bör kvinnor förvärvsarbeta? Attityder till kvinnor i Sverige, Tyskland och Italien [Should women be employed? Attitudes toward women in Sweden, Germany, and Italy]. In G. Ahrne & I. Persson (Eds.), *Familj, makt och jämställdhet* (SOU Report No. 13, pp. 7-30). Stockholm: Gotab.

Sundström, M. (1997b). Managing work and children: Part-time work and the family life cycle of Swedish women. In H. Blossfeld & C. Hakim (Eds.), *Between equalization and marginalization: Women working part-time in Europe and the United States of America* (pp. 272-288). London: Oxford University Press.

Sundström, M., & Duvander, A. (1998). Föräldraförsäkringen och jämställdheten mellan kvinnor och män [Parental leave and equality between women and men]. In I. Persson & E. Wadensjö (Eds.), *Välfärdens genusansikte* [The gender face of welfare] (SOU Report No. 13, pp. 69-91). Stockholm: Gotab.

Svenska Arbetsgivareföreningen [Svenska Employers' Federation].(1993). *Jämställdhet i arbetslivet* [Gender equality in work life]. Stockholm: Civiltryck.

Svenska Industritjänstemannaförbundet [Swedish Industrial White-Collar Workers' Union]. (1993). *Jämställdhet i SIF* [Gender equality in SIF]. Stockholm: Author.

Svensson, L. (1995). Politik för jämställdhet? [Policy for gender equality?]. *Social Vetenskaplig Tidskrift, 2*, 249-264.

Thörn, Y. (1997). Vardera arbetet, inte könet [Value the work, not the sex]. In A. Edam (Ed.), *Mot lika villkor* (pp. 176-191). Stockholm: Raben/Prisma.

Tre milj för sex timmar [Three billion crowns for 6 hours]. (1996, February 14). *Svenska Dagbladet*, p. 1.

Ulmanen, P. (1995). Kvinnorörelse i miniformat. In *Fria val? Om kön, makt och fritid* [On gender, power, and leisure time] (SOU Report No. 145, pp. 9-28). Stockholm: Gotab.

Vill ge facket mer makt [Wants to give unions more power]. (1998, July 10). *Arbetet Nyheterna*, p. 11.

Wadensjö, E. (1997). Arbetsinkomster för kvinnor med högre utbildning [Wage earnings for women with higher education]. In I. Persson & E. Wadensjö (Eds.), *Kvinnors och mäns löner: Varför så olika* (SOU Report No. 136, pp. 256-268). Stockholm: Gotab.

Wahl, A. (1992). *Könsstrukturer i organisationer* [Gender relations in organizations]. Stockholm: Ekonomiska forskningsinstitutet [Economic Research Institute].

Wahl, A. (1995). *Men's perceptions of women and management.* Stockholm: Ministry of Health and Social Affairs.

Wahl, A. (1997). Ledarstil, makt och kön [Leadership style, power, and gender]. In A. Nyberg & E. Sundin (Eds.), *Ledare, makt och kön* (SOU Report No. 135, pp. 109-134). Stockholm: Gotab.

Widerberg, K. (1993). Kvinnoperspektiv på rätten: Den svenska föräldraledighets-lagstiftningen som ett belysnande exempel [Women's perspective on justice: The Swedish parental-leave legislation as an illuminating example]. In L. Jakobsen & J. Karlsson (Eds.), *Jämställdhetsforskning* [Equality research] (Research Report No. 5, pp. 31-47). Karlstad, Sweden: Karlstad Högskola [Karlstad College].

PART III

Organizational Change and Gender Equity

Previous chapters have provided an overview of the situations of working parents and the development of workplace policies and programs designed to promote work-family balance and gender equity. This part of the book examines in closer detail the processes by which individual companies come to address work-family issues and the specific conditions under which organizational change is more likely to result in gender equitable work-family policies.

The key argument in this part is that adding on family benefits to existing organizational structures as a favor to parents is unlikely to help many parents achieve work-family balance or help organizations make much progress toward gender equity. Deeply held assumptions about the appropriate roles of men and women and about the structure of work life must be challenged if real progress toward helping mothers and fathers succeed in breadwinning and domestic roles is to occur.

In all, eight work organizations receive close scrutiny. In most settings, researchers report that the skills and contributions of women are undervalued, whereas men's desire to participate more in family life is not taken seriously. Recognition of both women's importance to organizational productivity and men's inner struggles to be loyal to work and family seems to be an important step in companies' ability to deal effectively with the needs of working parents.

Another issue that is raised in these case studies concerns the problems associated with treating working parents (especially mothers) as a special group with special needs for flexibility. When working parents are offered their own programs, other employees can become resentful. Instead, workplaces need to take for granted that all employees are likely to have responsibilities for caregiving and a desire for leave-taking (e.g., for caregiving of different relatives, continuing education, etc.) on and off throughout their work lives. All employees, regardless of parental status, have a need to lead a balanced life, with opportunities for leisure time activities, volunteering, and the development of social relationships outside of work. When employees are viewed as whole persons whose quality of life outside the workplace is regarded as affecting their motivation and productivity at the workplace, work organizations are more likely to develop universal policies for all employees to use.

In many of the work organizations studied, it was clear that the formal policies that were offered (or mandated by the government) to support working parents—such as flextime, parental leave, and reduced work hours—were not commonly used. This was not because employees did not need them but because they perceived that taking advantage of specific benefits and programs would create disadvantages for them in the workplace. This situation highlights the importance of examining and changing organizational culture in more basic ways and stresses the desirability of resolving work-family issues in the larger context of addressing strategic business concerns, such as efficiency and productivity. Significant change seems possible when traditional ways of working are problematized (especially the "long-hours culture" and measuring productivity by time at work rather than by performance). As long as parents (especially working mothers) are seen as the problem, progress toward gender equity will be slow.

The chapters in this part describe both forces that drive change and constraints on change in organizations. Some of these are external social forces, such as the society's specific ideology concerning gender, how competitive the economy is, and the scarcity of specialized workers. Other forces are internal, including the interests of top management, how valued highly trained women are, how interested employees are in gender equity, and how common it is for employees to practice egalitarian domestic arrangements. There appears to be a set of forces that initially encourages work organizations to consider change (e.g., problems with recruitment, retention, or productivity; demands placed by workers) and another set of forces that helps disseminate or obstruct change throughout the organization (e.g., attitudes of middle management, the nature of incentive systems). Beyond that, we could also look at the forces that help sustain or that can undermine organizational change once new norms and values have been established (e.g., financial constraints, changes in social policy).

Some of the chapters in this part report on how the researchers worked closely with company representatives not just in studying the organization but in developing pilot projects designed to bring about organizational change.

Bailyn, Rapoport, and Fletcher label this approach "collaborative, interactive action research." This appears to be a very promising approach to take because it helps researchers learn more about how companies function and about the barriers that make change difficult. From companies' perspectives, they gain knowledgeable consultants who bring a fresh perspective to some of the difficulties they are experiencing in enhancing the recruitment, retention, and productivity of working parents.

In one cultural setting, collaborative researchers deliberately incorporated their concerns about meeting legal requirements for equal employment opportunities for women in the company. In another setting, researchers realized they had to downplay their real interest in gender equity to secure the cooperation of the company, but by keeping it in mind, they were still able to propose changes that improved the situation of women. How researchers work with individual companies to bring about change clearly varies substantially from one cultural context to another and even within a particular society, most likely between different branches and areas of the economy. No one model of collaboration will likely fit all situations, but these researchers outline some important considerations that can be taken into account when undertaking action research designed to change organizational cultures to be both more productive and more gender equitable.

Altogether, these case studies improve our in-depth understanding of the processes of organizational change. They set the stage for the refinement of hypotheses and further research concerning factors influencing organizational cultures to be more gender equitable. They show that change in organizational cultures in the direction of gender equity is hard, but not impossible.

10

Moving Corporations in the United States Toward Gender Equity

A Cautionary Tale

LOTTE BAILYN

RHONA RAPOPORT

JOYCE K. FLETCHER

This chapter is a narrative of a collaborative, interactive action research project in one U.S. corporation in which work-family issues were used as a catalyst for organizational change toward increased gender equity. Our sense of an equitable society is one in which both sexes depend on family *and* on work for their sense of worth and identity; in which people and families regard the distribution of opportunities and constraints as fair; and in which all social institutions value and support both economic and domestic enterprise. It is important that both women and men be considered. Men's overidentification with work and occupation as a source of self-esteem feeds gender inequity just as the presumption that women alone are responsible for family and community does.

AUTHORS' NOTE: We want to acknowledge the contributions of the other members of the Xerox research team, including Deborah M. Kolb, Maureen Harvey, Susan Eaton, Robin Johnson, and Leslie Perlow.

The story begins by looking at what led up to this project, what actually happened during our involvement with this corporation, and what we learned about working with companies to promote work-family integration equitably for both sexes.

BACKGROUND

The project grew out of the Ford Foundation's Women's Program and its Women's Program Forum (established in 1986), which allowed the national and international donor community to discuss issues related to women's programs. In 1989, the forum provided an opportunity to examine the current debates about and possible responses to men's and women's growing needs for "balancing" their work and family responsibilities. These events, together with work on the Ford Foundation's own work-family program, reaffirmed that women were not being treated equitably with men in the workplace. There was pay inequity, inequitable mobility in work careers, continued gender stereotyping, and—important for our purposes—disincentives to using work-family programs and policies in ways that could decrease the inequities. Even in organizations that had well-developed work-family policies and benefits, men and women were inequitably treated, mainly by default. Such organizations were also losing the women whom they wanted to keep and thus began to realize that the work-family programs they had developed were not achieving the intended consequences. It became clear that, to increase gender equity in organizations, it is important that *both* men and women are enabled to achieve better "balances" between their needs and responsibilities in the workplace and their involvement in the family and the community.

The implication is that workplaces need to take on the integration of work-family issues as a strategic set of business concerns for all employees. Such a stance is quite contrary to the historical separation of work and family life since the industrial revolution, in which family concerns have been considered outside the purview of workplaces and gender equity merely a matter of opening employment opportunities to women (see Bowen, this volume). It is also contrary to companies' attempts to introduce family benefits and to evolve into "family-friendly" organizations. Such work-family policies and programs, introduced to support working women with children, are helpful to those who need the benefits. But they create inequities because they do not deal with the work situation. In contrast, our approach assumes that it is necessary not just to provide benefits but to change the structure and culture of the workplace, paying attention to both men's and women's roles. This is not an easy task, because it involves "breaking the mold" of existing ways of working and requires changing corporate structures and cultures (Bailyn, 1993). This approach, therefore, is not a story of easy success but a cautionary tale.

It was with these concerns in mind that the Ford Foundation agreed to fund an action research project whose ultimate aim was to develop ways to increase gender equity in American workplaces. Three corporations and three action research teams agreed to work together toward this goal. The companies were all leaders in the work-family field. Together with them, we agreed (a) to explore interconnections among current work-family policies and practices and other aspects of human resource policies, work structures, and corporate culture; (b) to identify barriers to implementing work-family policies in a gender equitable way, including gender stereotypes, constraints on men and women at different life phases, and the way work is organized; (c) to develop new practices to overcome these barriers in ways consonant with and integral to overall business objectives; and (d) to document the processes involved for broad public dissemination.

In this chapter, we present part of the case study of what happened when one research team worked with one company, the Xerox Corporation. First, we present the evidence that links work-family concerns to gender and explain how the division of work and family into separate, gendered, and adversarial spheres works against gender equity and also may not be in the best interest of organizations.

WORK-FAMILY CONCERNS AND GENDER

Although the difficulty of integrating work and family appears to be gender neutral, we found that, because of gender roles and expectations, its effects on men and women are often different. For example, requests for ad hoc, emergency flexibility have few career implications for those (mostly men) whose family needs are temporary and short term. On the other hand, reward systems that value "face time" and perfect attendance have significant career consequences for those (usually, at present, women) who have routine, ongoing family responsibilities and must end work at regular hours or use sick days to care for others.

In the same vein, expectations that women are, or should be, "family primary" portray women as unfit for the demands of organizational life. As a result, some women, especially those in professional or managerial positions, feel they have to hide their families. Thus, while men have family pictures on their desks, these women keep their desks clear of all family reminders. Indeed, one of the compliments frequently paid high-achieving women is that "You'd never even know she had a child." In other words, just as family-friendly policies are not gender neutral in their effect, neither are the demands of organizational life.

Although it is less politically correct than it used to be to suggest that women belong in the home and men belong at work, we found these attitudes and beliefs still alive and seriously influencing organizational practices. The deeply held, but not often expressed, belief that society works best when women stay at home and men go to work creates real problems for people who step out of ascribed gender roles. For example, when women do make the choice to focus primarily on work, there may actually be negative career consequences. One divisional manager, in explaining why one woman had failed a management review process, said,

> She probably thought it would be seen as positive that she was willing to sacrifice her family for work. But she has gone through two divorces and who knows who is taking care of those kids. . .that's not the kind of person we admire.

These women are caught in a classic double bind: The work culture expects them to subordinate families but punishes them for doing it.

When men try to step out of expected gender roles, they also experience a double bind. Although it is possible for men to be acclaimed for taking on some short-term family responsibility, it is far more difficult for them to use family policies for any long-term arrangements. Managers decide what requests for flexibility can be accommodated and often make these decisions based on perceived need. Assumptions about gender roles make it very difficult for men to make a strong case based on need, and many told us that they do not even try because they believe these long-term accommodations are, in reality, available only to women. As one technical supervisor noted, "Men here are seen as wimps by senior management if they talk about their desire to spend time with their families." Thus, men who want to be more involved in family and community and to share more of these responsibilities face significant organizational constraints in achieving this goal. Integrating work and family, then, is a different experience for women and for men, presenting different challenges and different organizational obstacles. The cultural separation of work and family by gender, as well as the narrow organizational definition of what constitutes a work-family "need," hinders women while seeming to support them. It also maintains the myth that the ideal worker devotes all to the company, which does not legitimate men's concerns for becoming equal parents.

Although both men and women spoke poignantly of the pain and unfairness of having to choose between career and family, we found that most do not challenge the gender roles that encourage men to give primary priority to their careers and women to their families. Indeed, these gender roles tend to be accepted at a very deep, often unconscious, level. One young man, for example, who was on the fast career track, spoke of how he wanted to spend more time with his two young children but feared that, if he was ever going to provide for them, he would have to make the same choice his father had and sacrifice time with his children to focus on his career. His sense of the appropriate masculine role seemed to dictate that, if forced to make a choice, it would have to be career. A young woman who had just passed up a promotion spoke of how "unreasonable" it was for her to even think of taking the job. As she put it,

> I chose to have three kids. I couldn't possibly do that job and stay sane. I chose to have these kids and now I have to take care of them. It's just not reasonable to take on a job like that with kids this age.

Her view of herself as a woman, and the current options open to her, made her feel she had to choose family. Thus, women are unfairly constrained in their ability to achieve in the workplace, and men are unfairly constrained in their ability to achieve in the family.

Our project challenged these deeply held assumptions that success, whether organizational, individual, or societal, relies on keeping the work and family spheres separate and distinct and, necessarily, a trade-off with each other. Strategically linking these spheres and viewing them as complementary can provide an alternative vision of an ideal worker, a successful organization, and a functional, equitable society. For example, at one of our sites, we challenged the image of the ideal worker by documenting the work practices of "integrated" individuals—people who were able, despite the cultural imperative to the contrary, to link the two arenas of work and family. (For complete details, see Fletcher, 1998; Fletcher, in press.) Our documentation of the work practices of these employees (many of whom were women) found that they used skills more often associated with the private, domestic sphere of life, such as sharing, nurturing, collaborating, and attending to the emotional context of situations. Because these skills are less valued, and often invisible, in the workplace or considered inappropriate to it, we created a language of competence to talk about these activities and the relational skills they required. We showed that linking these skills to those more strongly associated with, and more valued by, the public sphere of economic activity (e.g., rationality, linear thinking, autonomy, and independence) offers a new vision of an ideal worker as one who combines these characteristics.

We also question the assumption that society depends on the two spheres being separate and gendered. In fact, when we conducted surveys to determine the extent of employees' work-family concerns, we found that, at the level of individual experience, the assumption of separate spheres was more a myth than a reality. At every site, men and women recounted the ways in which their lives were interdependent blends of work and family, and they shared their desire to have good careers and good families. Some workers, because of their position, their financial resources, or their being defined as valuable employees, are able, at times, to manage this boundary on their own. The rest, including many working-class women and men and people of color, simmer with discontent. In all cases, energy and loyalty are diverted unnecessarily from the organization.

In our project, as discussed below, we challenged the assumption that work and family have to be entirely separate spheres by pointing out to individuals who cast these as issues of personal choice that there are in fact many ways in which they are interdependent and connected. For example, we pointed out to one management team that, by selecting as "top employees" only those who had skills associated with the public sphere (who were mostly male), they were inadvertently undermining the kind of skills and type of team orientation their corporate vision statement professed to need. With the manager who criticized the female employee for sacrificing family for her career, we pointed out that it is the organizational definition of commitment and the image of the "ideal worker" that are the problem. Expecting someone in a management review process to represent herself as someone other than this type of worker is unrealistic. Furthermore, to the extent that this definition of commitment has negative consequences for society (e.g., divorce, neglected children), managers and organizations have some responsibility to bear.

THE XEROX EXPERIMENTS

Our first interaction with Xerox was with a central group of human relations professionals in the corporation, augmented by a senior line manager soon to become vice president of human resources (though we did not know this at the time). In working with this group, we initially followed the quality method that was institutionalized at the company in the 1980s (Kearns & Nadler, 1992). This method, typical of total quality management (TQM), included procedures designed to help groups solve quality problems in a rational and well-specified manner. In this first meeting, there was an initial tension between those in the organization who were concerned about the provision of better work-family policies and programs (even though on paper their policies were already quite generous) and our view, supported by the senior line manager, that better policies on their own are not sufficient; we needed to look at the work itself and how it was accomplished. After an interesting and illuminating day of discussion, we came out with the following description of the current and the desired state of the organization:

> *Current State:* The culture and structure of the organization unnecessarily create conflict between work and family, which has negative consequences for the business and for the equitable treatment of employees.
>
> *Desired State:* The culture and structure capitalize on work-family issues as an opportunity to create innovative, productive, and equitable work practices in the organization.

Two things are important about this formulation. First, it emphasizes the culture and structure surrounding work, instead of policies that primarily help women. Second, it replaces the idea that work and family are necessarily adversarial (the either-or thinking of the current state) with the notion that it is possible to use work-family issues as a way of making work practices more productive *and* more gender equitable. This was quite a change from the current way of thinking.

Another aspect of that initial contact was also important. Gender equity was our ultimate goal; we wanted to use work-family concerns as a means to achieve a more gender equitable workplace. It quickly became apparent, however, that it would not be useful to use the term *gender equity* in our dealings with work sites. Its connotation seemed to be a mixture of pay equity and sexual harassment, both of which are legal issues and hence made the company very nervous. Gender issues, therefore, went underground, although, as will become clear, they played a significant role in our findings, and our work at the company had an impact on the way some people thought about gender. In our public dealings with the company, however, we emphasized that we were there to work collaboratively with work sites to see whether it would be possible to design different ways of working that would not hurt the business but would allow people to have a better integration between their work lives and their personal lives. In our minds, though not in those of our action partners, "work-family" was a proxy for gender equity. "Work-family" stood for the concrete, immediate, and "reachable" aspects of the work situation that connected the expectations, incentives, and assumptions about how work must be accomplished with the difficulty of achieving gender equity in the workplace.

Two beliefs underlie the methods we used. First, we wanted to get at what really mattered to people, and our method of data collection reflects this. Second, we were aware that the way we did this acted as an intervention. Indeed, we saw these early interventions on our part as an important beginning to the changes we hoped to be able to introduce in the organization.

Together with our initial liaison group from the company, we jointly devised a series of criteria for the selection of work sites to partner with. Our company partners then negotiated with the managers involved. Once on-site, we had to start the collaboration all over again with the managers and human resources people of that site.

Our first site was a product development division. We began by interviewing managers and engineers, observing them in meetings, and following them around during the workday. We were interested in the details of their work: what they did, how they did it, and whom they worked with. We also discussed with them their personal and family situations. We tried to surface the hidden assumptions that people were operating with, and, in the individual interviews, we were able to get people to talk about taboo topics.

As already indicated, we started the project with the belief that there was a significant correlation between people's personal lives and their experiences at work and that this somehow related to the issue of gender equity, but we were not sure how it worked. Our first analysis, and first feedback to management, dealt primarily with the work situation. We described the work culture as highly individualistic, as valuing the problem-solving aspects of the work while ignoring coordination and problem-prevention needs, and as oriented to long hours and face time—to "throwing time at problems." We also had discovered, and reported, that women engineers were not comfortable in this situation, and a number were thinking of leaving and finding work elsewhere.

The initial reaction of management was informative. They did not see the "work-family" connection of what we were saying, and they did not consider us experts on work process. Hence, they were not convinced that our analysis of the work situation was valid. But as we talked more with individual managers and explained the connections we were beginning to make, some began to see things in a different light. One manager in particular, who had not been at our joint meeting and with whom we therefore met individually to go over our results, saw the "revolutionary" character of what we were saying. He eventually even understood the connection to gender issues. It was he who explained to the vice president that telling a woman manager that she was valued and that one understood that she had to leave at 5:30 even though a meeting was continuing was actually discrimination because it reinforced her role as family caregiver and implied that her input was not necessary. Only stopping the meeting, he asserted, would be equitable. It was at this site, also, that the previously mentioned analysis of alternative ways of working was made.

In this division, we tried an experimental intervention with the software engineers of one particular product development team. This idea emerged from an interactive and collaborative attempt to find something that would lessen the number of hours and the stress the engineers were under while at the same time helping (rather than hindering) their ability to meet a very tight production schedule with limited resources. (For a full description of this experiment and its analysis, see Perlow, 1997.) Our initial suggestion was to limit the workweek artificially to some prespecified number, perhaps 40 or 50 hours of work. The thought was that, under those conditions, the group would still get their work done but would do so in a more efficient manner, working smarter rather than longer. Everyone turned down this suggestion summarily as impossible, given the highly ambitious, though many thought unrealistic, schedule that had been set for the group. Further analysis of why the long hours seemed so necessary showed that the engineers needed evening and weekend time to finish their individual deliverables (for which they were rewarded) because of the continuous interruptions during the normal workday. These interruptions, it turned out, consisted of both absolutely necessary interactions to coordinate the work (e.g., working with each other, having meetings) and unproductive encounters, often from managers asking for information and requiring elaborate presentations on how the work was proceeding. Moreover, even necessary interactions were not always urgent (i.e., they could be postponed to a time that was less disruptive to the engineer's individual work). On the basis of this analysis, the engineering group decided to experiment with a restructuring of their day into periods of independent work (quiet times) and periods of interdependent or interactive work. The result was a real win-win: It gave the engineers (and the managers) more control over their time and actually got the product to market on time.

This experiment was critical in a number of ways. First, it was clear that no individual accommodation to a particular person's time needs could have achieved this result. It had to be a collective decision and had to be followed by all in the group to help an individual engineer. Second, the main lesson that ensued stemmed from the new understanding the engineers arrived at about the nature of their work and the effect they have on each other. Because they could not interrupt each other during quiet times, they planned their work in more strategic ways by learning to distinguish between necessary interactions and unproductive interruptions and by becoming aware of their interdependencies and the effect they were having on each other's work. In other words, they learned to work more effectively, and, by doing so, they got the product out while easing the time and pressure crunch they were under.

At another work site, a customer administration center, the issues were quite different. This was a group of workers who interacted with customers by means of computers, scheduling installations and service, billing, and performing other administrative tasks. These clerical employees were highly dependent on their jobs to financially support themselves and their families. Long hours were not the problem here; indeed, days were regimented into a typical 9-to-5 routine, with a careful count of lateness and absence. What was difficult for these workers was the *rigidity* of these schedules. Commutes were long, and family obligations sometimes made this timetable difficult to reach, which had serious career consequences for those who were late or absent too often. Not surprisingly, it was the women employees who were most often caught in this bind.

Generous company policies to deal with such issues were already on the books, including flextime and the opportunity to work a compressed workweek. Very few people, however, were taking advantage of these opportunities. Through analysis of the initial set of interviews with employees, we surfaced a culture of individualism and control that not only prevented people from receiving permission for flexible schedules, and therefore stopped them from even asking for them, but also affected the entire way in which the organization worked. Managers, for example, felt they had to personally supervise all their workers or the work would not get done. The few people who did come earlier or stay later (the only form of flexibility that was used at all) led to the managers' workdays being necessarily lengthened. And those few employees who were given this permission were seen as especially needy—in other words, women with small children—with the result that others not only did not ask for such permission but felt keenly that the system was unfair.

Our feedback of this analysis to management and later to the entire division led to an intriguing result. At first resistant to the interpretation we had made, the division manager impulsively decided to permit an experiment during the full group meeting. Everyone could go on any flexible schedule they wanted to, as long as the work got done. This dramatic announcement to the whole division, which occurred spontaneously, led to a number of remarkable developments. First, almost everyone (men and women, with children or without, single or partnered) expressed an interest in a flexible schedule. Second, the supervisors, who had been the ones negotiating individually with anyone who asked to use these policies, found it impossible to continue in this manner and had to change their approach. They had to let their workers decide collectively how to get the work done and how to fit that in with their desired work schedules. This meant that, in the end, the groups began to function as self-managed teams, which had been a key business goal at the site that had previously eluded them.

The bottom lines of this experimental intervention were numerous: a 30% drop in absenteeism, increased customer service through elongated hours, realization by managers that their workers could work independently and did not need their continuous surveillance, less personal pressure on many employees, and an increased sense of fairness across gender and family status lines. These positive results all depended on a new collective understanding and legitimation of *all* employees' personal lives.

DISCUSSION

We have described some of what happened when we tried to use work-family issues as a catalyst for changes in work practices that would make the workplace more gender equitable. Since then, we have worked in many other organizations and have continued to learn about what it takes to move organizations toward gender equity. We have come to a number of conclusions from this work.

First, bringing about change in workplace practices to make a company more gender equitable is not easy. Beliefs about gender are deeply entrenched in the social fabric, and the extent to which they are embedded in work structures and cultures is generally unrecognized. To change an organization to be more gender equitable therefore engages layers of feelings and beliefs that are usually not necessary to challenge in other kinds of organizational change. Not only does this make change more difficult, but it also makes it easy for gender goals to get lost. This has happened to us in a number of instances, and we are still working on how to keep the change process aligned with the gender objectives.

Second, because gender is embedded in organizations in such a complicated way, the methods necessary to make progress are an elaborate interplay of intervention, analysis, and partnership. We have called what we do collaborative, interactive action research (CIAR). All elements, we feel, must occur together. To be *collaborative* means that we are colearners with partners at the work sites and that we all have expertise that is mutually acknowledged. We call this *fluid expertise,* because at different stages of the project, it moves back and forth between the researchers and the organizational partners. To be *interactive* implies that working together with our partners creates something new—new issues or unexpected resolutions. There are no predetermined outcomes of these interactions—we all share a goal but not necessarily the same perceptions—and there is no pressure to accept each other's frameworks. No one point of view need prevail. *Action* involves actually doing a demonstration project or an experiment, one that has face validity for the organization. It must be connected to an actual task that a work group is doing and accountable for. Since the experimental intervention must stay close to the actual work being done, it should engage a local site rather than attempt a change in the organization as a whole. Finally, *research* is an integral part of the process. It involves the collection, interpretation, and analysis of data. This conceptual task is done by the researchers and shared and elaborated on collaboratively with the organizational partners. By looking at the data through a gender lens, that is, by seeking the gender implications in the data and uncovering assumptions underlying work practices that have gender implications, the researchers and their action partners produce new knowledge.

As is obvious from the above, the CIAR approach is different from traditional research on organizations and from traditional ways of bringing about organizational change. But it is necessary, we believe, if the changes now occurring in organizations are to lead to greater gender equity.

In the long run, however, we have to move beyond the workplace if we wish for a truly equitable society. We must be concerned not only with enabling men and women to achieve better "balances" or integration in the workplace, but also with gender relations in domestic units and in society at large. The workplace is an important current leverage point for change, but the whole process is evolutionary, and changes will also have to occur in personal relationships, in the family, and in the community at large if we are to achieve the equitable society we all seek. Thus, we present a final and broader set of implications.

CONCLUSION

In the United States, the historically recent pattern of relationships between work and other spheres of life has three key elements. The first is the segregation of personal and family life from work life, with work taking priority, which increases the conflict between work and the rest of life. The second is the emphasis on individual achievement and material success. The third is the assumption that achievement requires individuals and companies to be ruthlessly competitive. Accepting these elements as conventional wisdom makes it possible to ignore the negative consequences of this pattern on family and community life.

This pattern is associated with serious marital and other family disruptions, concerns about what is happening to the next generation, pressures on elder care, and community problems. It also creates the gendered world as we know it, in which women are disadvantaged in the public arena and men are disadvantaged in their personal lives. We believe the relationship between work and personal life can be organized differently. In reporting on the study at Xerox, we have indicated other possibilities that are more gender equitable and that may have positive societal impact. However, as these other possibilities become understood, it is important that the gains are shared not only between employees and employers but also between both and communities (e.g., schools, children, health and family care, leisure).

Changing the way people in the United States view and act on the connections between work and nonwork life could have a profound effect on the rest of the world as well. Many developing countries are taking over the old conventional wisdom: segregating work and family life, with work taking priority; focusing on individual achievement and material success; and perceiving success as the consequence of ruthless competitiveness. Unfortunately, this pattern is being exported by the developed world at a time when some people in that world are beginning to recognize the costs of this way of valuing how we work and play, for individuals, for organizations, and for society.

REFERENCES

Bailyn, L. (1993). *Breaking the mold: Women, men, and time in the new corporate world.* New York: Free Press.
Fletcher, J. (1998). A feminist reconstruction of work. *Journal of Management Inquiry, 7,* 163-186.

Fletcher, J. (in press). *Disappearing the feminine: Relational practice, gender, and power in the new organization.* Cambridge, MA: MIT Press.

Kearns, D., & Nadler, D. (1992). *Prophets in the dark: How Xerox reinvented itself and beat back the Japanese.* New York: HarperBusiness.

Perlow, L. (1997). *Finding time: How corporations, individuals, and families can benefit from new work practices.* Ithaca, NY: Cornell University Press.

11

Organisational Change and Gender Equity

Case Studies From the United Kingdom

SUZAN LEWIS

Despite the focus in the United Kingdom on family-friendly policies, particularly directed at women (see Chapter 7 in this volume), there has been an emerging awareness in recent years that effective and gender equitable work-family solutions will require more fundamental organisational culture change (Hammond & Holton, 1992). *Organisational culture* refers to a deep level of shared beliefs and assumptions, which often operate unconsciously. They develop over time, embedded in the organisation's historical experiences, and are usually functional initially but may persist inappropriately (Pemberton, 1995). Multiple cultures may coexist within different parts of an organisation. Schein (1985) identified three operational levels of culture: artifacts, values, and assumptions. Formal work-family policies can be regarded as artifacts, that is, surface-level indicators of organisational intentions. Those intentions may or may not be articulated as the achievement of gender equity. To understand how these artifacts work in practice, it is necessary to go a stage further and examine the values and assumptions that underpin them.

EDITORS' NOTE: The author's use of British spellings has been retained.

This chapter examines some relationships between policies and organisational assumptions, as well as the processes of working toward more fundamental culture change. Case studies of two U.K. organisations, an accountancy firm and a county council, are presented. These two work organisations were developing in different ways and at different rates toward work-family practices that were more or less gender equitable, and they were experiencing the culture change that this entailed. The first case study on the accountancy firm highlights the ways in which fundamental values and assumptions can undermine initiatives to be more family friendly and gender equitable. The second case study on the county council examines the process of change within a specific context. Some of the lessons that can be learned from these two case studies are then discussed, and some issues for the future are highlighted.

THE ACCOUNTANCY FIRM

The first case study concerns the U.K. offices of an international firm of chartered accountants. The company was male dominated. There was only one woman in the senior management team (who were all partners in the firm) and a growing minority of professional women at more junior management levels. Professional staff based their fees on "chargeable hours," that is, the number of hours worked for a client. There was, however, a culture of working long hours, and not all of these hours could be charged to clients.

The company had developed a number of formal policies, designated as "policies for employees with family commitments," to prevent highly trained women from leaving the firm after having children. These policies included the provision for certain employees, at managers' discretion, to work reduced hours, with pro-rated benefits, and, in the case of senior employees, to retain a company car. Reduced hours were usually taken in the form of shorter days or 4-day workweeks, although other combinations, such as periods of working from home, were also possible. Part-time work or job sharing, career breaks, and extended maternity leave were also available, again at management discretion.

The case study, which has been described in more detail elsewhere (Lewis & Taylor, 1996), set out to examine the impact of these policies on employees and their families and on the organisation. In-depth, semistructured interviews were conducted with women working on the reduced-hours scheme and with other new mothers who were working 9 to 5 but, unlike most of their colleagues, were not working overtime. Only one man had taken advantage of the reduced-hours scheme, because of his wife's illness, and he declined to be interviewed. The women's line managers and the company's partners were also interviewed to examine the impact of the policies from their perspectives. Finally, interviews were carried out with higher-level managers who played a key role in the development and implementation of the policies. The next section examines the process of change, including factors leading up to the development of these policies, the actors involved, and the constraints that undermined the policies' impact on gender equity.

Driving Factors

Equal Opportunities for Women

The company had recently signed up as a member of a business-led campaign called Opportunity 2000, which aimed to enhance the representation of women at all levels of organisations and stressed the business case for equal opportunities. It was grounded in research in organisations in the United States, the United Kingdom, and elsewhere in Europe that identified four key aspects of good practice contributing to the successful implementation of equal opportunities and associated culture change (Hammond & Holton, 1992). These included (a) commitment from the top, (b) changing behaviour, (c) building ownership of the changes, and (d) making the necessary investment of resources. Membership in Opportunity 2000 signaled commitment at the highest level of the organisation, although there were no prescriptions about how the objectives should be achieved. The policies at this company were developed as a consequence of this commitment.

Recruitment and Retention

The drive to enhance opportunities for women in this male-dominated organisation stemmed mainly from a recognition that the loss of highly trained women after maternity leave was costly in terms of recruitment and training. The valuing of highly trained women has been an important driver of change in other British organisations and was a major factor in the accountancy firm. As more women with high levels of training and expertise left the organisation after having children, because they could not manage to combine child care with work as it was currently constructed, the firm became motivated to find new ways of retaining these women. On one hand, this represented a major culture change because it recognised the contributions that women made to the organisation. On the other hand, it was driven by pragmatic concerns, and women's careers and life cycles were seen as the "problem" to which a "solution" must be found. In this company, we found no parallel concern to enable highly trained men to modify work for family, except in extreme circumstances, and only limited awareness that men might wish to do so. Clearly, this was a consequence of men's not asking, or feeling that it was illegitimate to ask, for modifications to traditional working patterns. Men did not give work-family strain or the need for more flexibility as a reason for leaving the organisation. Perhaps an extreme example of the lack of awareness of these issues for men came from a senior manager and father of four young sons. When asked by the interviewer how he would respond if a male employee with family commitments asked to work reduced hours, he inquired incredulously, "But what would he do with the time?"

The valuing of highly skilled women employees also implied that other women might be expendable. Policies were available only at managers' discretion, and managers determined how essential an employee was to their department. Although some women in clerical positions were also permitted to use the reduced-hours scheme, many others were not allowed to do so and told us that they felt this was very unjust.

Predictably, because the initiatives were directed at women, almost all usage was by women. It was clear from the interviews with the senior managers that men were not expected to adjust their work for family.

Actors in the Process

The initiative was spearheaded by a woman partner. She, in turn, delegated the responsibility for developing policy and practice to the personnel department, where the policies were actually developed and monitored.

Constraints

The impact of the formal policies for employees with family commitments was constrained by organisational values and assumptions about the nature of time.

One assumption was that time spent in the workplace was an important indicator of commitment and productivity. The interviews revealed that, although some flexibility for women staff was being introduced into the firm by the work-family policies, those women who worked less than the long hours that were the norm were undervalued. They were defined as less productive and less committed than other staff. In this organisation, time was defined as a commodity to be managed and "given" to paid work and/or family. The prevailing belief was that time given to work symbolised productivity, commitment, and personal value. Thus, productivity and commitment tended to be defined in terms of hours spent at the office being seen working. As one senior male manager expressed, "Someone on reduced hours is less committed."

Even women who did not take advantage of reduced work hours but had negotiated to not put in any overtime were also negatively regarded, even if such hours could not be charged to clients. A male manager explained,

> Within an accountancy firm, career-wise, there can be an element of, you know, doing long hours, to be seen to be doing long hours. . . . I could quite easily see that your career in the office could be, well literally stopped, if you're not prepared to put the hours in . . . to get the work done.

According to the senior manager,

> We have also got a problem with commitment with women coming back five days. . . . They struggle in terms of giving outside 9 to 5 commitment. . . . It is difficult for them to go side by side with a male manager. . . . With a wife at home . . . [the male managers] are able to give that extra hour or two.

These reports from male managers contrasted with women's own reports of their productivity and efficiency, as well as reports from a minority of their managers. One woman working reduced hours said, "I would certainly say that I try to do as much in four days as some people might do in five days. I rarely take lunches. . . . I'm quite happy to work through lunch." Another woman in a similar situation said,

> In a way it's helped me, it's made me more conscious of what I've to do when, to help me sort out my work more than I did before. . . . Now I've got to have everything covered in advance, so I think it's made me more organised.

Some of the male managers acknowledged that reduced hours could make women more efficient, but this did not affect their attitude that employees working reduced hours lacked loyalty to the company. As one male senior manager said, "She's a good manager, but she won't be promoted. She doesn't have the commitment . . . doesn't put in the time."

The second assumption made in this organisation was that personal commitment was something that was finite and nonexpandable. This implied that if someone had commitments outside the workplace, this inevitably reduced his or her level of commitment at work. These assumptions clearly perpetuated gender inequity. As one manager stated about women, "They have other commitments. You can't be a wife and a mother and a manager and do them all well. Something has to give."

The impact of both these assumptions and the subsequent discourse was to obscure the beneficial impact that reduced hours had on employee efficiency. It also resulted in a low sense of entitlement to support for family demands. Any support became regarded as a favour.

Despite the discourse of time as a commodity, pockets of awareness were beginning to emerge throughout the organisation, suggesting a questioning of the dominant ethos. As one manager reflected, "We encourage people to work too long. They say 'it didn't do us any harm.' . . . The reality is that by encouraging long hours, you reward inefficiency."

The findings of the case study, especially concerning the long-hours culture and the emergent awareness of it as being counterproductive, were fed back to the company in a written report and presentation. Personnel resolved to try to raise awareness of the issues that were also highlighted in an in-house newsletter. Unfortunately, however, this idea was embraced more enthusiastically by the personnel department than by line managers and firm partners.

A follow-up of the organisation 2 years later revealed that the person who had been the driving force in the personnel department had left the firm. Although work-family initiatives continued to develop, initiatives to enhance awareness of the impact of the long-hours culture ceased when she left. Progress since then had been programmatic. Parental leave had been introduced, despite initial opposition from management, and the operation of the reduced-hours scheme had expanded, with all women going on maternity leave now being offered this, rather than having to negotiate with their supervisors. This represented a step forward in terms of enabling women to combine careers and motherhood. However, reduced hours remained an option only for women, which, in the context of the continuing valuing of long hours, did little to expand and build on the existing pockets of awareness that periods of reduced hours for all workers could benefit the firm.

THE COUNTY COUNCIL

The second case study involved a county council, a large local government employer in the south of England. The workforce was predominantly female, and there were women at all levels of management, except at the most senior level. The council employed people working in a range of local services.

This case study was carried out as part of a larger European project on good practice in relation to working time arrangements, equality between men and women, and job creation. Semistructured interviews were developed around a common set of questions used in organisations in five European Union countries. The council case study involved interviews with male and female employees working some form of part-time job or reduced hours. Union representatives, the principal personnel officer, and members of the senior management team were also interviewed. The focus of the interviews was not to evaluate the actual impact of the policies but to examine the process of change, driving factors, and constraints.

There was a range of family-oriented policies in this organisation, including career breaks, paternity leave, and child care assistance. Although the original focus was on the needs of women, there was now a concern that men, who were the minority in the work organisation, should not be overlooked. The principal personnel officer explained,

> We are in danger as an organisation of ignoring our male employees because they are quite small proportional to women, and I think it's important that men know what's on offer and feel entitled to approach us. So we now have a paternity information pack as well as a maternity information pack, which is one way of making sure that men . . . know about their entitlements.

The council had also developed a range of flexible working practices, including flextime, reduced hours, job sharing, and other forms of part-time work. In contrast to the accountancy firm, the flexible options at the council were used by men as well as women. Two thirds (66%) of women and one fifth (21%) of men worked part-time (including job sharing and reduced hours), and this occurred at all levels of the organisation. The flexible forms of work had been in place longer and were therefore more established at the council than at the accountancy firm. Managers were encouraged to consider the possibility of allowing all employees to work nonstandard hours in all jobs, to meet the needs of the organisation and the employees.

It was recognised that not only the employees but the organisation benefited from flexible work, and so it was not regarded as a favour to employees. Staff, both male and female, appeared to have a greater sense of entitlement to adjust work for family or other personal reasons than did those working at the accountancy firm. A male job-sharer at the council said,

> I appreciate the fact that you know they've been positive and supportive of my job share. . . . I believe that everyone automatically should have the right to job share if there is sufficient people to fill [all the jobs]. I think everyone should be entitled to it.

What are the factors associated with the more gender equitable culture at the council, and what was the process like that brought it about? Clearly, there are important inherent differences between a private-sector organisation like the accountancy firm, which provides services for a profit, and a public-sector organisation like the council, in which services have to be provided within a budget, not for a profit. The differences, however, go beyond this. Not all public-sector organisations are as flexible as the county council. There were a number of factors that facilitated the changes at this particular organisation, including both internal structural factors and external driving forces.

Internal Structural Factors Promoting Change

The council had historically offered part-time work because it had a large female workforce that wanted this type of work arrangement. The types of services provided by the council also leant themselves to being performed by employees working nonstandard work formats. For example, social workers could be "on call"; some services were offered in shifts around the clock; schools and academic services were based only on hours and months of the year that students were in school; and some agencies and government offices were extending their hours in response to increased consumer demand. These situations provided the foundation for the organisation to begin thinking about the possibility of expanding the offering of nonstandard work hours in place of traditionally full-time work.

External Forces Driving Change

Although the large female workforce, the council's experience with part-time work, and the structure of many of the jobs supervised by the council all provided a favourable context for the organisation to change its culture, they were not the driving forces. External forces driving change included equal employment opportunities legislation, financial constraints, and, rather surprisingly, antifraud initiatives.

Legislation

The implementation of equal opportunities legislation, including the Equal Pay Act and the Sex Discrimination Act in the 1970s, was the initial trigger to develop policies. Equal pay claims required workers to find a comparable group of the other sex within the same organisation. Local authorities such as the council were liable to equal pay claims because they were more likely than other employers to hire both women and men in a wide variety of occupations (e.g., from construction work to catering). This motivated the council to pay attention to equal pay and other equal opportunities issues (Lewis, 1996).

Financial Constraints

Paradoxically, financial constraints were a driving factor. The council had not been able to compete with the private sector in terms of pay, but good work-family policies and flexible working conditions had become powerful recruitment and retention tools, with little or no cost implications. As one manager said,

We have very little to offer in terms of cash incentives . . . but we have been able to recruit a steady stream of competent people over the years because we have been able to offer . . . part-time work, which is almost still unheard of in private practices.

A male employee agreed: "I've got nothing but praise for the County Council. . . . Even though the pay might not be as great as the private sector, the working conditions are just superb . . . even fathers get a few days' paternity leave." Company policies certainly helped retention, although one woman manager described the flexible working conditions less positively, as being "like golden handcuffs" binding her to the organisation.

The encouragement of employees' working reduced hours and part-time saved money, enabling the organisation to maintain the quality of services within the context of a severely reduced budget from central government, and without having to cut jobs.

Fraud Initiatives

An unexpected factor influencing the organisation to discourage people from working long hours was a national initiative to wipe out fraud in local authorities. A senior manager told us, "All local authorities have been told that they should look at people who don't take their leave. . . . The reason they gave us was that they found that people who don't take their leave are sometimes involved in fraud." The national antifraud initiative was taken up by the management team as an opportunity to challenge the assumption that long hours were positive and necessary.

Actors in the Process

In this organisation, support from management and support from employees were seen as important for the development of policy—as one senior manager said, "to empower people and get them to address the issue."

As was true in the accountancy firm, the development of policy at the council was located in the personnel department, with the principal personnel officer taking a leadership role. This person had more influence in the council work organisation than the personnel officer in the accountancy firm had. Traditionally, personnel officers have had little influence on organisational change (Liff & Cameron, 1997); however, a number of factors combined to make the council organisation an exception.

One important factor was that initiatives were undertaken by the most senior personnel officer. At the accountancy firm, responsibility was delegated to a junior personnel officer, and staff turnover at this level was high. The principal personnel officer at the council had been in the position long enough to develop and oversee the implementation of various initiatives. Furthermore, this personnel officer did not regard the policy on nonstandard work hours as an end in itself but as an initial stage in working toward more thorough culture change. Top management gave the personnel officer their support and at least an appearance of commitment, even though they did not take on a leadership role themselves. The organisation did not particularly consider gender equity a major priority, but there had been no attempt to block any of the personnel officer's initiatives, and this helped to gain wide acceptance of change. A champion at the top may therefore not be necessary if there is a sufficiently senior person leading the change and at least some support from the higher level. The personnel officer herself modelled the changes she promoted; she worked reduced work hours and supervised departmental personnel officers who also worked nonstandard hours themselves. These officers knew the issues and could help mainstream the initiatives throughout the organisation.

Unions were involved in the consultation process in developing and negotiating equal opportunities policies. Nevertheless, they were not widely seen as being among the key players, perhaps because unions could not come to an agreement on the issues.

Line management was a crucial layer that had to be convinced of the flexible working arrangement's value to the organisation. Line managers feared that part-time work would be disruptive. In changing the organisation, considerable emphasis was placed on encouraging line managers to be more flexible. The principal personnel officer said she decided to provide rewards for managers for being flexible, because they had told her this would help them pay attention to the issue. There was also a strategic use of examples of good practice, as stated by the principal personnel officer: "I think it makes more of an impact on line managers . . . if you point them in the direction of a different department who are already doing something. . . . They seem to know how it works." With experience, line managers learned that part-time work could be positive for the organisation, because of its association with increased efficiency. Many male managers who had initially been opposed to or disinterested in equal opportunities measures became more convinced when their own grown-up daughters experienced discrimination or a career block. According to the principal personnel officer, "Some male managers have . . . come to apologise and say, 'Look, I'm terribly sorry, I was never desperately supportive of this before, but I've realised why you're doing this; it's really useful, isn't it?' "

Once the policy was established, some individuals in key positions were empowered to request part-time or reduced-hours work. This highlighted the importance for the organisation of retaining valued skills and provided role models and examples of good practice to disseminate to other departments.

Men's interest in accommodating work for family also became legitimised in the process of men's requesting nonstandard hours.

Constraints

Pockets of the Long-Hours Culture

Unlike the managers at the accountancy firm, most senior managers at the council did not associate long hours with commitment. The flextime system tended to obscure the actual number of hours people worked anyway; some were always working earlier or later in the day. This created a greater emphasis on outcomes rather than inputs.

It was, however, still true in some departments that managers had trouble adjusting their expectations for employees with reduced work hours. A senior manager confided,

> I've got a number of people at the senior level who work less than a 37-hour week.
> . . . The reality is the organisation tends to ignore the fact they are working on a part-time basis . . . so they probably end up working harder, to be honest. . . .
> Periodically, one does have to take stock of what your expectations are of people in the context of what hours you pay them.

As at the accountancy firm, those working reduced hours at the county council felt they accomplished as much in reduced hours as they had in full-time work. However, this occurred often through an intensification of work effort. For example, the chief accountant at the council who worked reduced hours explained,

> There's things like not talking, not going off and making several cups of coffee.
> . . . I tend to steam through meetings, I organise meetings carefully. There's an agenda, we go through it, and I also tend to wind it up a bit faster.

Working reduced work hours helped decrease pressure on some workers, but it also lessened their pay. Some of the senior staff working less than full-time accepted that their cut in salary was the price they were forced to pay to legitimate shorter hours. According to the principal personnel officer, "Many people . . . will say to me, or say to each other in private, what you are really buying . . . is the right to go home with nothing on their conscience."

Although the long-hours culture that had undermined the attempts to be family friendly at the accountancy firm was less prevalent at the county council, it still existed in some departments. There was, however, an awareness that the long-hours culture was not a good thing, and there were efforts to eradicate it, through references to increased efficiency and productivity.

Financial Constraints

Financial issues can be constraints as well as drivers of change. Reduced hours of work resulted in reduced employee income, even if the employees' productivity remained the same. The salary cut was usually accepted by individuals because those working part-time wanted more time for nonwork activities and had the economic support from another part-time or full-time worker in their household. There was a recognition, however, that there was a danger in making assumptions that all employees were involved in families with two earners. If the council provided only part-time opportunities, it would disadvantage some families, especially those headed by single parents.

Policy as a Barrier to Culture Change

The county council, like the accountancy firm, began by implementing specific policies, waiting to address the need for culture change at a later stage. There was a recognition in the council that, in some cases, new policies could actually hold back progress. The principal personnel officer suggested, for example, that job-share policies could actually constrain progress toward challenging traditional working time: "I'm not a great fan of job-share . . . because I think it . . . perpetuates this straitjacket of the 37-hours workweek."

Impact of Gender Inequity in the Home

For organisations with a largely female workforce, an inequitable division of labour in the home could have repercussions at the workplace. Although the flexible work practices provided by the council gave them a competitive edge in recruitment, the practices could also encourage employee absenteeism if family care was not shared with employees' partners working in other organisations. The principal personnel officer explained, "Because we have relatively generous conditions for things like looking after sick children and so on, we have started to feel somewhat put upon. It's always our employees who shoulder the burden." This pattern of employee absence was seen as beginning to disadvantage the organisation, so the organisation was beginning to address some private work-family issues.

The principal personnel officer tried to get the organisation thinking about this issue by putting the topic of the domestic division of labour in the family as an agenda item in committee meetings. The council also took steps to get employees to request help from their partners. She explained,

Our position on leave for sick children is that we say you have this time off . . . if you are sure that no other provision can reasonably be made. . . . If it's the fourth time this year that the child has been ill and there's another adult in the household . . . not actually doing their share, we say . . . to the employee concerned, "We would like to be sympathetic here, but really, have you asked your husband to stay home?"

CONCLUSIONS

How generalisable or transferable are any implications that can be drawn from these two case studies? The differences between the contexts of each organisation highlight the difficulties in comparing work organisations across sectors. Intrinsic factors such as whether an organisation is male or female dominated and the nature of the services provided, as well as values and assumptions that make up culture, make meaningful comparison quite difficult. Even within the accountancy profession and within local government organisations, differences in circumstances and culture produce different outcomes with regard to gender equity. Clearly, it is important to address the issue of work and family integration, as well as gender equity, in the specific historic, economic, and social context of every specific organisation.

At the same time, however, there appear to be some tentative principles that can be derived from these two case studies that may have broader applicability. The first principle is the importance of clarifying the objectives of culture change. It is important to be clear that gender equity is an explicit goal if it is to be achieved. Inequity can be exacerbated if the goal is articulated as opportunities for women to act more like men or to be treated as special cases, while the male norms of long hours and continuous careers go unchallenged. It is also important to make clear that the objective is to find the best solution that will meet the needs of both the organisation and the employees, because this strategy has better potential to lead to mutual flexibility and to avoid the construction of flexible working arrangements as favours to which only selected employees are entitled. An explicit objective of bringing about organisational culture change will be more powerful than a goal of simply implementing formal policies, which can actually end up as barriers to more fundamental change.

The second principle is that strong and continuing leadership is important if culture change is to occur. It can come from the top or from another senior person; if it is delegated to someone with little influence or ownership of the initiatives, it will not be as successful. Initiatives driven by personnel or human resources departments are often marginalised and not perceived as key strategic business issues. However, under the right circumstances, change can be initiated from human resources departments if there is someone who has a high position in the company and is strongly committed to gender equity. Culture change takes time, and it helps to have continuity of leadership with a focus on continuing development.

The third principle is that it is essential to empower people at all levels of the organisation to participate in the change process. Top-down change can start the process, but the cooperation of line managers and the expectations of all employees help make the change take hold. Persistent encouragement of line managers to be flexible and the communication of good practice can be important, since line managers have the most discretion about employees' working arrangements.

The fourth principle is that the long-hours culture must be challenged. A culture of valuing long hours of work is prevalent in the United Kingdom, and this can undermine attempts by organisations to look at structuring work in different ways. It is important not only to question the assumption that long hours are necessary to demonstrate commitment and be productive but also to show that this assumption can actually be counterproductive. Questioning the long-hours culture, however, may not be enough. Fundamental psychological patterns and cultural values that equate self-worth with intense involvement in paid employment, mastery, and career success will create resistance to the goals of work-nonwork balance (Kofodimos, 1993). This highlights the importance of constantly rehearsing the business argument for a change in values. Windows of opportunities such as the antifraud initiative of the British government can be useful tools for challenging the valuing of long hours in the workplace for their own sake.

ISSUES FOR THE FUTURE

Two broader equity issues are raised in both case studies described in this chapter. The first concerns equitable pay. In both organisations, employees who worked less than full-time for family reasons reported themselves, and were reported by their managers, as being just as productive as they had been when working full-time. They achieved this by working more efficiently or by intensifying their efforts at work. Yet these employees received a cut in salary. Is it equitable to pay people more to take longer to do their work? This raises the issue of what is to be valued in an organisation—input (e.g., hours at work) or output (e.g., performance outcomes)?

The second broader issue concerns the gender-based division of labour in the home. The issues of gender equality in the workplace and in the home cannot be separated. This is an organisational issue, because family-friendly organisations that offer benefits to their employees can develop problems with absenteeism unless women and men in all companies equally share responsibility for dependent care. In some national contexts, social policy can play a role in encouraging shared responsibility—for example, by providing entitlement to both parents to take leave to care for a sick child. Even in these contexts, however, organisational cultures vary in the extent to which it is considered legitimate for men as well as women to reconcile work and family responsibilities (Haas & Hwang, 1995). A challenge for future research and practice is to determine how gender inequity at home can be addressed by work organisations so that organisations that are more flexible and gender equitable are not disadvantaged in relation to those with more traditional cultures.

REFERENCES

Haas, L., & Hwang, P. (1995). Corporate culture and men's use of family leave benefits in Sweden. *Family Relations, 44,* 28-36.

Hammond, V., & Holton, V. (1992). *A balanced workforce: Achieving cultural change for women—a comparative study.* Ashridge, UK: Ashridge Management Research Group.

Kofodimos, J. (1993). *Balancing act: How managers can integrate successful career and fulfilling personal lives.* San Francisco: Jossey-Bass.

Lewis, S. (1996). Work-family reconciliation and the law: Intrusion or empowerment? In S. Lewis & J. Lewis (Eds.), *The work-family challenge: Rethinking employment* (pp. 1-19). London: Sage.

Lewis, S., & Taylor, K. (1996). Evaluating the impact of family friendly employment policies: A case study. In S. Lewis & J. Lewis (Eds.), *The work-family challenge: Rethinking employment* (pp. 112-127). London: Sage.

Liff, S., & Cameron, I. (1997). Changing equality culture to move beyond "woman's problems." *Gender, Work, and Organization, 4,* 35-46.

Pemberton, C. (1995). Organizational culture and equalities work. In J. Shaw & D. Perrons (Eds.), *Making gender work: Managing equal opportunities* (pp. 108-123). Milton Keynes, UK: Open University Press.

Schein, E. (1985). *Organizational culture and leadership.* San Francisco: Jossey-Bass.

12

Organisational Change and Gender Equity
An Australian Case Study

GRAEME RUSSELL

DON EDGAR

Progress toward gender equity in the workplace, most commentators believe, is hindered by two tendencies: first, a lack of emphasis on gender equity as a strategic business issue, and second, a lack of emphasis on changing the culture of organisations. Interestingly, these are also two of the reasons given for why workers do not receive more help from companies in managing work and family roles. It is therefore essential to integrate gender equity and work-family issues into strategic thinking within organisations. This parallels arguments made earlier by Friedman (1991) and Friedman and Galinsky (1991) about the need for a focus on business benefits, integration, and changes in corporate culture.

It is this latter issue—changes in corporate culture—that has come in for the closest scrutiny recently. (See Bankert & Googins, 1996; Hammonds, 1996; Lewis, 1996; Rapoport & Bailyn, 1996; and other chapters in this volume.) A major theme running through Hammonds's (1996) *Business Week* article is the view that addressing work-family issues has limited value unless there is a strategic business focus. It is argued that strategic solutions involve building the "consideration of family issues into job design, work processes and organizational structures—just as one would consider marketing concerns, say, or

---

EDITORS' NOTE: The authors' use of British spellings has been retained.

engineering input" (p. 76). Another major theme in this article is the need to develop a supportive internal culture, especially one that demonstrates support from senior management. In the *Business Week* survey of 8,000 employees, "54% indicated their top brass do, in fact, demonstrate support for family balance" (p. 78).

The aim of this chapter is to describe the processes involved in developing a work-family strategy in one Australian work organisation. This organisation was chosen because of the active involvement of senior management and because clear links were established between gender equity and work-family issues throughout the process.

CASE STUDY OF AN
ORGANISATION IN CHANGE

The company we report on had approximately 6,000 employees (93% male) and operated in "the fiercely competitive and cyclic global minerals industry." The American-based company had always stressed the value of quality employees as a key to its competitive success. The company put great emphasis in its vision statement on "excellence through quality—creating value for customers, employees, shareholders and the community through innovation, technology and operational expertise." Though the managing director defended the company's focus on profit and safety, he emphasised the "people value" as central to achieving these goals: "People are the most important key to our success. Every employee will have equal opportunity in an environment that fosters communication, involvement and teamwork."

Such statements explain the starting point for this company's interest in developing a comprehensive work-family policy and in ensuring gender equity in job type and management level. First, the chief executive officer (CEO) had a clear appreciation of the centrality of a cooperative, committed, and participatory workforce for achieving business goals. Personnel or human resource matters were not regarded as "soft" add-ons to "harder" business concerns. Second, the company had a history of technological innovation, with a strong emphasis on clearheaded management practices that were prepared to change as circumstances demanded. Third, employees, customers, and shareholders were not seen as separate or unequal areas of focus; they were each seen as integral to the rationale for "excellence through quality."

Laying the Groundwork: Developing
an Employee Relations Strategy

In that vein, a brief history of the company's employee relations strategy is relevant. During the 1970s and 1980s, the typical union-versus-management industrial relations standoff had prevailed. Distrust was rife, and top-down management decisions often generated industrial strife. The company was attempting to improve quality performance and, like many others, explored the various management theories of the day in an attempt to reach "best practice" targets (e.g., total quality management, Deming's 14 principles, Shingo-SMED, Hoshin, Kaizen, etc.). One fad followed another, with little thought given to its suitability to the particular culture of the organisation (Bodi, Maggs, & Edgar, 1997). The result was a muddle of confusion. Workers distrusted the company's declared goals, believing that the true aim was downsizing.

Much of this came to a head in 1985 with a work stoppage in the mining group; they objected to the new company philosophy on individual and team development, which was "communicated" to all workers via a booklet, without union and employee involvement. Employees did not believe a word of it, because of the gulf they saw between what existed in front of them and what was described in the philosophy. The management approach had become known as the "ready, fire, aim" method, and the workers rebelled. As a result, management threw out all theories and agreed to develop a "blueprint for introducing change" with full worker participation.

The striking success of this process (during 1986-1987) as a model for later work-family policy development cannot be underestimated. Team participation and genuine reform based on employee-management cooperation resulted in a job redesign program, endorsed by secret ballot and ratified by the Australian Industrial Relations Commission in May 1987. The mining group developed a strategic plan, a vision and set of values, and key performance areas. Trust was built up to such an extent that, when two mines had to be consolidated into one, the implementation audit was awarded the Australian Quality Award for Outstanding Individual Quality Improvement Project in 1990. The management task force had actively involved all levels of employees, and decision making was data based and focused on the needs of its "customers"—the company's refineries.

Such an experience sent important messages throughout the organisation. Workers understood that management was genuinely interested in worker participation, that there were common interests at stake, and that teamwork was effective and here to stay. The processes learned in this period were applied to every new problem. A parallel effort had reduced serious injuries by 15% to 25% each year, and workers now believed that improved work practices and productivity did not imply job redundancies. The company's health report for 1990 claimed the following:

> Managers now understood that most people want to do a good job, most people are proud of achievement, most people want an opportunity to grow, and everybody needs training. Line managers had taken over a direct responsibility for

industrial relations, personnel, safety and training . . . and the new day-to-day process had created an "us"— with one agenda—rather than the traditional "them and us" with multiple agendas.

Getting Work-Family Issues
on the Corporate Agenda

These experiences had moved the company down the path to a "seamless organisation," further than most companies. The company had a well-developed work-site-specific and team-focused approach to training and education, and it enjoyed a high degree of employee trust in its stated "people value."

But not all was perfect. Almost all work sites still relied on an old-fashioned personnel approach, helping individuals to solve problems one at a time (e.g., wages, job design, leave arrangements, training, and gender equity issues), instead of developing a fully integrated human resources plan. Employee assistance programs (EAPs) were offered very piecemeal (apart from health services) and handled as "add-ons," via industrial chaplains, with little emphasis on preventive support. Industrial relations managers struggled somewhat reluctantly to find a new role for themselves. Despite a stated policy advocating equal opportunity, the dominant culture was technical-managerial and very male dominated; most managers were men and cynical about the place of women in such a "tough" technical organisation. Managers felt they were catering adequately to employees' work-family needs.

Only one work site had an integrated approach to human relations issues. This was one of the smelters, employing close to 800 people. Health services were closely linked with staff development, training, and the development of participatory management structures. This workplace offered several employee assistance programs, ranging from the usual health and safety topics to an assertiveness training program that was so successful that it was offered to employees' partners and local high school students. It had also set up a well-equipped gymnasium for health and fitness programs and an on-site child care centre for the children of employees. The development of this work site's approach to human relations relied heavily on the close relationship between the smelt plant manager and the psychologist in charge of the mental health services division. Together with senior staff, they developed a holistic approach to human resources based on the view that "the most modern equipment and technology mean nothing if we haven't got the best operators in the world. . . . Support to reach our full potential in this enterprise must come from a variety of sources, including our families." In a sense, this smelter was already well along in its acceptance of the need for more attention to work-family balance.

Decision to Undertake a Review

Two events precipitated the company's decision to undertake a comprehensive review of work-family and gender equity issues in the overall company. One was an intensive management seminar, during which Heather Carmody, the former director of the Australian Council for Equal Opportunity in Employment, addressed equal opportunity and family issues. The other event involved a presentation, given by Heather Carmody and Don Edgar, to a group of senior managers about their "New Links Workplace Initiative" (Edgar, 1997). They approached the company's CEO about making the company a pilot organisation in the initiative and found that he had already directed that a work-family committee be set up to investigate what might be done. He agreed to the company's involvement as one of the New Links Workplace companies in November 1992, and Don Edgar joined the company's work-family committee as an observer when it began meeting in 1993.

Implementing the Process

The establishment of the work-family committee was an important step in the development of the company's work-family policy. It was important that it was a central corporate committee, established by the CEO, and that it consisted of representatives nominated from each of the various work-site locations.

Committee members were chosen from the various work sites on the basis of strategic influence and cooperative spirit; they were individuals who were likely to avoid protecting work-site-based vested interests hostile to the initiative. The criteria for committee member selection proved to be both a weakness and a strength. The original work-family committee did not include the senior corporate personnel manager or any of the specific work-site personnel managers. Yet these clearly would be key people in any implementation plan; their understanding and acceptance of the problem of the work-family imbalance was crucial to any realistic policy action. Their intimate knowledge of the workplace, job-design issues, shift work, and continuous processing, along with their direct experience with interactions between employees, managers, and supervisors, proved helpful to the committee on many occasions. The work-family committee also lacked representation from work-site chaplains and medical professionals who were doing most of the day-to-day consultations with employees on work and family problems. These were curious omissions, because their understanding of and support for the planned work-family initiatives would also be essential for successful implementation. These choices were made because the CEO wanted "real action" and worried that some complacency existed among those already responsible for dealing with workers' family problems.

The corporate personnel manager was eventually added to the committee after several meetings because of his expressed interest and support and because his knowledge of the organisation's approach to its "people value" was essential. As time went on, some of the territoriality of the company's separate fiefdoms (work sites) was broken down as work-site managers compared notes on work practices, employee relations problems, and alternate solutions to work-family conflicts. The survey findings and subsequent discussions suggested more commonality than had been expected, and they gave a generally positive picture of the company's corporate values and management practices that brought the work-family committee members from different work sites together around agreed work-family goals.

The chair of the work-family committee was a senior mining manager from Western Australia who appeared initially reluctant to be taking on this "sideline" issue about which he "knew nothing." However, he was a true professional, imbued with the experience of Western Australia's strikes and the success of worker participation, and he extended this experience to his leadership on the committee. The selection of a senior Western Australian manager as chair of the committee was a strategic blow to the inherent east-west rivalry within the company, since the west was seen as taking a lead role in this issue. However, the appointment of someone from Western Australia made it obvious that this was a central, corporate committee, reporting directly to the CEO and his executive assistant, and was not being run by central office "bureaucrats" or "Melbourne people." Because of his strong engineering background and the equally strong planning focus of his Western Australian boss, the committee chair placed a strong emphasis on clarity of goals, objectives, and detailed implementation plans. Although this approach did not always go along well with the flexibility that is needed to develop a new work culture, one that would be truly responsive to a diverse workforce and its family-related needs, it gave a valuable structure to the committee's deliberations and implementation documents.

Some members did not want the observers (Edgar and Russell) to distract them from the fixed path they had already agreed on, which was to do a survey of employees' work-family needs and attitudes, on which a firm set of policies and implementation guidelines on work-family practices would be based. There had not yet been a wider discussion about the rationale for, or research on, a better balance between work and family, and opinions differed about what was already being done, what was feasible, and what might be acceptable or desirable. This group was also initially very reluctant to include gender equity and broader equal employment opportunity issues on the work-family agenda.

In the beginning, committee deliberations were affected by the problems of corporate federalism, and rivalries between the central head office and peripheral work-site locations were readily apparent (Handy, 1994). Only the one smelter described previously already had an excellent reputation for innovative work-family practices. Other company work sites expressed reservations about the approach that had been taken at the smelter. In committee meetings, despite the presence of Russell and Edgar, members openly discussed their scepticism that change in personnel policies would bring about any tangible benefits other than publicity. Uninformed about the purposes of a good survey, they worried that an employee survey might set up unrealistic hopes among employees that the company would solve "everyone's private family problems" and build gymnasiums and set up on-site child care centres at every work site. They were also concerned that the costs connected to new programs would threaten profits. Differences of opinion about the initiatives at the smelter and comments such as "in the west, we do things differently" often occurred at the committee's meetings. In retrospect, however, such exchanges became regarded as an important part of the learning process that eventually brought the group together around work-family goals.

The CEO kept out of the committee's discussions. The committee was delegated fully and entrusted with the task of identifying the nature of the work-family issues in the company. But it was clearly a committee reporting to him, and, as CEO, he would have final say on any statement of policy about work and family initiatives. The people value in the company was too central to allow any diminution by popular vote; its bottom-line profit motive was too important to permit slipping into catering to every employee whim. Consideration for the "bottom line" (profit) is a central issue in any human resources strategy and one on which some senior managers equivocate. Managers are sometimes swayed by social reformers' zeal to help improve employees' quality of life no matter the cost. This can involve maintaining equal opportunity employment, setting goals for recruitment of the underrepresented sex, offering employee assistance programs, establishing on-site child care, and implementing other work-family benefits. Senior managers are often hesitant to state openly that the company's chief aim is to make a profit or to stay in business.

In the new "membership" companies, employees become partners in the enterprise and are prized as its central assets rather than seen as expendable property. The best companies may well become, as Handy (1994) says, like clubs or fellowships of companions. This does not negate the fact that a business has to answer to its shareholders and its own future by turning a profit in the long run. The CEO of this company kept that firmly in mind while recognising that more flexibility and management sensitivity around family needs was desirable in its own right as well as for its potential positive effects on worker performance and profit making. The balance at work should be on the side of effective work; at home, it should be on the side of effective family relationships. The two were seen as going hand-in-hand, but the company's interests still came first, hard as that was to accept for some who wanted it to be otherwise.

Survey of Employee Work-Family Linkages

The central work-family committee agreed on the format of a comprehensive employee survey. It was to be a full population survey of all employees rather than a sample, because it was clear that there would be different findings for each of the different work-site locations. The survey would also collect information on employees' partners, the first attempt ever in Australia to investigate how employees' views of the work-family balance compared with partners at home, who might see it from another perspective. The survey covered the full range of work-family issues (e.g., impact of work on family life, impact of family commitments on work, assessment of current work-family culture) as well as equal employment issues (e.g., perceptions of gender equity in advancement opportunities, reports of discrimination). The survey process was influenced by the need for a central corporate policy on work and family issues as well as the need to work closely with the diverse workplace cultures within the various work-site locations. The survey work was conducted by a research team from Macquarie University (headed by Graeme Russell).

The *first step* was to pilot the questionnaire at every location with a small cross-section of employees. This was partly a strategy of clarifying the questions, but it was also a strategy of educating the workforce about the issues and informing the work sites about the main survey that was to come. Focus group discussions were held to check the validity of the questions and the responses obtained.

The *second step* involved conducting a comprehensive employee survey at every work-site location. These surveys were administered by the research team to groups during work time; the research team sorted out difficulties, assured workers of confidentiality, and immediately coded the questionnaires for analysis. Overall, 64% of all company employees completed the survey. A mail survey would not have had the same educational impact or as good a response rate. Employees' partners were asked to participate in the survey through notes in the company newsletter and by their partners who took questionnaires home. Partners' responses were mailed directly to the university. More than 800 partners completed questionnaires. It was estimated that this represented a 25% response rate.

The *third step* was to provide preliminary survey findings to the central committee, with suggested policy implications. The discussion of findings led to a clear realisation that company programs would have to vary by work-site location if the company's policy was going to respond adequately to the diverse work-family issues and needs that were uncovered. It was agreed that, in addition to information on the entire company, each work site would receive information on its own workforce, broken down by gender, age, and occupational group. The separate findings could then be compared with companywide data to identify commonalities and differences.

Key survey findings identifying employee needs and problems can be summarized briefly here. Although employees' overall needs for child care seemed to be met adequately in most locations, gaps were identified in emergency child care, in out-of-school-hours care, and in the flexibility of management responses to family emergencies. One surprise was that 16% of employees already had responsibility for an aging relative, with an additional 50% saying they would have elder care responsibilities within the next 10 years. The company's equal employment opportunity policy did not seem to be working effectively, because a large number of employees reported workplace harassment (because of gender, age, or nationality), and female workers often reported hostility from male workers, who thought they were "taking jobs from men." Despite its "people value" ideology, the company still expected employees, especially at the management level, to work long hours, train away from their home base, and attend meetings outside regular work hours. The impact of work pressure on individuals and family life was manifest in reports of absenteeism, decreased performance, and job dissatisfaction. There was no support for earlier committee fears that workers would expect too much from the company, such as costly child care centres or gymnasiums.

The *fourth step* involved conducting problem-solving focus groups to discuss work-family issues that could not be well articulated by a survey or left to senior management or research teams to identify. Nineteen groups were held across all work-site locations, including separate groups for partners of company employees. Focus group discussions were designed to identify problems that involved the family or the individual who had an identifiable potential impact on the business, even indirectly such as through reduced morale and commitment. These groups also discussed potential solutions that would provide benefits to the organisation and to employees.

The 10 problems most frequently identified by focus group members were the following:

1. A lack of flexibility in being able to take leave for family reasons

2. Discrimination on the basis of gender, age, disability, and ethnicity; the absence of equal employment opportunities; and the failure by many supervisors, especially male managers, to recognise this as a problem in the company

3. Stress resulting from work-family demands (the impact family has on work and the impact work demands have on family), especially for managers and supervisors

4. Problems with management or supervisor relationships, and perceived lack of openness, trust, flexibility, and people focus

5. Lack of flexibility in hours and days of work, as well as place of work

6. Child care problems for preschool-age children involving availability, hours, and costs

7. Lack of promotion opportunities

8. Expectations about working long hours and the assumption that employees have flexibility in their family lives that will enable them to accommodate work demands

9. The impact on family life of the demands of shift work and recent company changes (e.g., 12-hour shifts, annualised salaries, "flexi" call-ins)

10. High expectations of work performance but a lack of recognition of effort by management

This list shows that a number of different problems concerned employees and partners in this company; gender equity and equal employment opportunity were concerns, as was balancing work and family roles. Some focus group members mentioned the lack of company leadership on these issues and the lack of "balanced" role models in the organisation. All these issues are ones identified in the research literature as important to employees, and all concern basic elements of corporate culture. The focus group process adopted here was an effective vehicle to enable these issues to be named, argued about, and included on the work-family agenda.

The Community Scan

The New Links Workplace Project has the philosophy that employees live in and are part of a wider community and are not just moving between home and work. It follows that the solutions for work-family balance cannot be found only in the workplace or in individual homes. Employees need to live in a "family-friendly" community, in which services and resources support family life. Even the most family-friendly employer will have little impact on reducing parental or other family-related stress if the local community has few child care or elder care resources, if schools do not involve parents or offer after-school programs or counseling for problem students, and if there are few activities for teenagers or local support services for abuse victims, drug addicts, and alcoholics.

The New Links Workplace Project conducted a study in the Mandurah-Peel district of Western Australia, where some 70% of the company's employees resided. The community scan involved a relatively simple methodology. First, local data on existing family support services in the region were collated from official statistics and contacts with government departments. Second, a series of discussions was held with key service providers in the region involved in child care, elder care, social welfare, health, and education. Their subjective assessments of family problems in the region and perceived gaps in family support were then checked by a comprehensive but brief survey of every service organisation in the Mandurah region. They were asked to list their numbers of clients or places handled, fees, and waiting list numbers and then to write comments on their perception of unmet needs and current difficulties faced by families in the area. No mention was made of the company's involvement in the New Links Workplace Project so that false expectations about future action would not be raised. The results of this community scan were then compiled in a report for the company.

The community scan revealed a lack of certain key family support services that could be checked against what the company employees said they "needed." It also revealed what professional service providers, local government officials, schoolteachers, and other community people believed to be common family problems in the area that might resonate with the company findings.

The following are some examples of how information from the community scan corresponded with employment survey results:

- Community agencies and workers alike reported that costs of child care were a major difficulty for parents and that there was a shortage of emergency and after-school care in the area.

- The area lacked marriage counselling and family support services, yet almost three fourths of employees (72%) wanted access to family counselling and two fifths (42%) did not feel comfortable confiding family problems to their supervisor. The survey revealed that employees had problems that might be resolved with such services; one third (33%) of employees were not satisfied with their relationships because of work demands, and more than half (53%) frequently came home from work feeling stressed.

- The schools reported overwhelming problems relating to family breakdown, stress, "acting out behaviour," and a shortage of qualified guidance personnel. Company employees' children made up a large part of the area's school population. One third (33%) of employed parents said the job damaged their relationship with their children; 62% felt family education and parenting advice were important; and all agreed that after-school care was badly needed in the area.

- Elder care services were sparse in the region. Of the company's employees, 16% already had and 50% expected to soon have elder care responsibilities; 62% of this latter group wanted advice and information on how to deal with this new responsibility.

It became apparent that local community resources would vary in each work-site location, and this would change the character of "New Links" cooperative arrangements that could be established. The initial community scan became a model for other work-site locations to use to "scan" their own communities.

Developing Policy Guidelines

After the above projects were completed, the central corporate Committee on Family and Work developed a set of work-family policy guidelines. These were printed in an explanatory booklet for widespread circulation. A video was produced, starring the CEO and other key figures, to give the rationale for new work-family initiatives—the imprimatur of "the boss" within a dramatised, down-to-earth illustration of how the new and the old approaches might differ. Work-family teams were established at most work-site locations to help facilitate and monitor implementation of these guides. Briefly, the new guidelines involved the following:

- Temporary changes in working hours to accommodate important family commitments. (Impact on other team members must be taken into account, and the supervisor is responsible for negotiating the most mutually suitable approach.)

- Special leave for family needs, from a few hours to a full day or extended leave. (Leave could be taken as part of annual leave or from accrued sick leave. *Family* was very broadly defined and not limited to immediate household members.)

- One year of unpaid parental leave for either parent. (The company offered information and assistance for employees to return to work when desired.)

- Part-time work, job sharing, flexible hours, and home-based work. (These could be negotiated in consultation with the work-site personnel manager.)

- Programs to encourage respect for diversity and the elimination of harassment and discrimination.

- Development of "New Links" with community agencies, such as child care, elder care, youth support services, schools, and counselling services. (Better information about dependent care facilities and resources was to be compiled and made available through booklets and databases at each work-site location.)

Leadership and Integration With Business Strategies

A major outcome of this project was the implementation of a new company-wide strategic planning process on the goal of diversity involving all managers and area supervisors at all locations. The intention was to connect gender equity and broader equal employment opportunity issues with work-family and lifestyle issues. The following key elements were involved in this process:

1. A strategic diversity plan was developed and incorporated into the business plan at each work-site location. Senior managers developed this plan initially, and it was further refined through employee workshops.

2. Targets and measurable outcomes were set for specific groups (e.g., to increase the percentage of women from 6% to 20%, to exceed the current industry standard for the employment of women, to reflect the diversity of the community by the year 2005).

3. Specific strategies were developed to cover the following major components:

In regard to *recruitment,* strategies were designed to ensure greater diversity in the applicant pool for positions at all levels. It was recognised, however, that the company did not have enough information about the diversity in the populations from which they recruited. A need was also identified to review selection procedures (including interview training and interview panel composition).

In regard to *integration and retention,* the focus was on the attitudes and behaviours of the current workforce (e.g., to change the discriminatory behaviours of the male workforce) and on reviewing barriers associated with current work practices and job design. (Management was also concerned that work-family policies were not as effective as they were intended to be to ensure employment retention, and more attention was to be given to this issue.)

In regard to *advancement,* there was acknowledgment that targeting barriers to the advancement of women could result in a backlash and might not necessarily be in the long-term interests of women who wanted to be accepted and recognised within the organisation because they were the best person for the job rather than "because they are women." Therefore, the main emphasis was on strategies to ensure that the best people were given advancement and development opportunities and given support through mentoring and career planning. A major issue rarely addressed by these groups was the lack of diversity within the management groups aside from gender (e.g., the heavy emphasis on an engineering background).

In regard to *leadership,* strategies focused on establishing links between the goal of diversity and business plans. The outcome of this process was the identification of a need to define leadership behaviours and to audit these on a regular basis (both from within the management group and from reporting staff).

4. Diversity measures were included as part of mainstream business reports. These measures included employment diversity at each level of the organisation; the percentages of underrepresented groups who applied for each advertised position and what percentage were appointed; the percentage of underrepresented groups promoted in each level; average remuneration packages and salaries for underrepresented groups at each level; turnover rates for underrep-

resented groups; the number and nature of harassment or discrimination complaints; and assessment of employee knowledge and attitudes through surveys.

5. Senior management was held accountable for achieving diversity goals. Diversity targets and outcomes were incorporated into individual performance plans for direct reports to the CEO. Targets (in terms of numbers and completion dates) were set for the percentages of females to be employed at a particular location (e.g., 10%) and for the dates by which (a) managers would communicate the strategy to all employees, (b) all employees in their work area would participate in relevant training, and (c) human resource support systems (e.g., career development systems) would be in place. Targets ensured that managers conducted a thorough analysis of barriers (e.g., community views about which jobs were appropriate for males versus females) and put in place appropriate strategies to overcome these. Some organisations had taken this process further and had linked equal employment opportunity targets with reviews of management remuneration.

Key Aspects of the Organisational Change Process

This was a comprehensive change process that, at the time of this writing, had been in progress for 4 years. Outcomes were still being assessed, and there was no indication that work-family and gender equity issues were simply "the flavour of the month." Considering all that we know about this company, it is our view that the following were critical factors in ensuring the overall effectiveness of this process:

- Endorsement from the highest level in the company—the CEO
- High expectations for the leaders of the project to do the job well
- Operational credibility of work-family committee membership
- Recognising and subverting likely oppositional factors
- Using the survey-design process as an educational tool
- Using a broad approach in the analytic phase and including the full range of work and family/lifestyle issues and equal employment issues
- Insisting on balancing business goals with "people value"
- Using focus groups at every work-site location to determine which family issues were relevant to the employees
- Using the pilot survey and feedback on its findings as part of an educational strategy

- Including partners of employees in the survey and focusing on work-family stress experienced by senior managers

- Feeding back separate-location data to the work sites so that they could feel some "ownership" of the data and compare their issues with those of the rest of the corporation

- Using employee-based problem-solving groups to identify key issues and develop solutions based on effective business and employee/family outcomes

- Validating survey results through the community scan

- Identifying potential gaps and needs in local family support services

- Identifying through the community scan potential areas for company initiatives in building on and building up community resources that would help the company's work-family policy

- Acknowledging the links between work-family and gender equity issues

- Incorporating work-family and equal employment opportunity issues into mainstream business strategies

- Focusing on management accountability and incorporating work-family and gender equity issues into leadership skill development

CONCLUSIONS

Any organisational analysis of work-family and gender equity issues needs to take account of the diversity of factors that have an impact on employment behaviour and on an individual's ability to achieve a satisfactory balance between work life and family and personal life. These factors are located at various levels.

At the *individual* level, personal values and expectations around balance and lifestyle and the psychological impact they have vary markedly from one individual to another. At the *family* level, there are variations in employees' family situations, including their partners' needs for job and career, lack of flexibility in partners' jobs, quality of partner relationships, and degree of extended-family support. At the *community* level, individuals have differential access to social-network support and community resources that can address family needs, because communities (and societies) vary from one to another. It is sometimes argued that U.S. corporations have been impelled to address the work and family needs of their employees because government-funded community resources (e.g., child care) are inadequate. At the *organisational* level, individuals are affected by the nature of work (work design and work practices, degree of customer contact, etc.), rewards (outputs vs. time inputs), career structures and opportunities, supervisor and work-team support, employment conditions, and pay, as well as by work-family policies and practices.

The ultimate success of gender equity and work-family strategies in organisations rests with the extent to which changes occur in the culture of the workplace and the expectations managers and employees have about the behaviour that is rewarded. For most organisations, there is still considerable resistance to critically evaluating the way work is done, thus reducing the possibilities for employees to have greater flexibility. There is also opposition to the idea of challenging traditional role models and traditional definitions of success.

REFERENCES

Bankert, E., & Googins, B. (1996, July/August). Family-friendly—says who? *Across the Board,* pp. 45-49.

Bodi, A., Maggs, G., & Edgar, D. (1997). *When too much change is never enough.* Sydney: Woodslane.

Edgar, D. (1997). Developing the New Links Workplace: The future of family, work, and community relationships. In S. Dreman (Ed.), *The family on the threshold of the 21st century* (pp. 147-166). Hillsdale, NJ: Lawrence Erlbaum.

Friedman, D. (1991). *Linking work-family issues to the bottom line* (Report No. 962). New York: Conference Board.

Friedman, D., & Galinsky, E. (1991). Work and family trends. In S. Zedeck (Ed.), *Work and family.* New York: Jossey-Bass.

Hammonds, K. (1996, September 16). Balancing work and family. *Business Week,* pp. 74-80.

Handy, C. (1994). *The empty raincoat.* London: Hutchinson.

Lewis, S. (1996). Sense of entitlement, family-friendly policies, and gender. In H. Holt & I. Thaulow (Eds.), *The role of companies in reconciling working life and family life* (pp. 17-42). Copenhagen, Denmark: Danish National Institute of Social Research.

Rapoport, R., & Bailyn, L. (with Kolb, D., Fletcher, J., Friedman, D., Eaton, S., Harvey, M., & Miller, B.). (1996). *Relinking life and work: Toward a better future.* New York: Ford Foundation.

13

Organisational Cultures, Families, and Careers in Scandinavia

YVONNE DUE BILLING

For about three decades, it has been common for women in the Scandinavian countries to be in the labour market, and since the 1980s, women have been almost equally as likely as men to be in the labour force. The "breadwinner" role is no longer exclusively men's. Within the labour market, however, there is a pronounced horizontal and vertical gender-based division of labour, and a "career" is often described as incompatible for women if they have families. Women (mothers) are believed to be primarily oriented toward their families, whereas men (fathers) are believed to be primarily oriented toward their work. This way of thinking influences women's possibilities of having a career and reproduces gender inequity. Work organisations participate in this gender construction by encouraging mostly single women and married men to be career oriented.

In this chapter, I address how men and women come to push for organisational changes that make it easier to juggle family and career roles. The concepts of "exit," "voice," and "loyalty" are used to describe the career and family pathways of employees in three Scandinavian organisations. These concepts were originally developed by Hirschmann (1970) in his analysis of how organ-

---

EDITORS' NOTE: The author's use of British spellings has been retained.

isations react to external and internal market forces. I found these concepts helpful in analyzing people's reactions to the dilemma of combining work and family. (For further discussion, see Billing, 1991.)

"Exit" occurs when a person leaves the organisation, drops the career, or quits the marriage (or abstains from having a family and/or career). "Voice" can be complementary to exit or can become an alternative, especially when exit seems impossible. "Voice" implies that the person tries to change things, that he or she makes demands or protests against the conditions that cause strain. "Loyalty" is understood here as meeting the demands and needs of the family and/or the work organisation, whatever they are, without protest. Loyalty toward the family may result in postponing or even giving up a career. Loyalty to the work organisation can mean that work becomes a style of life that has effects on the time and energy remaining for family life. An individual can try to be loyal toward both the work organisation and the family, but this is difficult to manage. It can also be difficult to define loyalty. There are different degrees of loyalty; likewise, demands differ, and so do people's thresholds and needs. One person can choose to be loyal toward both the family and the work organisation, whereas another might exit an organisation to keep family loyalty intact.

Using these concepts of exit, voice, and loyalty, we can see how they affect individuals' career and family pathways and how they can influence the dynamics of organisational change. In the analysis to follow, I illustrate how there are differences in employees' use of the strategies of exit, voice, and loyalty, depending on the culture of the work organisation where they are employed, and how exit, voice, and loyalty can be ways to handle work-family conflict and to negotiate new family and organisational arrangements.

THE THREE CASE STUDIES

The three organisations were studied with several interests in mind. Two important purposes were to discover which social and organisational mechanisms facilitated or prevented women's attainment of managerial positions and to find out whether there were general patterns in how managers handled and combined their own personal work and family roles. The organisations studied were the Danish National Board of Social Welfare, Scandinavian Airline Systems, and the Danish Foreign Ministry. Fifty female and male managers were interviewed altogether. Only half of the female managers were married or cohabiting, whereas all but one of the men were married. Half of the female managers had children, but half of these were already grown; in contrast, all male managers still had young children at home. All female managers had hired housekeepers, compared with only one fourth of male managers. (For more information on the methodology of this study, see Billing & Alvesson, 1994.)

The Danish National Board
of Social Welfare

In the Danish National Board of Social Welfare, there was a common understanding that its members were not just organisational members but that they also had private lives and families that they valued. Family was understood broadly and could involve marriage or cohabiting relationships with or without children. The organisation was family oriented and committed to caretaking values. Families were talked about much in the organisation; children could be brought to work; and there were outings for families.

There was seemingly no difference in expectations for the two genders when they became parents. Fathers were regarded as being just as responsible for child care as mothers, no matter what occupational position the father or mother held. In this organisation, it looked bad if the male managers did not take parental leave or did not collect children from day care. Some of the men wanted to do this, but there were others who felt pressed to do so by the norms of the organisational culture. The latter group of men were also often married to career women, who voiced their demands to their husbands to do their share of the domestic work. If there were small children, fathers shared child care with their wives, delegated their share to a paid housekeeper, or did both.

The predominant family type among managers in this organisation was the dual-career family with children (at all ages). Only one female manager was single. Women in this organisation were not obligated to exit marriage or parenthood to have a career. The female managers at the Danish National Board of Social Welfare felt that they were pursuing a career on equal terms with their husbands. Male managers, however, sometimes voiced complaints about their situations because they felt they were not as positive as those of traditional men, who had wives to take care of all the domestic work. The female managers thought they benefited from living in dual-career families, whereas the male managers were much more ambivalent. Living in "egalitarian" relationships meant that male managers were on a par with female managers; both had to make sacrifices and to not travel too much.

The most common problem voiced by male and female managers living in dual-career families was a lack of time for private interests. For example, one male manager, married to a career woman, with two small children and a paid housekeeper said that he did not think he and his family spent enough time together. He did not take work home and tried to avoid working overtime to solve this situation, but when both he and his wife had to travel for business at the same time, they had to rely on grandparents and other relatives for child care. A female manager with two children, married to a husband with a career, said that her husband's time was more flexible than hers, so he did the shopping, cooking, and decision making about dinner, implying that her job prevented her from doing these tasks in her free time. This couple had a paid housekeeper but reported little time for friends.

Most research has found that lack of time is more of a problem for women than for men, because women tend to take on a double burden of work outside the home and most of the housework (e.g., Nieva & Gutek, 1981; Valdez & Gutek, 1987). A U.S. investigation of 3,600 married couples and 653 cohabiting couples showed that, even though the women were wage workers and did less housework than women who were not employed, they still took care of most of the housework. Among middle- and upper-class couples, women could delegate some domestic work to paid help (Diamond, 1987). In contrast, among managerial employees at the Danish National Board of Social Welfare, there seemed to be an equal sharing of the domestic work between husbands and wives, influenced by the fact that most individuals had spouses who were also pursuing careers. Although the spouses helped each other, both partners still felt that there was too little time for their children and that they had to prioritize their time to work everything out, even with paid housekeeping help.

Some female managers had been promoted at a later age than males, because they were part-timers when their children were young. At that point in time, their "loyalty" was directed toward their families, and careers had to wait. When the children grew older, these women voiced their demands to receive help from their spouses and children so that they could have time to have a career. They divorced their husbands (i.e., exited their marriages) if their husbands refused to consider their needs for a career. Divorces, however, were fairly rare in this organisation.

The predominant pattern for male and female employees at the Danish Board of Social Welfare was to be "loyal" toward both their families and the work organisation. Individuals who were very career oriented and had loyalty only toward the employer tended to exit this organisation. Employees had voiced their problems concerning lack of time for the family by occasionally refusing overtime work and travel abroad. This influenced the organisational culture, which had for some time been characterised as having considerable flexibility, a willingness to change, and empathy for family-oriented individuals. The Danish Board of Social Welfare consisted of many family-progressive women and men who had developed norms that paid attention to individuals' well-being within and outside of the organisation. The organisation was also committed to gender equity regarding promotions; there was an equal number of male and female managers.

Scandinavian Airline Systems

At Scandinavian Airline Systems, there was a much more conservative way of thinking about men and women. There was a manifest gendered division of labour, with women dominating the traditional jobs in the service area and men dominating the jobs in the technical areas and as pilots. Although there were a lot of free-time activities offered to organisational members, and the organisation liked to characterise itself as "one big family," the company in fact did not seem very concerned about people's family lives.

There were few female managers at this company; women held only 14% of all managerial posts, whereas their proportion of the total labour force was much higher, at 40%. The organisation tended to view how managers combined career and family as individuals' own private problems. Some women separated the work sphere and the private sphere to such an extent that they did not voice feelings about work at home or vice versa. For some, it was a difficult balance, to be regarded as equally loyal to work and to their families. Some women in dual-career families in this organisation experienced problems with their husbands when they earned higher wages or had higher-status jobs than their husbands did. These women tried to keep a low profile at home to make up for this, talking very little about their jobs and being very concerned about their husband's feelings. Other female managers lived in situations in which the couple shared housework but seemingly more for reasons of expediency rather than ideology. One said, "We do not make exact calculations of who is doing what. For instance, I don't mind not taking care of the car, and I probably cook the most. In return, he does the laundry and usually does the shopping." Only one female manager, with a young child, was married to a non-career-oriented man. He took care of most of the housework and collected the child from day care more often than she did. They did not have any problems with this arrangement; he was, however, often ridiculed in subtle ways by family, friends, and work colleagues who wondered "who wears the trousers in this family?"

All but one of the female managers had experienced delayed careers. The family was their highest priority when their children were young. When the children had grown older, the women's loyalty shifted toward the organisation, because of the high demands it placed on their time and energy. At this point, they voiced demands to their husbands, and sometimes their children, to help out more with domestic work. If the husband was not cooperative, the woman tended to exit the marriage. Often, women in these situations did not meet an "egalitarian" husband until their second or even third marriages.

At least one woman had used her voice to complain to the organisation about the demands placed on managers. One female manager said that, during her employment interview, she did not reveal to the organisation that she was divorced with two young children. She was convinced that if she had told the truth, she would not have been hired for the job as manager. When she was hired and on the job, she voiced concerns about the high demands for working overtime hours, and sometimes she took the children along with her to work if she could not get anyone to mind them.

The dominant pattern for the male managers at Scandinavian Airline Systems was that they were married to women who were totally loyal toward their husbands' careers. Wives took care of the family and did not have any ambitions for themselves with regard to careers (at least according to their husbands). If male managers' wives worked at all, it was part-time. It was therefore no problem for the male managers to be loyal toward the organisation because their wives had remained loyal to the family. There were hardly any conflicting demands made on them by their families.

The Danish Foreign Ministry

The Danish Foreign Ministry needed its employees to move from country to country. Earlier on, women tended to accompany their husbands who were employed in the ministry. But this had become a problem, because many male professionals nowadays were married to professional women who expected to use their skills in a career. The Foreign Ministry, however, could not guarantee that wives would obtain jobs abroad and could not guarantee that they would be able to get their former jobs back when they returned to Denmark. Consequently, some employees exited the organisation (or did not even consider entering it).

In general, though, once an employee had been promoted to the managerial level, it was not normal to exit the organisation, even if the family suffered. Loyalty toward the organisation was required at any price, and if there were problems coordinating the spheres of work and family, the family was the one that must adapt or pay the costs. There were many employees in this organisation who exited their marriages. The organisation was, in fact, informally known as the "Divorce Ministry" or the "Bachelor Ministry." One male manager said, "It is extremely rare to be still married to the same person if you have been here 10 to 15 years. It is not quite the same for women. Most of them are not married in the first place."

As indicated by this interviewee, women working for the Foreign Ministry had adapted much more than men to the demands of the job by abstaining from marriage and parenthood in order to be considered trustworthy and career oriented. Of the eight women interviewed, seven were single; all had a paid housekeeper, and two had older children. Although women made up 20% of the employees of this organisation, only 3% of managers were female.

"Voice" is beginning to be exercised in reaction to the antifamily atmosphere at the Foreign Ministry. An organisation of married couples has been formed in an effort to find ways to "save the family." Men's loyalty to the organisation was deteriorating, and they increasingly tended to exit the organisation if they could not get guarantees that their wives would get jobs at the same place where they were stationed.

DISCUSSION

As we have seen, these three organisations constructed women, men, and families differently. At the Danish Board of Social Welfare, the family was considered important for male and female managers and was not regarded as a problem but as a resource. Men were believed to be as nurturing as women, and when men had children, they were assumed to be responsible fathers who would be as interested as mothers in their children's lives and well-being. There were no women who had to exit the family because of the demands placed on them by the work organisation. Meanwhile, at Scandinavian Airline Systems, the family was something "private," something individuals took care of outside of their professional lives. The men who were married to women who willingly supported their careers were successful there because the organisation did not have to alter anything and no one voiced demands for any changes. In the Danish Foreign Ministry, the man's career had historically been considered more important than his wife's career aspirations, and women were expected to follow their husbands to postings abroad.

A study of these organisations revealed how change in corporate culture occurs. Individuals responded variously to the culture of the workplace: through their expressions of loyalty and disloyalty toward work and family, through their decisions to exit or remain in stressful jobs or unequal marriages, and through their willingness to voice their concerns about the inflexible work-places and spouses that would not support them in their work lives. For example, at the Danish Foreign Ministry, more couples were beginning to insist that the organisation support women in their career goals. This organisation was being confronted with people exiting and people voicing objections to the way things had been. At the Danish Board of Social Welfare, at which the numbers of male managers and female managers were even and male managers tended to have professional partners, the organisation was also pressured to be family friendly or to lose employees. It appears that organisations are more likely to change in a more family-friendly direction when the costs of the old pattern are too high for male (especially managerial) employees. The assumption made by Finkelstein (1981) that "family men" are more "manageable" in work organisations is no longer correct.

The majority of women in this study found it difficult to remain loyal to both their work organisations and their families. Some women chose to solve this dilemma by not marrying, by not having children (a form of exit), or both. Others chose to be loyal toward their families at one stage of their lives (i.e., when their children were young) and then to become more loyal toward their careers after their children were older. Women tried to influence their situations and reduce role stress by threatening to exit or actually exiting marriages in which husbands were not helpful and supportive and by threatening to leave or actually exiting organisations that were not family friendly. With any of these choices, however, women seemed to endure more costs than men. The majority of the female managers studied could not cope with a family alongside their careers, often choosing to remain single or waiting until their children were older to pursue a career. The pattern of female managers remaining unmarried or divorcing more often than male managers is one that has also been found in British, U.S., and Danish research studies (Bayes, 1987; Cahoon & Rowney, 1987; Carlsen & Toft, 1987; Diamond, 1987; Finkelstein, 1981; Harlan & Weiss, 1980; Nicholson & West, 1988).

One might ask if we can expect women to ever be as interested as men are in careers or if women can be as highly motivated as men to apply for and function in managerial jobs under the present conditions. (Further discussion of this issue can be found in Alvesson & Billing, 1997.) So far, women have often chosen to demonstrate more loyalty toward the family or to abstain from having a family if they wanted to pursue a career. But because of the difficulties for individuals to make adequate child care arrangements, find jobs in family-friendly organisations, or locate partners who are genuinely interested and willing to share equally in domestic work and child care, women have not had much of a free choice. It can also be difficult for some female managers who are confronted with their husbands' envy or resentment of their success; they cannot talk about their jobs at home; they feel they have to separate the work and family spheres because of their husbands' feelings. Cultural norms and expectations regarding male dominance and female subordination reinforce this pattern. Even when individual couples are able to negotiate an equitable division of domestic labour and when men support their wives' careers, couples are still faced with friends', colleagues', and relatives' more traditional norms and values. As more couples establish egalitarian domestic arrangements and survive the situation in which the wife has more status and earnings than the husband, cultural ideas about gender will be questioned and structures will eventually change.

Most workplaces have been designed by men, for men, and according to principles that accommodate traditional men who have supportive wives and well-functioning families. There are still organisations (like Scandinavian Air-line Systems in this study) that have changed little from this starting point; they see men solely as workers and not as nurturing fathers, even when the larger society itself has become more egalitarian in terms of values and norms. For example, the society (through legislative mandate) can make it possible for men to take parental leave, but the work organisation's informal rules can say that to do so creates so many problems that the man's career and the organisation itself would be placed in jeopardy.

There are many organisations, like the Danish Board of Social Welfare and, to some extent, the Danish Foreign Ministry in this study, that are learning to respond to the fact that women and men have loyalties to families as well as to their jobs. We might expect that, in the future, more organisations will see workers as having dual roles. Meanwhile, we can expect that individuals' choices regarding career and family will, to a large extent, be connected to the workplace culture (how flexible their jobs are, how much travel they need to do, how many hours a week they are expected to work) as well as to the culture of the larger society (whether day care is provided, if cultural values and norms portray children as a shared responsibility between mothers and fathers rather than as mothers' primary responsibility). Male dominance and gender inequality are preserved through organisational structures and socialisation processes, but these do not remain constant. One way of looking for evidence of change is to look for variations. This study showed how three Scandinavian work organisations vary in their outlook on work and family issues and on the subject of gender equity. It also revealed variations in how individual men and women in the 1990s value family life and careers. In many cases, it appears likely that organisations will need to be more attentive to these loyalties if they wish to keep their employees.

REFERENCES

Alvesson, M., & Billing, Y. (1997). *Understanding gender and organisational change.* London: Sage.

Bayes, J. (1987, July). *Do female managers in public bureaucracies manage with a different voice?* Paper presented at the 3rd International Interdisciplinary Congress on Women, Dublin, Ireland.

Billing, Y. (1991). *Køn, karriere, familie* [Gender, career, family]. Copenhagen, Denmark: Jurist og Økonomforbundets Forlag.

Billing, Y. D., & Alvesson, M. (1994). *Gender, managers, and organizations.* Berlin/ New York: de Gruyter.

Cahoon, A., & Rowney, J. (1987, July). *The interaction between worksite variables and personal characteristics for female managers.* Paper presented at the 3rd International Interdisciplinary Congress on Women, Dublin, Ireland.

Carlsen, A., & Toft, L. (1987). *Køn og ledelse* [Gender and leadership]. Copenhagen, Denmark: Forlaget Politiske Studier.

Diamond, E. (1987). Theories of career development and the reality of women at work. In B. Gutek & L. Larwood (Eds.), *Women's career development* (pp. 15-27). Newbury Park, CA: Sage.

Finkelstein, C. (1981). Women managers: Career patterns and changes in the United States. In C. Epstein & R. Coser (Eds.), *Access to power: Cross-national studies of women and elites* (pp. 193-210). London: Allen and Unwin.

Harlan, A., & Weiss, C. (1980). *Moving up: Women in managerial careers. Third progress report.* Wellesley, MA: Wellesley Center for Research on Women.

Hirschmann, A. (1970). *Exit, voice, and loyalty: Responses to declines in forms, organizations, and states.* Cambridge, MA: Harvard University Press.

Nicholson, N., & West, M. (1988). *Managerial job change: Men and women in transition.* Cambridge, UK: Cambridge University Press.

Nieva, V., & Gutek, B. (1981). Sex effects on evaluation. *Academy of Management Review, 5,* 267-276.

Valdez, R., & Gutek, B. (1987). Family roles: A help or a hindrance for working women. In B. Gutek & L. Larwood (Eds.), *Women's career development.* Newbury Park, CA: Sage.

14

Swedish Parents at a Multinational Conglomerate

CLARISSA KUGELBERG

How are Swedish parents seen in working life? Are mothers seen in a different way from fathers, parents in administration seen differently from parents in production? Do men and women see themselves as entitled to adjust their work to their family needs? Can they take advantage of their legal rights to take parental leave, work part-time, and stay at home to care for their children when they are ill? What strategies do men and women develop to balance family life and working life? These questions led me to use fieldwork methods to intensively study parents in one particular work organisation, a food production company with just over 300 employees.

In this chapter, I present and discuss how motherhood and fatherhood were considered and constructed at this company. I also discuss variations in the ways mothers and fathers were regarded, and I relate these variations to differences in work subcultures and the philosophy of those in top management positions. Although the focus of attention was on parents working at one particular company, this study offers insight into how Swedish companies are or are not adjusting to broader cultural demands for gender equality and for family-friendly workplaces. These adjustments result from conflicts and negotiation between the company-based discourse and the experience-based discourses evident among production and administrative workplaces.

EDITORS' NOTE: The author's use of British spellings has been retained.

STUDY METHODS

To study this company, I spent 50 days at the workplace over 6 months' time. The interview was the main tool used for collecting empirical data; participant observation and group interviews were conducted to obtain in-depth insight into work-family issues. More than 100 individual interviews were conducted, for up to an hour each. At first, I interviewed everyone I met, but gradually my knowledge grew and my work became more systematic, so I progressed to interviewing only fathers and mothers with school-age children and their managers. Forty interviews were with parents of preschool-age children and 40 were with parents of school-age children. I also interviewed parents' managers, workmates, and union leaders.

The interviews were guided by a list of themes and questions to be discussed. I tried to give the informants plenty of opportunity to develop their own reflections and considerations by pursuing their images and descriptions. Consequently, the different topics and experiences men and women brought up led the conversation throughout the interviews, with the list of themes being used as a reminder so that all the necessary issues would be addressed. My growing insights into the work organisation helped me over time to construct new questions more closely related to the concrete situation at that workplace. These interviews were recorded and transcribed.

Three group interviews with employees were also conducted at the company, one with fathers in administration, one with fathers working in production in the warehouse, and one with mothers in administration. The stories from men and women, and workers and managers, gave me different perspectives on the same episodes and arrangements. Thus, my analysis derives from the narratives of many people in different positions and with different experiences.

THE COMPANY

I purposely chose a company that employed an equal number of men and women and had production as well as administrative workers. The company was situated in a midsized town in central Sweden. It began as a privately owned, locally based industry. The company's production processes began to be modernised through automation and computerization, and, in 1971, the company became part of a multinational conglomerate based in Switzerland. The head and general management of the company were located in Stockholm.

Before the company became part of a multinational conglomerate, absenteeism among the staff was high. As technology reduced the number of jobs available, the new management became more negative about absenteeism. The economic recession that had gripped Sweden beginning in the early 1990s had had a heavy impact on the town; the town's unemployment figures had been among the highest in the country. Individuals with high absenteeism could thus easily be replaced from the ranks of the unemployed.

Before 1971, and to some degree even before the recession took hold in 1991, staying at home with one's child once in a while was not considered a problem. By the mid-1990s, however, it was far less accepted for employees to take time off from work for any reason. The presence of employees at work was a high priority for management, since it had an overall aim of increasing productivity at the same time as reducing staff. Managers reported that this meant women with small children might have difficulties getting a job in the future.

There were few women with high management positions in this company, and the lower down in the organisational hierarchy you looked, the more women were found. There were also gaps between men's and women's incomes, with men receiving more pay. The biggest gaps were between men and women in high positions; the lower the position, the smaller the income difference. In these respects, the situation in this company was similar to the Swedish labour market as a whole (Baude, 1992; Blomqvist, 1994; Forsberg, 1992; Roman, 1994; Statistiska Centralbyrån, 1993; Wahl, 1996).

Some departments were dominated by women while others were dominated by men. Women were seen as more suitable for some jobs (e.g., in human resources) and men more suitable for others (e.g., specialised jobs involving grinding and roasting). Feminist researchers name this process "gender coding," and they have shown that this process permeates Swedish working life to a great extent (Baude, 1992; Kyle, 1979; Roman, 1994). The process of gender stereotyping was a force that the female managers in human resources considered when recruiting. One told me that, before employing a woman, they always imagined how she would be received in the company—they tried to place women where they would not be too harshly received.

There were also examples in this company of departments that were integrated, and it was considered positive for there to be both men and women in a department. Women were believed to bring in a familiar and friendly feeling. One supervisor expressed this by saying that, ever since a woman was employed in his unit, they have become more "like a family"; when there were just men, they were just a team of workers.

There were three different unions at the company, but none of them admitted to working with issues concerning equality between men and women. They did not see any need for this. Gender segregation in terms of jobs was not seen as a matter of inequality but as a natural consequence of individuals' attitudes toward and participation in work. They believed that individuals who were continually present, worked full-time, and took on heavy jobs could qualify for more remunerative positions. To combine motherhood with a job was seen as mothers' private problems. The same conclusions have been reached in other research studies (Lindgren, 1985; Widerberg, 1991). The unions had not been encouraged by their members to take action on women's behalf; they had also not been contacted when employees demanded the right to take parental leave. Leave-taking was always arranged by the employee's direct supervisor, who contacted the company's department of human resources.

TWO DIFFERENT DISCOURSES

I was surprised to discover that the company had a formal human resources policy that seemed to be more sympathetic toward parents than the policy of my own workplace (a public research centre). However, the stories related by the employees about how mothers and fathers struggled to combine work and family presented a different image of what the company policy was. From the conversations about parenthood with the employees, it became apparent that there were two different and coexisting discourses in this company. They were sometimes intermingled within the same conversation, sometimes segregated in different conversations.

The Company Discourse

The "company-based discourse" emanated predominantly from managers and union leaders. It was founded on the conglomerate's goals and ideology concerning the continuous struggle to raise productivity, increase economic profits, and make the company survive in the competition anticipated both inside and outside the conglomerate. Norms and values concerning working hours and employees' behaviour were embedded within this discourse. What first struck me visiting the company was the fast working pace. Everybody seemed to be in their place, nobody met over a cup of coffee, and I saw women having lunch at their desks. During interviews, this impression was confirmed by people's stories about their own situation and about workmates and subordinates.

The parent was defined as the mother in the company-based discourse, and the cultural construction of the concept of woman included not just the mother but also the potential mother. Interviews with female employees in administration and management confirmed the close ties between "woman" and "mother" in the cultural construction of woman at the workplace. They told me that, when applying for the job, they were asked if they intended to have babies. Young women reported that having children would make them less appealing as employees. Mothers' responsibilities for their children and their need for parental leave and part-time work were considered to be problematic because they forced a departure from the company's norm that employees should be able to work overtime and stay accessible when work demanded it.

Women's typical way of coping with parenthood was central to the company's view of women as deviant from the ideal worker. Women stayed away on parental leave to care for their infants for 1 or 1½ years—a huge amount of time when even a month's leave was seen as a long period, long enough to risk losing one's job to somebody else.

Part-time work was not seen as being possible to combine with a high-pressure job, because such jobs demanded much more than full-time commitment; the responsibility such jobs entailed was also regarded as impossible to divide between two people (e.g., through a job-sharing scheme). To work part-time was seen as emphasising that the person did not want to have a career; it demonstrated that the worker wanted to split his or her life into job time and free time.

Overtime work was also highly valued. The company's conception of work involved not just being there full-time but also working overtime regularly at different periods, such as at the end of a budget period. Overtime had become a way of life, and working overtime was a way of stressing that you were loyal to the company.

Research in organisations in Sweden and in other Western countries shows that the length of the working day is often used to define the loyalty and productivity of an employee. Full-time work and doing plenty of overtime work are associated with loyalty, devotion, and competence, whereas part-time work is associated with restricted loyalty and less productivity (Bailyn, 1993; Haas & Hwang, 1995; Lewis, 1996). Swedish research on management shows that leaders in organisations must work long hours and give priority to work before other commitments such as the family (Asplund, 1984; Edlund, Ahltorp, Andersson, & Kleppestø, 1990; Wahl, 1996).

The Experience-Based Discourse

The second discourse prevalent in this company, which I call the "experience-based discourse," was anchored in employees' experiences of work. In this discourse, parenthood had a different meaning from that in the company-based discourse. When women talked about their experiences as mothers, they viewed the work situation from a perspective that related work to the needs of their children and their own needs as mothers. This discourse was composed of stories about men's and women's daily work. "Woman" in this discourse was associated with hard work and loyalty. There were also stories about hardworking fathers with small children whose care for their children was a part of their working life. Although these were recurrent themes, there were also variations in the experience-based discourse. These variations were related to the informants' own personal experiences and personalities, as well as to the charac-

teristics of work and the organisation and the management philosophy of
employees' immediate superiors.

Intermingling of Discourses

As mentioned above, the company-based discourse was found particularly in
the stories by managers and union leaders. In the stories of managers and
union leaders, however, the two discourses were sometimes intermingled
within the same conversation, especially when female managers were informants.

The following quote shows how a female manager mixed the discourses in
her interview. She was the supervisor of 13 people in the human resources
department and had, at the same time, the main responsibility for staff matters
for 300 employees. She had two school-age children and worked 75% time
(30 hours a week). She complained,

> Our director once said to me that it is a privilege for us to work part-time. He sees
> this as a gift to us from the firm, while I think that most of us who work part-time
> think, "Well, I work 75%, but I also get 75% of a full-time salary." Many think
> to themselves, now she leaves to go home at 3 o'clock, what a relief. You are
> lucky. But I only get 75% of a full salary. When I leave at 3 o'clock, I have worked
> hard to finish a job somebody else might sit working on for 2 more hours. That
> is the price you have to pay to be able to leave work at 3 o'clock with a good
> conscience.

This manager then changed context, from the perspective of a mother to the
perspective of a manager, and through this change the meaning of the concept
"mother of small children" was transformed:

> No woman is happy to stay at home when her children are ill. Everyone gets a
> bad conscience, although they shouldn't. But then you have to recognise the fact
> that the employer takes an economic loss. That's the fact and you can't deny that
> such is correct economic thinking. The woman costs more money and her
> presence is more unreliable; we know that she is away more often, that we know.

We can see that she held opposing assumptions. In the cultural construction
of "mother" from the company-based (manager's) discourse, the mother was an
economic loss for the company, whereas in the experienced-based (mother's)
discourse, she was seen as a person who worked hard for a part-time salary.
Because her statements were attached to different contexts, the contradiction
between them was not openly revealed.

In another female middle-level manager's discourse, the divergent perspectives were explicitly opposed and described as an insoluble dilemma for her as she consciously viewed the problem from both the experienced-based and the company-based discourses:

Being women, I think that we have a right to be part-time . . . but I find it troublesome to have an employee who is absent to care for sick children, although I myself am a mother. I can't say that one should not employ mothers with small children, but I can realise that small companies can have a real problem. One cannot be blamed for having a child who is often ill, but as manager and mother, you feel somewhat divided. You are happy that your own children are healthy.

It was very difficult to figure out a way to equally consider both perspectives when managing work. The mother's justified right to stay at home with her children was put in opposition to getting the job done and the demands that the management placed on her department for fulfilling work goals.

The union leaders' stories also contained both discourses. Although they were advocates for the workers in the company, they also used the words of the company-based discourse when discussing the company's circumstances, painting an image of women as a problem. In their daily work, union leaders participated on committees with management to consider wage negotiations, security issues, and so on. The union leaders based their arguments on the company-based discourse to get on speaking terms with the management. The management in Foucault's (1991) perspective is the dominant actor who sets the rules for communication by imposing its discourse as the frame of reference and the basis for the discussions.

Even some managers would occasionally speak about women and work from the perspectives of both discourses. The view of women as deviating from the norm of a good worker was prominent in most of the interviews that I had with managers, but not all. Although some recognised that it was problematic for a woman to have a career, others felt that women were fully capable of becoming successful in careers. These managers had experienced this themselves, and they had promoted women who had been working part-time. They acknowledged that women could be hardworking and efficient. Although some managers in the organisation saw women's tendency to work part-time and take parental leave as problematic, others saw it as a chance to reexamine the organisation and possibly give another employee a chance to learn something new. This in turn could lead to opportunities for positive organisational changes. It is too much to call this redefinition of working mothers' situation a great change in the ideology of the company, but it showed that there was variation in the views of women, and this could affect the conditions for women at work.

VARIATIONS IN DISCOURSES
WITHIN DIFFERENT UNITS

As previously mentioned, both the company-based discourse and the experience-based discourse existed in this company, as two undercurrents, expressed in the stories and statements made at formal and informal levels. Attitudes and behaviours associated with motherhood and fatherhood were shaped by the stories about daily work, by parents' daily actions in regard to combining work and family roles, and by the interplay between employees and their managers. Over time, shared assumptions of parents' rights and duties developed and formed possibilities and restrictions. There were variations in attitudes toward parents and work, however, between the administrative section of the company and the production area. These variations related to the character of work and organisation in each area. Variations were also observed within the production area regarding whether the work was organised in terms of assembly-line production or in teams.

The Production Line

When the assembly line was used for production, managers' views of the company ideology and management philosophy strongly influenced their subordinates' views of rights and duties. These managers orchestrated the interplay between management's decisions concerning the unit and the unit's internal culture regarding parenting and work. The importance of middle managers for parents' opportunities to successfully combine work and family has been recognised in other studies (Holt & Thaulow, 1996).

Production-line work was characterised by huge machines requiring large investments. The supervisors discussed the increasing pressure to keep up with the competition in the global market. The weak economic situation in Sweden was blamed for staff reductions; this in turn had increased the burden on remaining workers and had led to a stress on avoiding absenteeism. Absence had immediate consequences and affected all workers; a replacement had to take over the machines, and fewer replacements meant less time for rest breaks for the machine drivers. The supervisors of both shifts described parents as problematic in regard to planned output and the need to reduce absenteeism. One said, "Parental leave can cause me trouble. Many have children and someone must stay at home when a child is ill, but the machines cannot stop. Those who are present have to take the burden for the others."

The struggle to survive economically was placed in opposition to workers' needs to reduce their work hours or to stay at home when their children were ill. Supervisors told stories of how they had helped make arrangements for mothers' and fathers' situations, which showed some understanding for parents' needs, but these stories were mixed with remarks that showed irritation about parents' staying home with ill children and the problems this created for units trying to reach productivity goals. Production lines avoided recruiting women with small children to reduce conflict between company goals and employee needs.

Those who were away from work caring for children saw themselves as pushing their jobs onto their workmates, especially if they were away several times. They experienced displeasure from both supervisors and workmates without small children. Substitutes were not hired automatically when an employee was on parental leave; the situation was assessed each time. The silent agreement on the factory line was that parents were not really entitled to take parental leave, which was confirmed by parents' limited practice of taking leave and by their stories about how they experienced supervisors' reactions when telling them about their desire to take parental leave. When a woman returned from a long parental leave after childbirth, she could be assigned different, less desirable work tasks, which has also been found in other studies (Haas, 1992; Widerberg, 1991). Many mothers felt supervisors had no right to complain when they occasionally took time off because they usually complied when supervisors asked them to work overtime.

There was one less automatised department at the factory that was an exception to this pattern. It was a department dominated by women, many of whom had small children. The supervisor did not describe parents' leave-taking as a problem but as a basis for his efforts to plan the work. When planning and organising the work, he considered the fact that many workers had small children and used this as an opportunity to reorganise the staff in relation to what was determined to be the most urgent product according to production goals. A major difference between the situation in this department and that in other production areas of the company was that here the women felt entitled to be away, knowing that the responsibility for getting the work done was not theirs alone but a shared responsibility.

Work Teams in Production

In production, some workers were organised into teams, which were typically male dominated, and machines did not control the work in the same way that they did on the machine lines. The maintenance unit, for example, in which there were only men, was made up of trained electricians and repairers who were among the best-paid workers. In this unit, the supervisors' leadership was based on a trust in the workers. There was an implicit agreement that the workers were free to organise their work themselves as long as they were willing to take responsibility for it; this often meant they had to work overtime. The agreement was based on the work team's collective responsibility for work, so when one was away, the others did his job. In return, they had the freedom to stay away from work when they needed to. When a worker accompanied his child to the health centre, he could do this without taking formal leave.

One supervisor said that he did not pay attention to whether an employee was a parent with small children or not, but implicit in his story was the assumption that maintenance job workers were male. He admitted that parenthood would cause problems when it came to female employees. "Here, everybody backs up each other," other supervisors said, and subordinates confirmed this image of the unit. They said it was common to be on leave to care for an ill child; "we let children come first." One supervisor told me that he had to take leave when his children were ill because his wife's job made it difficult for her to do so.

The workers experienced the jobs' being organised into work teams as giving them a lot of autonomy, because as long as they did what they had to, the supervisors did not interfere. They told me that it was mandatory to stay at work until the machines were in order; therefore, they were prepared to work overtime. On the other hand, this gave them the opportunity to later take time off in compensation ("comp time"). By cooperating, working overtime, and discussing which one of them could take leave, a system of mutual trust was created within the work team. Although none of the workers were away for reasons having to do with children very often, the ambience that characterised some of the male work teams in this company was probably a new phenomenon. In a study of food industries in the 1980s, supervisors in male units were said to show a lack of understanding for men's needs (Baude, 1992).

The way these supervisors led these work teams has many similarities with modern management philosophy, in which more responsibilities are distributed to smaller independent production units. Research on women in work life has indicated that nonhierarchical organisations with a decentralised decision-making process can enlarge women's possibilities of combining work with family responsibilities (Blomqvist, 1994; Roman, 1994). My research indicates that this is also true for men with family responsibilities and that such organisations can exist as small units in larger organisations that on the whole are hierarchically structured.

Men's using time off for family purposes was not regarded as a productivity issue on these teams because their large amount of overtime and hard work, as well as the work team's sense of collective responsibility, more than compensated for men's taking time off.

Administration and Management

Jobs in the administrative part of the company were different from those in production. Salaried employees and clerks had more individualised responsibilities, whereas production workers tended to be part of a group or team. This meant that when salaried employees who had been away several days returned to work, they found that the piles of paper on their desks had grown. There was talk about the need for backup, which meant that several people should be able to do the work when someone was absent. However, the development of a backup system was hindered by staff reductions, fewer people managing a growing workload, and the increasing specialisation of the work.

Another difference between production and administration was that production workers could leave their jobs behind when they went home for the day or stayed at home with a sick child, whereas administrative workers, who were typically mothers, sometimes could not. Production was a never-ending process with the aim of producing a certain amount of goods, but the work of an absent worker was taken over by workmates; it did not await the worker's return. In contrast, the nature of administrative work, for most salaried employees, meant that their work only increased during their absence. Although they could postpone some work for a day or two, it would wait for them, and, to meet a deadline, sometimes they would have to work at home or go in over the weekend.

The situation for mothers in administrative jobs in this company corresponded well with that described by other researchers of Swedish workers involved in administration and management (Holt, 1994; Kaul, 1991; Lundén Jacoby & Näsman, 1989; Widerberg, 1991). They found that women were responsible for their individual jobs even when they were away; colleagues would take over only the most urgent tasks. This negatively affected their colleagues and increased their own burden when they returned to work. To avoid missing work, mothers would arrange for sick children to be cared for by relatives or take turns with their spouses staying home.

There were variations in management's ways of leading the work and coping with mothers' needs in the administrative departments. Some managers considered parents' special needs when organising work, whereas others regarded parents' rights regarding parental leave and part-time work as problems for the organisation. One mother compared experiences from two departments in which she had worked. She told me that the first department lacked any sense of understanding for parents' needs. In the second department, to which she was sent after she returned from parental leave, she encountered much more understanding; she worked 75% time, and her boss and workmates considered this to be her indisputable right, as was staying at home when her daughter was ill. She blamed the first department's position on men who did not understand women's needs. She believed that men had different experiences from women and that the absence of parents in a department created a different worldview from that pervading in a department in which there were parents and many women. I heard about other variations in company responses to working mothers. Some mothers experienced feelings of discomfort in phoning their male boss to say that they were staying at home with their child, whereas others talked about understanding male and female colleagues who told them to go home when they stayed over the limit of their formal working hours. Some women reported that female and male managers tried to find them suitable forms of part-time work and flexible working hours. Even in the most "understanding" departments, however, there could be certain assumptions about what kind of leave was legitimate for mothers to take.

THE COGNITIVE FRAME
OF MOTHERHOOD

Pregnancy was not looked on as a reason for staying away from work, except for exceptional cases such as illness or when someone had a physically tough job. Neither the women themselves nor the people around them seemed to consider a pregnant woman as somebody who needed more rest and care. This was also found in a Norwegian study of pregnancy (Heiberg Endresen, 1991). Heiberg Endresen attributes this to women's own intentions to not let pregnancy, as the gender-separating reality it is, affect other people's views of them. Letting pregnancy affect their behaviour would make women deviate from the ideal norm of a good worker and the ideal that men and women should have equal roles. In the company I studied, several women who were pregnant for the second time actually worked longer hours than they had before they became pregnant so that they could qualify for a higher level of monetary compensation during parental leave.

Motherhood, unlike pregnancy, affected all women's work and most women's careers. When making decisions about work, they weighed their own intentions to spend more time with their children against the company's view of mothers. Becoming a mother started a complex process by which the woman's identity was transformed. Taking parental leave and then working part-time have become "normal" stages of Swedish women's life course (Asplund, 1984; Blomqvist, 1994; Kugelberg, 1987; Lundén Jacoby & Näsman, 1989; Roman, 1994).

The main reasons women gave for working part-time was to have time for their children, time to be together with their family, and time for doing household work in peace. Long days at the day care centre were said to make children tired. Most mothers had taken all of their parental leave and had gone into part-time jobs after returning to work. Only a few had shared parental leave with their spouses, but when a child was sick, the spouses discussed who should stay at home. Many of the women had difficulties staying at home without notice; for many, it was as difficult as it was for their husbands. This difficulty, however, was contributing to making staying at home to care for a sick child a negotiable responsibility between mothers and fathers.

Several women gave examples of how cooperation helped them manage to work part-time. Through women's part-time work and cooperation, the meaning of work time was changed. Some part-time administrative jobs were organised into work teams, in which the whole work team's hours, rather than the individual's hours, formed the relevant base for the discussion of productivity. Moreover, the meaning of *work time* was broadened; it included not only the duration of work but also the time it took to arrange and participate in cooperation. This approach seemed similar to the way work was managed in some male-dominated production teams.

Women in part-time administrative jobs did work overtime. At certain periods, such as when the accounts needed to be balanced, most of them were expected to do so. Overtime was so common that many part-time working women's actual work hours came close to full-time. This was especially true for women at middle and higher administrative levels. The label of "part-timer" concealed the fact that a woman had done a good job, often having worked overtime or having returned to work at night to complete a project. Some women said they paid dearly for being entitled to leave earlier at least some days.

THE COGNITIVE FRAME FOR FATHERHOOD

When asking about the situation for fathers in this company, I first got the impression that very few fathers let their fatherhood affect work and that parenthood was women's domain. It appeared that a male employee was assumed to be a man with full-time employment, strongly engaged in his job, and available for work when needed. However, over time, I gained insights about the caregiving work fathers were involved in and gained a new impression—that fatherhood affected fathers' time at work, too.

Just as women did, men considered their possibilities and interpreted their managers' views about parenting as they made decisions about how they would combine work and family roles. In administration, there were actually few fathers with small children, and only a few of these had taken parental leave. Although most of them had taken daddy days (10 days off immediately after childbirth or adoption), some said that they had not had time to take all the days due to them within the 2 months of eligibility because of a heavy workload. None of the fathers with small children worked part-time, and they had never imagined this alternative; their jobs were such, they said, that part-time was unthinkable. Part-time work was seen as indicating that you split your life into job time and free time and that you did not want to have a real career. Several fathers said that they had not taken leave because of the risk of it affecting them negatively. The difficulties of men's taking parental leave have been shown to be greater in the private sector than in the public sector (Haas, 1992; Riksförsäkringsverket, 1993; Statens Offentliga Utredningar, 1982a).

Men gave several reasons for not taking leave. They said their work burden would grow while they were away because nobody would do their tasks while they were gone. These men talked about the burden of a growing workload just as women did; the difference was that men's overtime was anchored in a full-time job, whereas most women's overtime was tied to a part-time job. Men also cited economic reasons for not taking parental leave; the household would lose too much money if the man, as the better-paid wage earner in the family, stayed at home. Men also stressed that their wives wanted to take all the leave and then work part-time. They said that, if their wives had not wanted this, they would have considered staying at home.

All these motives have also been found in other studies as explanations for why mothers so often take all or most of the parental leave (Falkenberg, 1990; Haas, 1992; Hwang, 1985; Lundén Jacoby & Näsman, 1989; Statens Offentliga Utredningar, 1982a, 1982b). These explanations can be seen as reinforcing cultural conventions of mothers and fathers in working life. Men are still considered to be the main breadwinners, and the women are still seen as mainly responsible for the children and family. Women feel more entitled than men to adjust their work to family responsibilities.

However, behind the conventional image of the father appeared another image. The father of small children was beginning to practice his fatherhood in new ways that affected his job. I found many examples of fathers who talked about their children with workmates. Men took part in the care of sick children and organised their work so that they could accompany their children to the dentist or doctor for a checkup. To do this, they often did not take formal parental leave but instead used comp time (formally or informally) for overtime they had worked. Men who had responsibility for organising their own work could leave the workplace in the middle of the day and catch up on work later. This was an approach to time that other people sometimes had; the primary aim was to do the job well and to take the responsibility for this yourself.

Few fathers had openly exposed themselves as fathers with family responsibilities, but some had, and they were seen as worth their weight in gold in the eyes of women. Most parenting tasks performed by men that affected their work involved staying home when a child was sick, taking a few hours' leave to take the child for a health checkup, or taking a day off when the children had vacation from school. Fathers stressed that it was good to have a balance of free time to use for the care of their children. One father said,

We have tried to share the care when the children are sick. I phone my boss, and there are no problems. Nobody has harassed me or made me feel I have let them down. I always bring the children to medical checkups and such things. It is easier for me because I can take comp time off, I never take overtime work in pay. The free time is so good to have when there is school vacation, for medical checks, etc. It is good for those sorts of things. My wife can't, she doesn't have this kind of overtime.

When I compared the older generation of fathers with the younger, I found that ways of practising fatherhood had changed. Middle-aged men told me that, when they had small children, it was unthinkable for a man to take parental leave. It was only during the last few years that fathers in this company had started to take parental leave to stay at home with their newborn children, despite the fact that the law had been in force since 1974. It was also only recently that fathers had started to take leave to stay at home when a child was sick, even though they have also had this right for many years.

In a story about a young man in midcareer who openly admitted the extent of his parental responsibility, the cognitive frames of the discourses for fathers at the company with small children are evident. He was spoken about with respect and almost a little awe:

We have a new guy in the marketing department, a young man, around 28 years old. He has a rather high-pressure job in the company, being a marketing manager, but he has taken a lot of responsibility for his children. He started by saying that he doesn't work longer than 4 o'clock, because he must fetch his daughter [at the day care centre]. This was indisputable and everybody was very surprised and assumed that he would not stay long—that was their attitude. He was much more challenging than I ever was.

The image of men as unaffected by fatherhood, which was a basic tenet within the company-based discourse, was thus opposed by fathers' actual practices. The younger fathers' increasing involvement in the care of their children had not, however, negatively affected attitudes toward employing fathers in the workforce. Male applicants for jobs were not yet asked if they had or planned to have children.

COPING WITH CONTRADICTIONS

I have analysed the interviews with the employees at the company as two different discourses. In both, there were assumptions about parenthood, and those constituted what I call the cognitive frames for motherhood and fatherhood at the company. These cognitive frames contain cultural assumptions and views about parenthood and the associations, definitions, and strategies that motherhood and fatherhood generate both in the daily interplay between colleagues and bosses and in discussions about the company and its future. I have shown that motherhood and fatherhood gave rise to different associations, and I claimed that this gave women and men different situations in the company. This meant that they faced different expectations from bosses and colleagues; they were evaluated differently and were met with different attitudes. When interpreting others' expectations and evaluations, mothers and fathers shaped their images of their entitlements and duties in regard to work and parenting. I have also shown that cognitive frames differed between departments; the interaction in every department constituted a specific variation of the company's culture, and this gave parents different situations in which to work. Managers' ideologies and the type of work organisation that predominated had great influence.

The image of the mother as a "productivity problem" was part of the culture in this company. It appeared at the workplace in the form of serious and joking comments about how women were treated and in stories about what women saw and heard about how others were treated. The human resources department promoted family-friendly policies toward women by facilitating part-time jobs for them as well as flexible working hours and less exposed positions. At the same time, this put women in a special category defined by their special needs, which reinforced the view of women as problematic. Every woman had to show herself, the management, her supervisors, and her colleagues that she was competent and could manage her work; as one woman said, "Women must be twice as competent as men working at the same level." This was especially true for women in mid-level and high-level positions.

Women coped with this in a number of ways. Many had a "pragmatic" strategy, whereas others struggled against the view of women as problematic. The pragmatic strategy meant accepting offers of adjusting work hours to meet needs to take care of families, accepting being labelled as a part-timer with special needs, working fewer hours per day, and/or taking positions in departments with a more understanding attitude toward mothers. The pragmatic adjustment to the difficulties intertwining different domains was expressed in statements such as "One must not have too high ambitions," "It is not possible to have two careers in one family," and "Children give you new priorities." These statements expressed an adjustment to the view of women as subordinated to men in the labour market and to the view of women as principally responsible for children. This adjustment also reflected some women's strong identification with motherhood and their adherence to the belief that mothers and children being together was important.

Another way of coping with the contradictions was by using the strategy of constantly balancing opposing claims. One woman manager said, "It is like balancing on a knife edge." There was the danger of not managing the work *and* the fear of not giving children what they needed. This way of coping seemed to be a common reaction of women in higher positions and of women who worked in production departments in which they were met with suspicion and criticism when they stayed home with sick children or when they left in the afternoon to fetch their children. Women coped by working hard and working overtime to try to erase negative associations of motherhood and part-time work. Office workers came back in the evenings or on the weekends to finish what they had not been able to do when staying home with sick children. By this, they showed others and themselves their capacities; they got credit from others and raised their self-esteem.

I regarded their hard work as a type of protest against the negative associations of motherhood and part-time work, but it could equally be regarded as acceptance of the negative view of women constituted within the company-based discourse. Such an interpretation would indicate that women themselves saw their work as being of lesser value, which correlates well with the analyses by Herlin (1980) and Lindgren (1985), who studied women at male-dominated workplaces and found that women undervalue their own work.

Fatherhood was not assumed to affect working life and individual fathers' jobs in the company-based discourse. If you studied only this discourse, you would not find many signs of new assumptions, but they existed in the stories of men's daily work. Some fathers in administration and in production had abandoned conventional practice by taking parental leave to care for their children when they were sick or to accompany them to health checkups. Fathers brought their concerns for their children to the workplace when planning for their work. The "new father" had appeared at this workplace, and this I interpreted as a transformation of the cultural construction of fatherhood.

For men with small children, there was a balance to be maintained between the conventional male role, which included working overtime, and the modern father role, which valued taking part in the family. In administration and management, the father had to achieve a balance between exposing himself as disloyal to the company and not sharing the responsibility for the children. When fathers were away, their workload piled up. A man who refused overtime and left a meeting, saying that he had to fetch his child at the day care centre, ran the risk of being defined as somebody whom the company could not trust. He departed from the image of a male employee as defined in the company-based discourse. On the other hand, if the father let the child stay at the day care centre too long, he could be defined by his wife and children as not trustworthy.

Men in this company balanced employment and fatherhood through two strategies that were already part of the company culture— taking out "comp time" and relying on work-team members to make up the slack. Using these strategies became men's way of handling contradictory perceptions, a way of being loyal to both sides. Fathers demonstrated their loyalty to the company by being willing to work overtime, and this overtime generated for fathers time they could use to care for children. Being a cooperative member of a production unit work team that took collective responsibility for getting work done was also a sign of loyalty to the company; at the same time, this cooperation could also generate goodwill for fathers to use to ask others to stand in for them when they wanted to stay home on leave. By using comp time or taking advantage of the work-team format, a "new fatherhood" was being constituted in this work organisation.

REFERENCES

Asplund, G. (1984). *Karriärens villkor: Män, kvinnor och ledarship* [Career conditions: Men, women, and leadership]. Stockholm: Bokförlaget Trevi.

Bailyn, L. (1993). *Breaking the mold: Women, men, and time in the new corporate world.* New York: Free Press.

Baude, A. (1992). *Kvinnans plats på jobbet* [Woman's place at work]. Stockholm: SNS Förlag.

Blomqvist, M. (1994). *Könshierarkier i gugning: Kvinnor i kunskapsföretag* [Gender hierarchies challenged: Women in knowledge-intensive companies]. Uppsala, Sweden: Acta Universitatis Upsaliensis.

Edlund, C., Ahltorp, B., Andersson, G., & Kleppestø, S. (1990). *Karriärer i kläm: Om chefen, familjen och företaget* [Careers in a squeeze: On managers, families, and companies]. Stockholm: Norstedts.

Falkenberg, E. (1990). *Far till 100%* [100% fathers]. Stockholm: Tjänstemännens Centralorganisationen [White-Collar Workers Central Organisation].

Forsberg, G. (1992). Kvinnor och män i arbetslivet [Women and men in work life]. In J. Acker, A. Baude, U. Björnberg, E. Dahlström, G. Forsberg, L. Gonäs, H. Holter, & A. Nilsson (Eds.), *Kvinnors och mäns liv och arbete* [Women's and men's life and work] (pp. 108-153). Stockholm: SNS Förlag.

Foucault, M. (1991). *L'ordre du discours* [The order of discourse]. Paris: Gallimard.

Haas, L. (1992). *Equal parenthood and social policy: A study of parental leave in Sweden.* Albany: State University of New York Press.

Haas, L., & Hwang, P. (1995). Fatherhood and corporate culture in Sweden. *Family Relations, 44,* 28-36.

Heiberg Endresen, A. (1991, October). *Pregnancy and gender in two generations.* Paper for the symposium Growing Into the Future, Institute for Future Studies and Education, Stockholm.

Herlin, H. (1980). *25 kvinnor om jämställdheten i statsförvaltningen* [25 women on equality in state government] (Report No. 13). Stockholm: Arbetslivcentrum [Work Life Centre].

Holt, H. (1994). *Foraeldre på arbejdspladsen: En analyse af tilpasningsmulighderne mellem arbejdsliv og familieliv i kvinde- og mandesfag* [Parents at work: An analysis of the preconditions for conciliation between work and family in female and male jobs]. Copenhagen, Denmark: Social Forsknings Instituttet [Social Research Institute].

Holt, H., & Thaulow, I. (1996). Strategies to make companies more responsive to the need of families. In H. Holt & I. Thaulow (Eds.), *Reconciling work and family life: An international perspective on the role of companies* (pp. 65-87). Copenhagen, Denmark: Social Forsknings Instituttet.

Hwang, C. P. (1985). *Småbarnspappor* [Fathers of small children]. Stockholm: Natur och Kultur.

Kaul, H. (1991). Who cares? Gender inequality and care leave in the Nordic countries. *Acta Sociologica, 34,* 115-125.

Kugelberg, C. (1987). *Allt eller inget: Barn, omsorg och förvärvsarbete* [All or nothing: Children, child care, and employment]. Stockholm: Carlssons.

Kyle, G. (1979). *Gästarbeterska i manssamhället: Studier om industriarbetande kvinnors villkor i Sverige* [Guest worker in male society: Studies on women industrial workers in Sweden]. Stockholm: Publica.

Lewis, J. (1996). Sense of entitlement, family-friendly policies, and gender. In H. Holt & I. Thaulow (Eds.), *Reconciliation of work and family life: An international perspective on the role of companies* (pp. 17-42). Copenhagen, Denmark: Social Forsknings Instituttet.

Lindgren, G. (1985). *Kamrater, kollegor och kvinnor: En studie av könssegregeringsprocessen i två mansdominerande organisationer* [Comrades, colleagues, and women: A study of the gender segregation process in two male-dominated organisations] (Research report). Umeå, Sweden: Umeå University, Department of Sociology.

Lundén Jacoby, A., & Näsman, E. (1989). *Mamma, pappa, jobb: Föräldrar och barn om arbetets villkor* [Mommy, daddy, job: Parents and children on the conditions of work]. Stockholm: Arbetslivcentrum [Swedish Centre for Working Life].

Riksförsäkringsverket. (1993). *Vilka pappor kom hem? En rapport om uttaget av föräldrapenning 1989 och 1990 för barn födda 1989* [Which fathers came home? A report on the use of parental leave in 1989 and 1990 for children born in 1989] (Statistical report). Stockholm: Author.

Roman, C. (1994). *Lika på olika villkor: Könssegregering i kunskapsföretag* [Equal on unequal terms: Gender segregation in knowledge-intensive companies]. Stockholm: Symposium.

Statens Offentliga Utredningar. (1982a). *Enklare föräldraförsäkring: Betänkande från föräldraförsäkringsutredningen* [Simpler parental leave: Thoughts from the commission on parental insurance] (Report No. 36). Stockholm: Socialdepartementet.

Statens Offentliga Utredningar. (1982b). *Förvärvsarbete och föräldraskap* [Employment and parenthood]. Stockholm: Arbetsmarknadsdepartementet [Labour Market Department].

Statistiska Centralbyrån [Central Bureau of Statistics]. (1993). *På tal om kvinnor och män* [Talking about women and men]. Stockholm: Author.

Wahl, A. (1996). Företagsledning som konstruktion av manlighet [Management as a construction of masculinity]. *Kvinnovetenskaplig Tidskrift, 17,* 15-29.

Widerberg, K. (1991). Reforms for women, on male terms: The example of the Swedish legislation on parental leave. *International Journal of the Sociology of Law, 19,* 27-44.

15

Conclusion

GRAEME RUSSELL

PHILIP HWANG

LINDA L. HAAS

OVERVIEW

This has been an ambitious exploration of the linkages between gender equity, work-family balance, and organizational change. It has been ambitious for several reasons. First, it focuses on three fundamental issues in industrialized societies—gender equity, work-family balance, and organizational change—whose outcomes have a direct bearing on individual, family, workplace, and community well-being. Second, it seeks to integrate the perspectives of a diverse group of scholars and policymakers from several countries. Third, it pulls together what we can learn from the "results" of different mixes of policy, government and organizational interventions, community and workplace values, and workforce demographics. As was argued in the introduction, it is by adopting an international perspective that we are better able to understand, and therefore make recommendations for, strategies to change the cultural values and norms of work organizations to facilitate gender equity and work-life balance.

This work is also unique in its emphasis on work organizations. Very little research has focused on the responses of individual organizations to either gender equity or work and family, and there is an almost total absence of organizationally based research that examines links between gender equity and work-family issues. A major reason for this lack of research, of course, was that, until recently, few organizations demonstrated any formal interest in work-family issues. In a major shift in orientation, workplace responses to work and family concerns have become an important interest of private- and public-sector organizations in most Western countries. And, as was pointed out by Friedman (1991), "Thousands of companies have responded to the family needs of workers despite the limited body of research available" (p. 9). The analyses provided in this volume go partway to addressing this imbalance. Indeed, a major argument to be made below is that even greater emphasis needs to be given to analyses and interventions at the organizational level. Research on the Swedish government's policy, reported in this volume, demonstrates how such policy is limited in its success unless work organizations actively promote work-family balance for both male and female employees.

This chapter summarizes the key findings and recommendations of the book with regard to four issues:

1. What is the current status of gender equity in both paid work and family life?

2. What have been the most common and effective approaches to policies and programs?

3. What organizational strategies have been particularly effective in facilitating change?

4. Where to from here? What are the future directions for research, policy making, and practice?

WHAT IS THE CURRENT STATUS OF GENDER EQUITY IN BOTH PAID WORK AND FAMILY LIFE?

Outcomes

Trends evident in the four countries are remarkably similar despite very different public policy orientations and social forces (e.g., demands for labor). In all countries, there has been a significant increase in the past 20 years in the percentages of women in the paid workforce, especially women with younger dependent children, and in the number of dual-worker families. The percentages of women in the paid workforce are as follows: United States, 60%; United Kingdom, 59%; Australia, 54%; and Sweden, 76%. Whether or not women are in the paid workforce, however, generally still depends very much on the ages of their children. Again, Sweden provides the exception. When women have children under 5 or under school-age, their participation rates are United States, approximately 50%; United Kingdom, 45%; Australia, 39%; and Sweden, 79%. It is also the case that women, on average, work fewer hours and are more likely than men to be in part-time and casual positions. In the United States, 24% of employed mothers work part-time, compared with only 4% of fathers; in the United Kingdom, approximately 40% of employed mothers work part-time, compared with approximately 10% of fathers; in Australia, 43% of employed women work part-time, compared with 11% of employed men; and in Sweden, 40% of employed mothers compared with 9% of fathers work part-time.

In contrast, labor force participation rates for men are much higher, and there is little evidence of there being variations according to the age of children. Fathers are also much more likely to work longer hours than women and to work more overtime. In the United Kingdom, fathers spend about double the number of hours that mothers do on paid work, and they work the longest hours of any fathers in the European Union (an average of 47 hours a week). Increases in the working hours of fathers have been noted as a major concern in all four countries.

As was noted by Haas and Hwang in Chapter 9, gender equity in breadwinning and economic independence depends not simply on having equal access to employment but on achieving equality in access to the full range of jobs, especially those with higher earning potential. The data from all four countries demonstrate that there has been a shift in the percentages of women in higher-status professional and managerial jobs, especially in the public sector, indicating that the focus on equal employment opportunity policies has had some impact. Nevertheless, a substantial gender gap remains.

The gender gap is especially evident in more senior positions in private-sector organizations. For example, in the United States, Australia, and Sweden, women make up only approximately 10% of those in more senior or executive management positions in corporations. Marked gender segregation is also a characteristic of the broader workforce, with women dominating clerical and service jobs and men dominating technical, mechanical, plant, and operator positions. As was reported in Chapter 9, in 1996 in Sweden, only 10% of employed women and 8% of employed men worked in gender-neutral jobs. These differences in occupations are reflected in the relative earnings of women and men. Considering women's pay as a percentage of the average income of men, full-time working women earn about 70% of what men earn in the United States and the United Kingdom; in Australia and Sweden (where trade unions have played a more important role), women earn about 80% of men's pay.

An equivalent gender gap remains between men's and women's participation in domestic life. Analyses presented for all countries indicate that there have been recent small increases in the amount of time fathers spend on household tasks and on child care (but, perhaps, more in play) and a reduction in the amount of time mothers spend (perhaps families are employing outside help). Overall, however, women are still spending more time on all tasks (paid work and domestic work combined), and domestic labor is still divided along traditional lines.

Analyses conducted in both the United Kingdom and Australia contain the clear message that there has not been a major renegotiation of domestic roles and that there is no "new man." Although this may be the case when involvement in all domestic tasks is considered, there is still an indication that there has been a more general shift toward men having a greater interest in fatherhood and that they have a greater psychological investment in this part of their lives (Russell, 1998). Findings from Sweden indicate that public policies advocating that fathers share in the responsibilities of caring for their children can have a major impact on the behavior of men.

There are several possible explanations for the current gaps in gender equity both in occupational status (and earnings) and in responsibility taken for family life (e.g., taking extended leave to care for children or reducing work commitments for a period of time). Two key issues stand out from the analyses presented in the various chapters. The first issue concerns what has been called "the gender contract," while the second relates to assumptions about the nature of work and how commitment is demonstrated (e.g., by working long hours, having a full-time job). Haas and Hwang in Chapter 9 detail the nature of the gender contract, as it operates in Swedish society, and how it can be used to explain current gender gaps. There are three key assumptions: (a) Men should have more power than women; (b) the roles of men and women are different (and in some societies, this is associated with a belief that mothers should be the primary caregivers of young children); and (c) men's roles and ways of thinking should have greater value than women's (supporting gender differences in pay rates for jobs dominated by one sex or the other). It was argued that these assumptions influence decision making within families to support sex segregation in the workforce. Partners would be expected to negotiate their particular work-family arrangements based on the assumption that it is more important for women to combine work with child care and that it is more important for men to be continuously employed and pursue job advancement. As many authors in this volume have noted, reducing the gender gap in decision-making and child care responsibilities in the family is a necessary condition to achieve equality in the workplace. At the same time, however, it is obvious that substantial changes need to be made in assumptions in the workplace to enable both women and men with family responsibilities to have equal employment opportunities. Factors associated with the nature of work are considered further below.

Mothers' and Fathers' Experiences in the Workplace

A major strength of this volume is the inclusion of several comprehensive and well-designed studies that provide current historical perspectives on the experiences mothers and fathers have in the workplace. We now have reasonable knowledge of the difficulties parents experience in balancing their work and family commitments and how this varies for mothers and fathers. Understanding these processes and the impacts they have on the workplace and on individual and family well-being provides directions for governments and organizations to develop more appropriate policies.

The study reported by Galinsky and Swanberg (Chapter 2) is particularly valuable because it includes a large, randomly selected representative sample and enables comparisons to be made over a 20-year period. Their findings reflect what has been noted and publicly debated in many countries but, as yet, has not been as well documented through research findings. They reported that, compared to 20 years ago, U.S. mothers and fathers are working longer hours and are under greater pressure to work harder. At home, mothers are spending about the same amount of time with their children, but they have reduced the time they spend on household tasks and on personal activities. Fathers, on the other hand, have increased the amount of time spent on household tasks and in caring for children. Like mothers, they too have reduced their time on personal activities. Parents of today are also experiencing greater difficulties in balancing their work-family commitments and are seeking options that will enable them to achieve a better balance.

An important finding from this research is that the degree of work-family support workplaces provide to employed parents *does* matter. Employees who reported greater support in terms of flexible work arrangements, supervisor support, supportiveness of the workplace culture, and positive coworker relations experienced lower levels of job burnout and less negative spillover from the job to home. Nevertheless, as was noted by Galinsky and Swanberg, their findings show quite clearly that a supportive workplace by itself is not enough. They conclude that job demands and the demands of life off the job (e.g., difficulties with child care) need to be manageable to ensure high levels of personal and family well-being as well as effective job performance.

In contrast to the data presented for other countries, Brannen (Chapter 3) focuses much more on the experiences of employed mothers in the United Kingdom, mainly because of an absence of research on fathers. Findings indicate that mothers reduce the amount of time spent on housework and personal social activities while attempting to create "quality time" for their children, often excluding their partners in the process. Struggling to juggle competing priorities and feelings of guilt are also themes in this chapter. It is pointed out that the evidence is quite mixed regarding the impact of combining employment and family life on stress and role strain for mothers, and it is argued that mental health outcomes for women are "mediated rather than determined by features of their employment situation and by the nature of their domestic and child care responsibilities."

Australian findings presented by Glezer and Wolcott (Chapter 4) reveal that, overall, Australian parents coped well with their work and family commitments. Forty-five percent of working men and 52% of working women reported a good balance between work and family priorities, and close to 60% of both mothers and fathers felt that work had a positive impact on their self-esteem. For women, being employed and having family commitments appeared to have a positive impact on their satisfaction with life as a whole. Only a minority felt that work had a negative impact on their relationships with their partner (33% of the men and 25% of the women) or their children (40% of both mothers and fathers) or on the level of energy they had for family life. Factors found to be related to lower levels of work-family spillover were similar to those reported by Galinsky and Swanberg: satisfaction with working hours, a low degree of pressure and stress in life, being older (with older children), feeling in control over their lives, and an absence of financial difficulties (especially for women).

The Swedish dual-breadwinner study reported by Björnberg (Chapter 5) provides additional insights into the experiences of employed parents with 5-year-old children. There are some common themes with other chapters. Mothers reported lower levels of psychological well-being than fathers, as well as more "home stress" associated with difficulties experienced in balancing work and family commitments. Interestingly, "home stress" for women was not associated with work demands but was, instead, related to the amount of conflict in the family (financial, housework, and child rearing) and whether they felt they had control in their role as a parent. The lack of impact of work demands is likely explained by the finding that 87% of women had already made some form of adjustment in their work behavior in response to their family commitments (e.g., reduced their hours of work, changed to a more family-friendly job, reduced their overtime, or avoided taking on more responsibility at work).

Findings reported for fathers reveal yet again the impact that social expectations can have. Although smaller in number than women, 62% of fathers still said that they had made significant adjustments to their workplace behavior (reduced hours, reduced overtime, etc.) to accommodate their work and family needs. Björnberg indicates that there is a significant group of Swedish fathers, especially those in higher-status jobs with more higher education and greater workplace flexibility, who are active in developing themselves as fathers. It is possible that these men have recognized the personal advantages of caring for children (e.g., to gain insights into themselves) and that this experience will lead to the development of social skills necessary for success in their jobs.

Although government involvement in supporting working parents in Sweden and elsewhere is obviously a major contributor to facilitating the dual-breadwinner model (e.g., through funding of child care), analyses presented in this volume show that policies and practices adopted by private and public sectors are of critical importance. Both of these strategies are discussed below.

WHAT HAVE BEEN THE MOST COMMON AND INNOVATIVE APPROACHES TO POLICIES AND PROGRAMS?

Governments

In the United States, there has been little evidence of government intervention and more emphasis on expecting working parents to take responsibility for combining work and family. The government does subsidize some poor single mothers' needs for child care to facilitate their employment and removal from the welfare rolls. Since 1993, about one half of American workers (who work for businesses with 50 or more employees) are entitled to take up to 12 weeks off every 2 years for family or personal medical leave, but this is unpaid. Widespread access to government-subsidized child care and paid parental leave is lacking, but there is little demand for these as government supports. The American tradition that views government involvement in private lives as intrusive and harmful prevents the government from being seen as an important provider of family-friendly programs and policies.

The government, however, has recognized that there are high numbers of employed mothers in the labor market, and it has urged companies to take a more active role in providing work-family benefits. Consequently, many large companies have taken a business interest in providing work-family benefits as part of more general strategies to become employers of choice. So far, however, the benefits that have been offered are largely superficial (e.g., child care referral) and cosmetic (flextime). Many are offered only under "managerial discretion," which means that work-family benefits become favors that employees must ask for, at the risk of appearing uninterested in their jobs.

In the United Kingdom, in comparison with the United States, fewer mothers of young children are in full-time paid work, partly because of a widely held belief that maternal employment has a negative impact on the well-being of children. Until quite recently, there has been little evidence of government intervention (e.g., through subsidized child care or paid parental leave). However, since more mothers have entered the labor force and a more liberal political party came into power, greater interest in developing child care and parental leave has been shown by the government. There is still little concern about changing men's roles, and work-family issues are seen (as they are in the United States) as a woman's issue and are not yet directly linked with concerns about gender equity in employment opportunities. As in the United States, some companies provide benefits to employees, but often at the discretion of immediate supervisors. Many workers are involved in jobs with no job security, which locks them out of company benefit programs and will likely make them ineligible for any new government programs.

Recent trends in Australia also show an increase in the number of employed mothers with young children, with little government intervention to mandate financial support for working parents. However, subsidies for child care have increased substantially in recent years, and unpaid parental leave is widely available. The initial impetus for workplace changes to support working parents came from the efforts of trade unions (e.g., the *Parental Leave* test case in the Industrial Relations Commission). In contrast to the United States and the United Kingdom, however, stronger links are evident between policies aimed at ensuring gender equity in employment opportunities for women and work-family initiatives. A number of regional and national laws concerning discrimination, affirmative action, and human rights have been used to improve the situation of women, along with collective bargaining agreements that have resulted in industrial tribunals. Australia's decision to ratify UN and International Labour Organisation directives in regard to work-family policy has also been a driving force affecting equal employment opportunity policy, as have a number of government-sponsored task forces and their resulting reports. Leading Australian companies have attained national recognition for their establishment of model work-family policies. Like the other two countries, however, in public policies, little attention has been paid to fathers and their involvement in family life.

As has become quite clear by now, Sweden is more "advanced" than the others in the extent to which the government has mandated family-friendly policies and programs and demonstrated a commitment to the goal of gender equity. Interestingly though, work-family policies (e.g., providing subsidized high-quality child care) have been partly driven by a strong concern for the well-being of children. Another differentiating feature of Sweden is the emphasis placed on changing men's roles to facilitate gender equity in both breadwinning and caregiving responsibilities. Although all other countries considered here emphasize gender equity in paid work, none has this equally critical emphasis on men being equal partners at home.

But even in Sweden, the government can only go so far in helping working parents if work organizations remain opposed to actively supporting fathers and mothers in their efforts to combine work and family roles. As Bowen suggests in Chapter 6, governments need to work in partnership with work organizations to promote work-family balance and equal employment opportunity for women.

Work organizations themselves must take more leadership in initiating change if gender equity is to be achieved.

Organizational Policies and Programs

Authors in this book, as well as other commentators (e.g., Bankert & Googins, 1996; Cooper & Lewis, 1995; Haas & Hwang, 1995; Lewis, 1996; Russell, James, & Watson, 1988), agree that there are two major limitations of organizational work-family approaches adopted up till now. The first is that initiatives have been targeted at women with child care responsibilities. "In the early 80's, the explanation for why work/family was becoming such a visible issue was focused mostly on the increase of women in the work force" (Bankert & Googins, 1996, p. 47). This is despite evidence that men are also seeking solutions to their need to balance work and family roles and knowledge that workers need flexible employment conditions for a wide array of issues in addition to child care (e.g., elder care).

The second limitation is that work-family programs are offered and regarded as employee fringe "benefits," designed to facilitate individual solutions to work-family conflicts. As such, they can be offered and then taken away, as economic circumstances change. Individuals may feel that taking benefits marks them as less committed to the workplace. The emphasis on individual solutions to work-family conflict also keeps work organizations from considering how work-family issues should receive more attention as part of strategic business concerns.

Some of the chapters in the volume discuss the availability of work-family benefits. In their national survey of employed parents in the United States, Galinsky and Swanberg (Chapter 2) report that a majority of parents say they can easily take time off during the day to attend to family matters and that they have the flexibility to take time off for sick children. Most report access to maternity leave and paternity leave. Although about two fifths say they have access to flextime, only about one fifth receive help with child care or elder care referrals, and fewer still get any financial assistance with these needs. Only services for elder care had increased significantly over time.

In contrast to the findings for the United States, Brannen and Lewis (Chapter 7) indicate that, in the United Kingdom, "family-friendly" practices are increasing. Nevertheless, they are not widespread and are more likely to be offered by public-sector and large organizations. Three practices were reported to be relatively common (but were usually provided on a discretionary basis): enhanced maternity leave (offered by 23% of employers), leave to care for sick children (approximately 25%), and paternity leave (69%). Much less common were career breaks, child care, flexible hours, and job sharing.

In Australia, family-friendly policies listed in advocacy documents (e.g., Wolcott, 1996; Work and Family Unit, 1994) include relocation assistance, child care (centers and referral, emergency), family support (youth clubs, family leave, parenting seminars, respite care for people who have family members with disabilities), care for dependent adults (elder care resource and referral services), flexible work and leave arrangements (flexible hours, flexible working year, career breaks, job sharing, permanent part-time work, home-based work), and other family-friendly measures (flexible salary packages, work and family information). Australian data on how many organizations currently offer these types of services and programs, however, are not currently available.

Analyses conducted in the United States, the United Kingdom, and Australia show that many workers lack formal access to any work-family services or programs because they are part of a growing portion of the contingent labor force that lacks job security; these individuals work on contract, short term, or when called. This is part of an international trend referred to as "casualization." In Australia, for example, the proportion of casual employees increased from 15% in 1984 to 26% in 1996. Part-time employees in Sweden, in contrast, are more likely to have equity in access to work-family policies and programs.

Haas and Hwang (Chapter 9) focus more on broader policies and programs available and mandated in Sweden, such as child care and parental leave, as well as a policy that has been advocated for more than 20 years—a 6-hour workday for all employees, who are paid for 7 or 8 hours. Although this practice is not yet widespread, findings show that many organizations have experimented with this policy, resulting in positive outcomes for organizations, employees, and their families. Haas and Hwang also report that a very small number of companies have provided managers with allowances to purchase cleaning, laundry, and ironing assistance as a way of helping dual-career couples manage their work and family commitments.

Although parental leave is mandated in Sweden and there is a strong emphasis on advocating that both women and men take leave, there is still a significant gender gap in take-up rates. Haas and Hwang argue that a major reason for this outcome is the failure of organizations to adopt "active measures" to encourage men to use their parental-leave rights, despite this being enshrined in the equality law. In two separate studies (both with approximately 200 companies) reported in their chapter, it was found that (a) only 14% of the companies tried to make it easier for fathers to take parental leave and (b) only 3% were actively helping male employees to balance work and family.

Haas and Hwang conclude that Swedish companies have been slow to initiate their own policies and programs to reduce work-family conflicts and to enhance gender equity. Companies still base their policies on the traditional gender contract that reinforces male dominance in all spheres of public and private life.

It is clear from all research reviewed in this section that the most significant challenges and opportunities for change are at the level of the organization.

Organizations With Innovative Policies and Programs

One of the major gaps in both the gender equity and work-family areas is the lack of high quality evaluation data; therefore, statements about effectiveness are somewhat limited. Nevertheless, all countries included here have various award systems or surveys aimed at identifying those organizations performing well in providing work-family policies and programs. Bowen (Chapter 6) reviews U.S. findings showing that only 5% of organizations in the United States offer "cutting edge" work-family strategies. Cutting edge strategies included child care and elder care assistance, reimbursement accounts, alternative work schedules, information and referral services, paid personal days for child and family responsibilities, fitness centers, stress-management and family life education programs, and extending benefits to partners of employees in cohabiting or same-sex couples.

Brannen and Lewis (Chapter 7) provided examples of "principles of good practice" in U.K. organizations. In the area of child care and other care, they identified several public- and private-sector organizations—particularly those with a high number of female employees—that provided extensive child care facilities and career breaks of up to 5 years to enable employees to care for children. Brannen and Lewis argue that good practice regarding flexibility calls for policies and practices that either "enhance employee autonomy or normalise ways of working," enabling employees to have control over balancing their work and family commitments, with mutual benefits to employees and employers. The example they provide is a supermarket chain that enables employees to swap shifts with other workers from the same or different departments without the involvement of management. This is to overcome the common practice of flexibility options being offered only at the discretion of managers.

Some U.K. companies have challenged the view that work-family integration is solely a woman's issue and have tackled the long-hours culture (with the emphasis on "face" time). In one organization, flexible work options were promoted to a broader group of employees, and there was an emphasis on the value of achieving a healthy balance between work and life (beyond family) for individuals and for the organization. In another organization, a number of innovative initiatives were put in place (e.g., a new parents' program for staff and their partners, a parenting consultation service, and a work-family consultation service for managers) that challenge the idea that family matters should not be of concern to the workplace and recognize that men have work-family integration concerns as well.

In the final example provided by Brannen and Lewis, an organization conducted a campaign to challenge the belief that it is necessary to work long hours to show commitment. This included "Go Home on Time Days"; encouraging employees to work smarter, not harder (with tips about how to achieve this, such as evaluation of the need for meetings); and a series of management training programs to encourage a better work-life balance.

Squirchuk and Bourke (Chapter 8) highlight innovative policies and programs in a large insurance company. Based on a survey of employee needs and an analysis of associated business opportunities (e.g., to be an "employer of choice"), the organization implemented a range of family-friendly leave policies, including 6 weeks' paid parental leave for the primary caregiver and expanded opportunities for part-time work, job sharing, and working from home. An evaluation of the impact of these policies has revealed positive outcomes for employees and for the business. These include high take-up of parental leave, even by men, and an increase in return to work after maternity leave and in retention rates.

Like several other Australian organizations, this insurance company aligned its work-family strategies with others aimed at enhancing gender equity (e.g., reduced hierarchical and occupational segregation and improved pay equity, management awareness programs, and antiharassment and affirmative action programs). Findings reported in the chapter indicate that, as a result, the number of women in management positions has increased significantly; more women have moved into traditionally male sales and service positions; and there has been an increase in the number of managers in part-time positions. This is an important case study because it shows that, with a combined focus on equity in work and family (e.g., paid parental leave) and gender equity in employment, changes are possible in both domains. It should be noted, however, that there are still major gaps in gender equity in several areas of employment, especially in management positions.

Data on the effectiveness of the implementation of government-mandated parental leave for Swedish men are provided by Haas and Hwang (Chapter 9). They argue that there are three stages in Swedish companies' response to men's interest in taking parental leave. Only about 3% of companies provide active support, while about one third "passively oppose" men's leave-taking; the rest provide support conditional on the circumstances. In the most supportive organizations, the corporate culture actively facilitated men to participate more in child care, and it had become the company's responsibility (not the employee's) to work out ways for men to take parental leave. Important, too, it is argued by the authors that in these more advanced companies, leadership came from the top (e.g., from young managers who were themselves fathers or from older men concerned that younger men should have more contact with their children than they had), and this was based both on ideological concerns (e.g., valuing the welfare of families) and business concerns (e.g., companies recognized that there were productivity gains in having men take parental leave). These companies were also more likely to institute other workplace changes that are critical to ensure effective outcomes. These included cross-training and job rotation, flattened hierarchies, autonomous work teams, job autonomy, measuring productivity by outputs (performance) rather than inputs (work hours), and alternative career paths for specialists and managers.

Common to most examples of companies that have been innovative in implementing policies are two themes. First, there is an emphasis on both employee and business benefits of addressing work-family issues, and second, there is a recognition that better outcomes are achieved if there is a focus on work practices, leadership, and organizational culture. Business issues and organizational culture are major issues addressed in the next section.

ORGANIZATIONAL CHANGE

What Are the Business Arguments?

As has become clear in this volume, organizations have changed, and work-family is now an issue they are being proactive about rather than reactive (see also Friedman, Christensen, & DeGroot, 1998). The better organizations are also striving to be publicly recognized for their achievements, by seeking nominations for the many corporate work-family awards. Various reasons for the responses of companies in different countries have been provided.

Overwhelmingly, reasons provided have focused on *changes in the demographics* of the present and potential workforces. The most common demographic change noted concerns the family responsibilities of workers, especially women with preschool-age children. Although the focus has been on women and dependent children, it has also been widely recognized that this is also an issue for those with elder care responsibilities (it is estimated that 15% to 20% of workers have such responsibilities) or responsibilities for the long-term ill or individuals with disabilities.

The potential impact on men has also been noted, especially those with employed partners. This means that there are proportionally more people in the current workforce (women and men) with dependent care responsibilities that will potentially create conflicts and influence their employment behavior. Various authors in this volume note the different ways family responsibilities can influence employment. Concerns about work-family conflict and responsibilities for dependent care partners' career aspirations can influence (a) whether individuals take a job or are willing to relocate within the same company, (b) whether they are willing to leave a job, (c) whether they are present or absent on a particular day, (d) the level of their work commitment, and (e) their ability to concentrate and focus on particular work tasks.

A second major change commonly discussed concerns *the increased diversity in family and individual lifestyles and changing values.* The diversity in family lifestyles is now widely recognized. There is evidence (see Cooper & Lewis, 1995) that more people are seeking balanced lives and high levels of satisfaction from both their paid work and their family and community lives. Findings presented here also argue that increasing numbers of workers are prepared to trade career advancement for better work-family balance.

Pressure from unions and government policies has also helped motivate organizations to address work and family issues. This has especially been the case in both Sweden and Australia, but less so in the United Kingdom and the United States.

These demographic, social, and political changes have been shown to create several business-related pressures in organizations to respond to work-family issues. One concern is *to reduce productivity losses associated with dependent care.* This is one of the most common arguments found in the volume and elsewhere in the literature: Employees are frequently absent because of dependent care responsibilities (Friedman & Galinsky, 1991; VandenHeuvel, 1993), and unwanted turnover is often an outcome of difficulties in finding suitable care for dependents. Another important concern is *to reduce productivity losses associated with a lack of balance.* Findings presented in this volume show that people with family responsibilities who work in unresponsive organizations are more likely to experience stress and reduced quality of life. It is assumed that this leads to a reduction in productivity and increased risks of workplace accidents; however, more research is needed.

A focus on work and family has also been seen as presenting opportunities for organizations. Such a focus can provide *an incentive to increase workers' motivation and commitment* and thus get higher levels of productivity from the current labor pool, especially during a period of downsizing and reduced career opportunities with flatter organizations. It can also serve *as a way of attracting and retaining the best-quality people* and *enable the best-quality people to advance* in an organization. It has been recognized that barriers to women's advancement in corporations include having to take time out for dependent care responsibilities, lack of flexibility in career structures, and traditional rules and work practices based on assumptions of the male-breadwinner model. Another argument evident in the analyses presented in this volume is the potential impact that involvement in family life has on *personal development and skills* that are needed in the workplace. As was argued by Haas and Hwang (Chapter 9), companies that actively support fathers' leave-taking recognize that this experience can help men develop skills and self-confidence that in turn will enhance their work productivity. Finally, companies can *obtain community recognition* by being seen as "good" corporate citizens or caring organizations, resulting in greater customer loyalty and business growth.

Factors Facilitating Organizational Change

Arguments presented here also challenge the extent to which organizations have become family friendly and point to the broader systemic and organizational issues that need to be addressed for this to be achieved. In this volume, we have emphasized integrating work-family issues into strategic thinking within organizations. This parallels arguments made earlier by Friedman (1991) and Friedman and Galinsky (1991) about the need for a focus on business benefits, integration, and culture change. Friedman and Galinsky argued that organizations tend to go through three stages in their responses to family needs: (a) a programmatic approach, involving identification of needs and program development (especially with a focus on dependent care needs); (b) an integrated approach, when family needs are seen as business issues and there is an attempt to integrate a range of work-family policies (especially flexible work arrangements); and (c) changing the corporate culture, in which the emphasis is on developing a supportive, family-friendly organizational culture.

It is this latter issue—changes in corporate culture—that has come in for the closest scrutiny recently. The emphasis given to this issue is a particular strength of this book and is consistent with other recent analyses. These themes are also taken up by Bankert and Googins (1996). They argue that there is a growing list of policies and programs (on paper) that appears to indicate corporate commitment to work-family balance; however, organizational cultures have not changed much at all. They argue that success with work-family concerns "depends on a combination of top-management support, buy-in to the business case, ownership throughout the organisation, and a willingness to go after the necessary culture change" (p. 46).

Major contributors to this debate have been Bailyn, Rapoport, and Fletcher (Chapter 10). They see work-family as a driver for organizational change to improve gender equity. They maintain that "family-friendly benefits" can be useful for women with young children, but they can also lead to an increase in inequities between employees. Like others, they argue that, for effective change to occur, the need for integration of work and family for women and men has to be incorporated into organizations as a strategic business issue. It is necessary to "change the structure and culture of the workplace, paying attention to both men's and women's roles."

The broad aims of the project described in Chapter 10 at a large manufacturing and service corporation were to (a) explore interconnections between work-family policies and practices and work practices and culture, (b) identify barriers to implementing work-family policies in a gender equitable way, and

(c) develop new business-focused practices that overcome identified barriers. They found that work-family policies were not being applied in a gender equitable way (e.g., using various policies had different career implications for women and men) and that assumptions about gender (and what is appropriate for women and men) were "embedded in work structures and cultures" to an extent that is not currently recognized. Their work involved challenging organizations about their work practices based on the assumptions that work and family are separate spheres and that success (individual, organizational, and societal) depends on ensuring that work and family are kept separate and distinct. As they point out, "integrated" employees can be more effective in their jobs through the use of a combined set of skills, including those more usually associated with domestic life (e.g., nurturing, addressing emotions) and those traditionally valued by workplaces (e.g., autonomy, linear thinking).

Implementing effective organizational change to ensure gender equity, they conclude, is much more difficult than anticipated, especially because there is a need to challenge a diversity of feelings, beliefs, and assumptions about gender. Indeed, they found that they could not use "gender equity" when conducting their work, and "work-family" became a proxy for gender equity. Strategies they report as being effective included moving away from seeing work and family as adversarial toward "the notion that it is possible to use work-family issues as a way of making work practices more productive *and* more gender equitable" and involving employees directly in analyzing work-related problems to develop more effective work practices. The focus was clearly on developing creative solutions to work-related problems on the basis of an acceptance of the legitimacy of taking account of employees' personal lives. The fundamental issue addressed was "What is it about the way work gets done around here that makes it difficult (or easy) for you to integrate your work and personal life?" Positive outcomes associated with their interventions were also reported, such as reduction in absenteeism and stress, improvements in worker autonomy, and perceived fairness.

Two very different U.K. case studies (involving an accountancy firm and a county council) illustrating the process of organizational change are presented by Lewis (Chapter 11). While arguing that it is problematic to make meaningful comparisons between organizations, especially because of differences in the historical, economic, and social contexts of different organizations, Lewis highlights some general principles of organizational change evident from the two studies. First, it is important to clarify the objectives of change, especially to have explicit objectives for gender equity, for developing solutions to meet the needs of both employees and organizations (to avoid the assumptions that flexible work practices are favors), and for changing key elements of the culture. Second, strong and continuing leadership is needed—either from senior management or from key line or operational managers. Initiatives driven by human resources departments are often marginalized and are not seen as strategic business issues. Third, it is necessary to empower people at all levels to ensure that they feel a sense of entitlement to varying their working arrangements to meet family needs. Fourth, there is a need to address the culture of working long hours and to question the assumption that working long hours is a demonstration of commitment. Moreover, the emphasis needs to shift away from valuing and rewarding inputs (hours) to valuing outcomes.

The approach taken by Billing (Chapter 13) is yet another approach to identifying key factors in organizational change. The focus here is on data obtained from interviews with female and male managers in three Scandinavian organizations—a social welfare board, an airline, and a foreign ministry. This analysis demonstrated how different organizational values and expectations about work and family influence gender equity outcomes. At the social welfare board, people having private lives was accepted and valued, and both females and males were expected to be involved in family life and to take parental leave regardless of occupational position. There was also a strong commitment to gender equity in promotions, which was reflected in the finding of equal numbers of male and female managers. At the airline, in contrast, the family was considered to be a private matter, and the organization had work practices and expectations that supported the male-breadwinner model. Understandably then, men were much more likely to advance than women were. Billing also provides an interesting analysis of how the responses of individuals can change the corporate culture of an organization. She describes how different people responded to work practices and expectations, by displaying loyalty or disloyalty to work or family, by deciding whether to leave or remain in an organization and cope with difficult jobs (or leave their marriages to invest more energy in work), and by their preparedness to express their concerns about inflexible work practices.

Kugelberg (Chapter 14) presents another approach to analyzing organizational change in a different industry sector (food production). In this company, there were few women in senior management positions, and there was a significant gap in average incomes for males and females. Kugelberg's analysis showed that there were two different discourses about work and family issues that resulted in women and men having to cope with contradictions between company and individual expectations. The company discourse, reflected in the views of managers and union leaders, focused on raising productivity and economic survival in an increasingly competitive marketplace; it also emphasized expectations about a job being a full-time commitment and employees being accessible when needed by the company (e.g., to work overtime). The traditional breadwinner model (with women assumed to have primary responsibility for children) was also reflected in the company discourse. The second, experience-based, discourse concerned employees' day-to-day experiences in responding to different needs—children's, their own, and the workplace's.

Differences in attitudes toward work and family were also found between administration and production areas of the company and between different areas of production, which points to the importance of considering organizational subcultures. Shift supervisors in the production area viewed parents as being "problematic" because of their right to take leave. They wanted maximum attendance to ensure achievement of output levels and so that they could remain competitive in the global market. This contrasted with the experiences of employees in production units organized as work teams. In these groups, there was a system of mutual trust and an "implicit agreement that the workers were free to organise their work themselves as long as they were willing to take responsibility for it." Workers in teams were able to take time off to attend to family commitments when they needed to. Work demands and expectations were different again in the administrative area (e.g., where taking leave meant that work simply piled up). Women and men encountered different expectations from their bosses (again along more traditional gender lines, with mothers being seen as a "productivity problem"—even though there was evidence that younger men were increasingly interested in fatherhood), and these shaped their views about entitlements and responsibilities in both work and family.

A further example of organizational change, in a vastly different industry sector (a male-dominated mining company), is presented by Russell and Edgar (Chapter 12). They reviewed a wide range of factors found to facilitate the change process, many of which are consistent with those noted in other chapters. The first factor was endorsement from the highest level, or *leadership.* The CEO in their study had high expectations for project leaders, focused on work-life balance issues for senior managers, insisted on management accountability, and incorporated work-family and gender equity issues into leadership skill development. The second factor was *integration with business;* this granted operational credibility for those leading the process of change and encouraged integration of work-family issues into business strategies and other corporate policies. The third factor involved *addressing barriers to change;* this meant identifying and addressing the major workplace and attitudinal barriers, challenging traditional assumptions about gender roles, and accepting that many men as well as women are seeking a better balance. The fourth factor related to an *emphasis on research;* data collection was used as a way to inform and educate employees as well as management, and findings were shared with different work sites. The fifth factor was *employee involvement* at every stage—from problem solving to identifying key issues and developing solutions based on effective business and employee/family outcomes. These solutions were designed to be based on mutual trust and to have the potential to increase creativity and employee effectiveness. The last factor was insistence on *including the full range of issues;* this meant acknowledging that work and family are not separate spheres. It also involved taking up the full range of work and family/lifestyle issues and equal employment issues; adopting a broader approach that included employees' partners and their local communities; and acknowledging the links between work-family and gender equity issues and the need to provide gender equity in work practices and expectations as well as work and family commitments.

THE FUTURE

Those who have monitored the development of work-family initiatives in organizations and who have had a parallel concern for gender equity at work and at home should recognize the significance of the research and analyses presented in this book. This volume has advanced our knowledge of the ways in which governments and organizations can facilitate employees to balance their work and family roles, increase organizational effectiveness, and produce better outcomes in terms of gender equity and individual, family, and community well-being. It is clear that several key shifts have begun and will need to continue in the future to ensure that better outcomes are achieved for all concerned. These are summarized below.

First, there has been a shift from a narrow focus on work and family to an acceptance that work, family, personal, and community commitments all need to be considered. Second, there is now much more emphasis given to dependent care issues beyond regular daily care for preschool-age children. This includes concern for the care of elderly and disabled relatives and the recognition of the need for emergency or backup child care (e.g., for school-age children). Third, more organizations are now recognizing that work-family is an issue for men as well as for women. Analyses presented here, however, indicate that it is still problematic for organizations and senior managers to accept that more men are seeking to be active fathers and welcome initiatives that will facilitate this change. Fourth, there is a clear move away from work and family being seen as only an issue of social justice and/or a benefit for employees. The fundamental driver for organizations is now the impact that work-family initiatives and strategies have on business outcomes. Cost-benefit analyses and research into the evaluation of the impact of work-family initiatives are becoming more common, as are arguments about the positive impact that skills learned in the domestic sphere can have on workplaces.

Fifth, there is a shift from policies and programs to a focus on changing work practices and organization to enable employees to have control over how, when, and where they work. Changing the culture as well as work practices and expectations of managers is now seen as being much more critical than having a raft of "family-friendly" policies and practices. Sixth, the initial focus on the impact that family demands have on work (e.g., attendance) has been extended to include the consideration of the impact that work has on individual stress and on relationship and family well-being. The fundamental argument now concerns the extent to which initiatives address the underlying causes of the tension between work and family and whether, indeed, the approaches add value to businesses and are strategic in their focus. Seventh, rather than work-family and gender equity issues being seen as separate, many organizations are actively addressing the links between the two.

Future approaches need to develop responses to work and family issues from a strategic business perspective and to take account of the increasing globalization of organizations. They need to be based on the premise that, unless employees can relate the business advantages of such programs to their day-to-day work experiences, utilization rates and improvements in individual and organizational effectiveness will not occur. Yet there is very little discussion in the literature about the process of identifying problems and developing solutions that enhance both individual and organizational well-being—chapters included in this volume, of course, provide the exception. A process is needed to analyze the potential impact of work-family issues on employment behavior and business outcomes. The process needs to be based on the assumption that employees are both capable and motivated to develop solutions that can result in mutual benefits to families and corporations.

The approaches outlined by Bailyn, Rapoport, and Fletcher (Chapter 10) and by Russell and Edgar (Chapter 12) illustrate how employees can be involved in bringing about organizational change. Although their approach may not be possible to take in every research situation, these researchers make a strong case for a type of research that Bailyn et al. have labeled "collaborative, interactive action research" (CIAR). Collaboration is established between the researchers and the workplace partners; both are assumed to have expertise and to be able to learn from each other. From the interaction between researchers and workplace partners, new issues and resolutions emerge. Although a common goal is assumed, frameworks and perceptions would be expected to be different. Proposals for action or change need to be relevant to a particular group, "to be connected to an actual task that the work group is doing and accountable for." Data collection and analysis are central components of the process. The aim is to reveal new knowledge and to examine the data through a "gender lens, that is, by seeking the gender implications in the data and uncovering assumptions underlying work practices that have gender implications."

REFERENCES

Bankert, E., & Googins, B. (1996, July/August). Family-friendly—says who? *Across the Board,* pp. 45-49.

Cooper, C., & Lewis, S. (1995). *Beyond family friendly organisations.* London: Demos.

Friedman, D. (1991). *Linking work-family issues to the bottom line* (Report No. 962). New York: Conference Board.

Friedman, D., & Galinsky, E. (1991). Work and family trends. In S. Zedeck (Ed.), *Work and family* (pp. 168-207). San Francisco: Jossey-Bass.

Friedman, S., Christensen, P., & DeGroot, J. (1998, November/December). Work and life: The end of the zero-sum game. *Harvard Business Review,* pp. 119-120.

Haas, L., & Hwang, P. (1995). Fatherhood and corporate culture in Sweden. *Family Relations, 44,* 28-36.

Lewis, S. (1996). Sense of entitlement, family friendly policies, and gender. In H. Holt & I. Thaulow (Eds.), *The role of companies in reconciling working life and family life* (pp. 17-42). Copenhagen, Denmark: Danish National Institute of Social Research.

Russell, G. (1998). Primary caregiving fathers. In M. E. Lamb (Ed.), *Nontraditional families* (pp. 57-81). Hillsdale, NJ: Lawrence Erlbaum.

Russell, G., James, D., & Watson, J. (1988). Work/family policies: The changing role of fathers and the presumption of shared responsibility for parenting. *Australian Journal of Social Issues, 23,* 249-267.

VandenHeuvel, A. (1993). *When roles overlap: Workers with family responsibilities* (Monograph No. 14). Melbourne: Australian Institute of Family Studies; Canberra, Australia: Department of Industrial Relations, Work and Family Unit.

Wolcott, I. (1996). *A nice place to work: Small business and workers with family responsibilities.* Canberra, Australia: Department of Industrial Relations, Work and Family Unit.

Work and Family Unit. (1994). *The workplace guide to work and family.* Canberra: Commonwealth of Australia.

Author Index

Subject Index

Affirmative Action Act (1986) (Australia), 123-124
Age, youngest child:
  Australia, 45, 51, 52f
  United Kingdom, 32
Allied Dunbar (U.K.), 110
AMP Limited (Australia), 127-129
Anti-Discrimination Act (1977) (Australia), 123
Asda Stores (U.K.), 111

Barclays Technology Services (U.K.), 112-113
Benefits:
  Australia, 53
  for corporations, 105, 107-108, 256-257
  for homosexuals, 107
  fringe, 22
  social security, 53
  United States, 22
British Broadcasting Corporation, 107

Carmody, Heather, 201
Child care, Australia:
  and labor force participation, 45, 50, 51, 52f

programs/policy, 120, 121-122
  youngest child age, 45, 51, 52f
Child care, Sweden:
  and labor force participation, 57, 60-61, 64-67, 68-69, 71-72
  attitudes toward, 57, 60-61, 64-67
  child well-being, 133-134
  programs/policy, 133-135
  subsidized, 57, 60-61, 64-66
Child care, United Kingdom:
  and labor force participation, 32, 37, 38-39
  and organizational change, 192-193, 194-195
  programs/policy, 100-101, 102, 109-111
  youngest child age, 32
Child care, United States, 19-20, 24-25
Clinton, Bill, 84
Collaborative/interactive action research (CIAR), 167, 177
Community resources, Australia, 206-208
Compensation, United States, 22
Continuous employment:
  Australia, 50-51
  United Kingdom, 29-30, 31
Coworker relations, United States, 23
Culture:
  Australia, 7

About the Contributors

Lotte Bailyn, PhD, is the T. Wilson Professor of Management at Massachusetts Institute of Technology (MIT), Sloan School of Management, in Cambridge, Massachusetts. From 1995 to 1997, she was the Matina S. Horner Distinguished Visiting Professor at Radcliffe's Public Policy Institute. Her latest book, *Breaking the Mold: Women, Men, and Time in the New Corporate World* (1993), sets out the hypothesis that by challenging the assumptions in which current work practices are embedded, it is possible to meet the goals of both business productivity and employees' family and community concerns, and to do so in ways that are equitable for men and women. The book spells out the contours of how this might be done, and her current work in corporate settings has supported this basic proposition. Some of this work is detailed in *Relinking Life and Work: Toward a Better Future* (1996), of which she is a coauthor. Other recent publications in related areas include "Changing the Conditions of Work: Responding to Increasing Work Force Diversity and New Family Patterns," in Kochan and Useem's *Transforming Organizations* (1992); "Challenging the Last Boundary: Reconnecting Work and Family," in Arthur and Rousseau's *The Boundaryless Career: A New Employment Principle for a New Organizational Era* (with J. Fletcher, 1996); "Beyond Work and Family: Adventures on the Fault Line"; and "The Impact of Corporate Culture on Work-Family Integration" in Parasuraman and Greenhaus's *Work and Family in a Changing World: A Multiple Stakeholder Perspective* (1997).

Yvonne Due Billing, PhD, is Associate Professor in the Department of Sociology at University of Copenhagen, Denmark. Her specialty areas include organizational sociology, gender, careers, family, and leadership. Currently, she is working on a book about gender and trade unions. She has published the following books in English: *Understanding Gender and Organisations* (with M. Alvesson, Sage, 1997) and *Gender, Managers, and Organizations* (with M. Alvesson, 1994). Related articles she has published include "Gender and Bureaucracy" (*Gender, Work, and Organizations,* 1994); "Starting a Business: An Attractive Alternative to a Traditional Career in an Organization" (*Nutek,* 1996); and "Gender and Organization" (with M. Alvesson, *Organization Studies,* 1992).

Ulla Björnberg, PhD, is Professor of Sociology at Göteborg University in Göteborg, Sweden. She leads a research program called "Family Relations in Modern Society: Development of Theory and Methods in Sociological Research on Families." She has been engaged in several international projects on family policy and family life in Eastern and Western Europe. In her studies, she has focused on reconciliation of employment and family life with a perspective of gender and class. At present, she is studying subsistence strategies of lone mothers and negotiations about distribution of money, time, and domestic work in dual-earner couples. Recent publications include "Family Orientation Among Men: A Process of Change in Sweden" in Drew and Mahon's *Reconciling Family and Working Life* (1998); "Dual Earner Families: Perspectives on Gender and Policy" in Commaille and De Singly's *The European Family* (1997); "Negotiations About Family Responsibilities Within Dual-Earner Families: Theoretical Perspectives" (with A. Kollind) in Holmer and Karlsson's *Work: Quo Vadis? Re-thinking the Question of Work* (1997); "Single Mothers in Sweden: Supported Workers Who Mother" in Duncan and Edwards's *Single Mothers in an International Context: Mothers or Workers?* (1997); "Well-Being Among Swedish Employed Mothers With Preschool Children" in Chesney et al.'s *Women, Stress, and Heart Disease* (1998); and "Family Change and Family Policy in Sweden" in Alestalo and Flora's *Family Change and Family Policy in the Scandinavian Welfare States* (in press).

Juliet Bourke, LLM, is a lawyer working as Senior Policy Officer in the Legislation and Policy Division of the New South Wales Attorney General's Department in Sydney, Australia. She commenced legal practice in the late 1980s and now advises the New South Wales government on human rights and discrimination law (with a particular emphasis on women's employment). She represented the New South Wales Attorney General on the committee he and the Minister for Women established in 1996 to consider gender bias in the legal profession, and she subsequently coauthored the report *Gender Bias and the Law: Women Working in the Legal Profession. Report of the Implementation Committee* (1996). Her Master of Laws honors' thesis, *Professional Women: Balancing Careers and Family Responsibilities*, is currently being published as a monograph by the UNSW Industrial Relations Research Centre, and she has published a number of papers on work and family issues. She is currently developing the New South Wales government's proposal to prohibit discrimination in employment on the basis of caregiving responsibilities. She is also an industry consultant on workplace flexibility with Work+Life Strategies, in collaboration with Graeme Russell.

Gary L. Bowen, PhD, ACSW, is Kenan Distinguished Professor in the School of Social Work at the University of North Carolina at Chapel Hill. He has consulted extensively with all branches of the armed forces on how structural and dynamic aspects of the military environment influence the adaptation of service members and their families. He presently serves as a consultant to Communities in School, Inc., the largest stay-in-school network in the United States, where he works on behalf of students at risk of school failure. He teaches courses in the School of Social Work on family stress, coping, and social support and on the evaluation of practice. He is the author, coauthor, or coeditor of more than 150 publications, including the books *Navigating the Marital Journey* (1991), *The Work and Family Interface: Toward a Contextual Effects Perspective* (1995), and *The Organization Family: Work and Family Linkages in the U.S. Military* (1989) and the articles "Effects of Organizational Culture on Fatherhood" in Bozett and Hanson's *Cultural Variations in American Fatherhood* (1991) and "The Effects of Leader Support in the Work Unit on the Relationship Between Work Spillover and Family Adaptation" (*Journal of Family and Economic Issues,* 1998).

Julia Brannen, PhD, is Professor in the Sociology of the Family at the University of London and a Senior Researcher at Thomas Coram Research Unit, Institute of Education, University of London, in Great Britain. She also codirects the Work-Life Research Centre. Her research interests include the relationship between employment and family life, children's and young people's experience of households and family life, and methodology. She is a coeditor of the new *International Journal of Social Research Methodology: Theory and Practice.* Her recently authored or coauthored publications relating to the work-life field include *Employment and Family Life: A UK Review 1980-94* (1994); *Mothers, Fathers, and Employment: Parents and the Labour Market in Britain 1984-1994* (1997); "Employment and Family Lives: Equalities and Inequalities" in Drew, Emerek, and Mahon's *Women, Work, and the Family in Europe* (1998); "The Polarisation and Intensification of Parental Employment: Consequences for Children, Families, and the Community" (*Work, Family, and Community,* 1998); and "Caring for Children" in Walby's *New Agendas for Women* (1999).

Don Edgar received a master's degree in education from the University of Melbourne in Australia and a PhD from Stanford University in California. He works as a consultant to business on work-life policies and programs and conducts research on the links between education, training, business, and community change in regional Australia. He is also Adjunct Professor at the Centre for Workplace Culture Change, Royal Melbourne Institute of Technology, in Melbourne. He was the director of the Australian Institute of Family Studies for 14 years; he has also been Professor and Research Associate at the University of Chicago and Reader in Sociology at La Trobe University. He is the author or editor of 14 books, the latest being *Men, Mateship, Marriage* (1998) and *When Too Much Change Is Never Enough* (1998). He is currently working on a book titled *Linking the Future,* which examines changes in the family, community, and workplace culture. He is a member of the International Family Policy Forum and Australia's UNESCO Social Science Committee.

Joyce K. Fletcher, DBA, is Professor of Management at the Center for Gender in Organizations at Simmons Graduate School of Management in Boston. She is also a Research Scholar at the Jean Baker Miller Training Institute at the Wellesley College Center for Women, in Wellesley, Massachusetts. Her research uses feminist theory to study organizational phenomena, especially as they relate to organizational change and transformation. As a teacher, consultant, and researcher, her professional practice is focused on exploring how gendered assumptions about learning and organizational effectiveness affect issues such as management education, leadership, gender equity, and the integration of work and personal life. She is a frequent speaker at national and international conferences and has published in both management and education journals. Recent publications include "Relational Practice: A Feminist Reconstruction of Work" (*Journal of Management Inquiry,* 1998); "Unexpected Connections: Considering Employees' Personal Lives Can Revitalize Your Business" (with L. Bailyn and D. Kolb, *Sloan Management Review,* 1997); and "Personal Development in the New Organization: A Relationship Approach to Developing the Protean Work" in Hall's *The Career Is Dead: Long Live the Career* (1996). Her new book is titled *Disappearing Acts: Gender, Power, and Relational Practice at Work* (1999).

Ellen Galinsky, MA, is the President and Cofounder of the Families and Work Institute, a nonprofit organization in New York City that addresses the changing nature of work and family life. She is currently overseeing the following studies: the National Study of the Changing Workforce, a nationally representative study of the U.S. workforce; the Early Childhood Public Engagement Campaign, designed to increase awareness about the importance of the first years of life; the 1998 Business Work-Life Study, on the trends and prevalence of business initiatives that support the family and personal life of employees; and *Ahead of the Curve: What Business Is Doing for New and Expectant Parents,* a report on how business is supporting families from pregnancy through the first few years of children's lives. In addition, she has directed studies on child care in eight states and is a past president of the National Association for the Education of Young Children. She has served as an adviser on work and family issues to the U.S. Departments of Health and Human Services, Education, and Labor. She has also served as an adviser to many states on their early education and care initiatives and on work and family issues. She is the author of more than 20 books and reports (including *The Six Stages of Parenthood* and *The Preschool Years*) and has published more than 85 articles in academic journals, academic books, and magazines. Her latest book, *Ask the Children* (1999), investigates how children feel about their working parents.

Helen Glezer, MA, is Senior Research Fellow at the Australian Institute of Family Studies in Melbourne, Australia. She is Project Manager of the Australian Family Life Course Study, a national longitudinal survey of 2,700 Australians ages 25-70, currently being conducted by the Australian Institute of Family Studies. Her main research focuses on demographic changes in family formation patterns, changing family values, and work and family issues. Currently, she is working with Ilene Wolcott on a book on work and family issues across the life course. Relevant publications include *Maternity Leave in Australia: Employee and Employer Experiences* (1988); *Work and Family Life: Achieving Integration* (with I. Wolcott, 1995); and *Pathway Between Paid Work and Parenting* (1996). Published papers include "Bridging Paid and Unpaid Work: Strategies for the Future" and "Work and Family: Work Values, Preferences, and Practice" (with I. Wolcott, 1998).

Linda L. Haas, PhD, is Professor of Sociology and Adjunct Professor of Women's Studies at Indiana University-Indianapolis. She teaches courses on the sociology of the family, gender and society, families and social policy, women and work, and research methods. She is a former Director of the Women's Studies Program at Indiana University-Indianapolis. She regularly serves as a consultant to social service agencies, companies, and governments on issues related to the well-being of youth and women. Her research activities have focused on work-family linkages in industrial societies, with an emphasis on Sweden. She has conducted research on egalitarian marriages; women in engineering; girls' and young women's attitudes toward the future; the gender-based division of labor for breadwinning, housework, and child care; parental leave; families and social policy; and the impact of corporate culture on fatherhood (the latter in collaboration with Philip Hwang). She has published several chapters in edited books and texts, as well as articles in several different journals devoted to gender studies. She is the author of *Equal Parenthood and Social Policy: A Study of Parental Leave in Sweden* (1992). Other recent publications include "Corporate Culture and Fathers' Use of Family Leave Benefits in Sweden" (with P. Hwang, *Family Relations*, 1995); "Families and Social Policy in Sweden" (*Journal of Family and Economic Issues*, 1996); and "Families and Work" in Sussman et al.'s *Handbook of Marriage and the Family* (1999).

Philip Hwang, PhD, is Professor of Applied Psychology at Göteborg University in Göteborg, Sweden. His interests center on child development and parenting. He is currently overseeing the following studies: Stability and Change in Family Relationships, a 15-year prospective longitudinal study of Swedish families; the Impact of Postnatal Depression on Mothers and Their Families, a transcultural study; and Work and Family: The Role of Unions for the Promotion of Equality Between Men and Women and the Impact of the Workplace on Men's Involvement with Children (together with Linda Haas). Until recently, he was the Associate Editor of the *International Journal of Behavioral Development.* He is the author or coauthor of seven books, including *Child Care in Context* (1993); *Images of Childhood* (1996); and *Faderskap* [Fatherhood] (1998). Other recent publications include "Corporate Culture and Fathers' Use of Family Leave Benefits in Sweden" (with L. Haas, *Family Relations,* 1995); "The Effects of Day Care on the Development of Cognitive Abilities in Eight-Year-Olds: A Longitudinal Study" (with A. Broberg, H. Wessels, and M. Lamb, *Developmental Psychology,* 1997); and "Father Involvement: Stability and Perceptions" (with M. Lamb, *International Journal of Behavioral Development, 1997).*

Clarissa Kugelberg, PhD, is a Research Fellow at the Institute for Housing Research, Uppsala University. She has been engaged in research and teaching on work and family issues, including changes in the welfare state and its significance for reconciliation of work and family; parents' cultural orientations to child care and upbringing; changes in gender aspects of parenting and parenthood; and the culture and practices of workplaces and their impact on men and women with children. She is presently involved in research on the orientations of young men and women to family life and working life, which is part of a cross-national project with participants from five countries. Publications include "From Poor Relief to Parents' Insurance: Swedish Family Policy in the 20th Century" in Çernigoj & Lewis's *Balancing Employment and Family Life: The Role of Employers Centre for Welfare Studies* (1997); "Föräldraskap på en svensk arbetplats i diskurs och handling" [Parenthood in a Swedish Workplace in Discourse and Practice] in Thurén and Sundman's *Kvinnor, män och andra sorter: Genusantropologiska frågor* [Women, men, and other kinds:

Studies in gender anthropology] (1997); "Imagens culturais dos jovens suecos acerca do inicio da vida adulta" (*Sociologia: Problemas e Practicas,* 1998); and *Perceptions of Fatherhood and Motherhood: Swedish Working Parents With Young Children* (1999).

Suzan Lewis, PhD, is Reader in Psychology at the Manchester Metropolitan University, Manchester, U.K. She is also a codirector of the Work-Life Research Centre and coeditor of the journal *Community, Work, and Family.* She is an organizational psychologist and carries out research in areas relating to work, family, and the community. Her recent publications include "Family Friendly Policies: Organisational Culture Change or Playing Around at the Margins?" (in *Gender, Work, and Organization,* 1997); "Work, Family, and Well Being: Can the Law Help?" (with J. Lewis, *Criminological and Legal Psychology,* 1997); "Balancing the Work-Home Interface: A European Perspective" (with C. Cooper, *Human Resource Management Review,* 1995); *The Work-Family Challenge* (with J. Lewis, 1996); and *Caring to Work: Accounts of Parents Combining Employment With the Care of Disabled Children* (with C. Kagan & P. Heaton, 1998). Her recent research projects include a five-country European study of young adults' orientations to work and family in the post-job-security age, a study of employed parents of disabled children, the development of a work-life benchmark framework, and a study of the impact of organizational change on families.

Rhona Rapoport is Director of the Institute of Family and Environmental Research, a nonprofit educational trust located in London. She is currently Distinguished Fellow at the Center for Organizational Change at the Simmons Graduate School of Management in Boston. Born in Cape Town, she received a PhD in Sociology from the London School of Economics. For the past 40 years, she has conducted research, taught, and engaged in consulting work in England, the United States, South Africa, and other countries. She has been on the staff of Harvard University and the Tavistock Institute of Human Relations and was a visiting professor at the University of California, Santa Barbara. Many publications—some in collaboration with her husband, Robert—have emerged from her work, including *Dual-Career Families; Fathers, Mothers, and Society;* and *Leisure and the Family Life Cycle.* For the past 15 years, she has been a consultant to the Ford Foundation, where she has helped to evaluate affirmative action programs and conduct research on work and family issues involving organizational transformation. She has also been a consultant to public- and private-sector organizations, including the Vienna Center for Research Documentation in the Social Sciences, British Aerospace, British Gas, a British political party, Lichfield Partnership, and the Gender Program of the Consultative Group on International Agriculture Research. A major concern in her work is the issue of equity between men and women, which has led to involvement in action research projects in the United States, the United Kingdom, and South Africa.

Graeme Russell, PhD, is Associate Professor in Psychology at Macquarie University, New South Wales, Australia, where he teaches organizational change. He specializes in the areas of work-family, fatherhood, gender equity, diversity, equal employment opportunity, and family relationships. He is the Director of Work and Life Strategies, a group that provides advice to organizations on work-family strategies, diversity, and gender equity issues. He is also the leader of a research group conducting a study of the theoretical and applied aspects of "Men's Role in Parenting" (funded by the Australian government). Publications include *The Changing Role of Fathers* (1983); *A Practical Guide for Fathers* (1983); "Fathers as Caregivers" in Lamb's *Non-Traditional Families: Parenting and Child Development* (1998); "Workers With Family Responsibilities: Adopting a Wider Family Outlook" (*Australian Journal of Ageing,* 1994); "Co-Parenting in Early School Aged Children: An Examination of Mother-Father Independence Within Families" (with A. Russell, *Developmental Psychology,* 1994); and "The Influence of Parents and Family Context on Children's Involvement in Household Tasks" (with Antill, Goodnow, & Cotton, *Sex Roles,* 1996).

Rohan Squirchuk is Managing Director of the Council for Equal Opportunity in Employment Limited, located in Sydney, Australia. Her experience and employment have covered a broad range of responsibilities, especially in the fields of equal employment opportunity, affirmative action for women, and valuing and managing diversity in federal, state, and local government organizations as well as organizations in the tertiary and private sectors. Providing expert assistance for the rapid resolution of workplace harassment complaints, with a focus on getting employees back to work with the least disruption, has been a feature of her work for many years. She has acted as an expert witness in sexual harassment and discrimination cases heard at the New South Wales Equal Opportunity Tribunal and at the New South Wales Industrial Commission. She also has a part-time statutory appointment as a legal member of the New South Wales Mental Health Review Tribunal, which is a quasi-judicial body. She is on the boards of Swinburne University's National Centre for Women and the Centre for Employment and Labour Relations Law at Melbourne University. Her MA is from the University of Otago in New Zealand, and her bachelor of law degree is from the University of New South Wales in Australia. She is currently enrolled in a master of law and management program at the Australian Graduate School of Management.

Jennifer E. Swanberg, PhD, is currently Director of Training and Learning of CASAWORKS for Families, at the Center on Addiction and Substance Abuse at Columbia University in New York. In her previous job at the Families and Work Institute, she was one of three authors of the 1997 National Study of the Changing Workforce and was active in the institute's research on work-life supports for low-income employees and on employer supports for new and expectant parents. In addition to her work at the Center on Addiction and Substance Abuse at Columbia University, she is an Associate Professor at City University of New York's Hunter College School of Social Work. She has presented extensively on the work and family needs of lower-wage workers, including an interview on National Public Radio's Morning Edition. She has a master's degree in Human Service Management and a doctorate in social welfare policy from the Florence Heller School at Brandeis University. Her doctoral research, which was done in collaboration with the Center for Work and Family at Boston University, focused on the work-family needs of low-wage workers. Prior to working at the Families and Work Institute, she was on the faculty of Wheelock College and worked as a research and policy consultant focusing on work-family issues. She has lectured extensively and appeared on numerous radio and television programs in the United States, Canada, and the United Kingdom.

Ilene Wolcott, M.Ed., is Senior Research Fellow at the Australian Institute of Family Studies in Melbourne. She has been a member of the staff of the institute since it was established in 1980. Her major research focus is in family support, with specific attention to work and family issues. Recent publications include *Families in Later Life: Dimensions of Retirement* (1998); *Work and Family Life: Achieving Integration* (with Helen Glezer, 1995); *A Matter of Give and Take: Small Business Views of Work and Family* (1993); and *A Nice Place to Work: Small Business and Family Responsibilities* (1996). She has been a member of the Australian Financial Review/Business Council of Australia and was on the Australian Chamber of Commerce and Industry Corporate Work and Family Awards selection committee between 1995 and 1998. She is currently working on another work and family book based on the 1996 Australian Family Life Course Study with Helen Glezer.